REED ANTHONY,
COWMAN

An Autobiography

ANDY ADAMS

Reed Anthony, Cowman

Andy Adams

© 1st World Library – Literary Society, 2006
PO Box 2211
Fairfield, IA 52556
www.1stworldlibrary.org
First Edition

LCCN: 2006905690

Softcover ISBN: 1-4218-2119-2
Hardcover ISBN: 1-4218-2019-6
eBook ISBN: 1-4218-2219-9

Purchase *"Reed Anthony, Cowman"*
as a traditional bound book at:
www.1stWorldLibrary.org/purchase.asp?ISBN=1-4218-2119-2

1st World Library Literary Society is a nonprofit
organization dedicated to promoting literacy by:

- Creating a free internet library accessible from any computer worldwide.
- Hosting writing competitions and offering book publishing scholarships.

**Readers interested in supporting literacy
through sponsorship, donations or
membership please contact:
literacy@1stworldlibrary.org
Check us out at: www.1stworldlibrary.ORG
and start downloading free ebooks today.**

Reed Anthony, Cowman
contributed by Tim, Ed & Rodney
in support of
1st World Library Literary Society

TO

CAPTAIN JOHN T. LYTLE

SECRETARY OF THE TEXAS CATTLE
RAISERS' ASSOCIATION
FORT WORTH, TEXAS

CONTENTS

CHAPTER I

IN RETROSPECT

I can truthfully say that my entire life has been spent with cattle. Even during my four years' service in the Confederate army, the greater portion was spent with the commissary department, in charge of its beef supplies. I was wounded early in the second year of the war and disabled as a soldier, but rather than remain at home I accepted a menial position under a quartermaster. Those were strenuous times. During Lee's invasion of Pennsylvania we followed in the wake of the army with over a thousand cattle, and after Gettysburg we led the retreat with double that number. Near the close of the war we frequently had no cattle to hold, and I became little more than a camp-follower.

I was born in the Shenandoah Valley, northern Virginia, May 3, 1840. My father was a thrifty planter and stockman, owned a few slaves, and as early as I can remember fed cattle every winter for the eastern markets. Grandfather Anthony, who died before I was born, was a Scotchman who had emigrated to the Old Dominion at an early day, and acquired several large tracts of land on an affluent of the Shenandoah. On my paternal side I never knew any of my ancestors, but have good cause to believe they were adventurers. My mother's maiden name was Reed; she was of a gentle family, who were able to trace their forbears beyond the colonial days, even to the gentry of England. Generations of good birth were reflected in my mother; and across a rough and eventful life I can distinctly remember the refinement of her manners, her courtesy to guests, her kindness to child and slave.

My boyhood days were happy ones. I attended a subscription school several miles from home, riding back and forth on a pony. The studies were elementary, and though I never distinguished myself in my classes, I was always ready to race my pony, and never refused to play truant when the swimming was good. Evidently my father never intended any of his boys for a professional career, though it was an earnest hope of my mother that all of us should receive a college education. My elder brother and I early developed business instincts, buying calves and accompanying our father on his trading expeditions. Once during a vacation, when we were about twelve and ten years old, both of us crossed the mountains with him into what is now West Virginia, where he bought about two hundred young steers and drove them back to our home in the valley. I must have been blessed with an unfailing memory; over fifty years have passed since that, my first trip from home, yet I remember it vividly - can recall conversations between my father and the sellers as they haggled over the cattle. I remember the money, gold and silver, with which to pay for the steers, was carried by my father in ordinary saddle-bags thrown across his saddle. As occasion demanded, frequently the funds were carried by a negro man of ours, and at night, when among acquaintances, the heavy saddle-bags were thrown into a corner, every one aware of their contents.

But the great event of my boyhood was a trip to Baltimore. There was no railroad at the time, and as that was our market for fat cattle, it was necessary to drive the entire way. My father had made the trip yearly since I could remember, the distance being nearly two hundred miles, and generally carrying as many as one hundred and fifty big beeves. They traveled slowly, pasturing or feeding grain on the way, in order that the cattle should arrive at the market in salable condition. One horse was allowed with the herd, and on another my father rode, far in advance, to engage pasture or feed and shelter for his men. When on the road a boy always led a gentle ox in the lead of the beeves; negro men walked on either flank, and the horseman brought up the rear. I used to envy the boy leading the ox, even though he was a darky. The negro boys on our plantation always pleaded with "Mars" John, my father, for the privilege; and when one of them had made the trip to Baltimore as a toll boy he easily outranked us younger whites. I must have made application for the position when I was about seven years old, for it seemed an age before my request was granted. My brother, only two years older than I, had made the trip twice, and when I was twelve the great opportunity came. My father had nearly two hundred cattle to go to market that year, and the start was made one morning early in June. I can distinctly see my mother standing on the veranda of our home as I led the herd by with a big red ox, trembling with fear that at the final moment her permission might be withdrawn and that I should have to remain behind. But she never interfered with my father, who took great pains to teach his boys everything practical in the cattle business.

It took us twenty days to reach Baltimore. We always started early in the morning, allowing the beeves to graze and rest along the road, and securing good pastures for them at night. Several times it rained, making the road soft, but I stripped off my shoes and took it barefooted through the mud. The lead ox was a fine, big fellow, each horn tipped with a brass knob, and he and I set the pace, which was scarcely that of a snail. The days were long, I grew desperately hungry between meals, and the novelty of leading that ox soon lost its romance. But I was determined not to show that I was tired or hungry, and frequently, when my father was with us and offered to take me up behind him on his horse, I spurned his offer and trudged on till the end of the day. The mere driving of the beeves would have been monotonous, but the constant change of scene kept us in good spirits, and our darkies always crooned old songs when the road passed through woodlands. After the beeves were marketed we spent a day in the city, and my father took my brother and me to the theatre. Although the world was unfolding rather rapidly for a country boy of twelve, it was with difficulty that I was made to understand that what we had witnessed on the stage was but mimicry.

The third day after reaching the city we started on our return. The proceeds from the sale of the cattle were sent home by boat. With only two horses, each of which carried double, and walking turn about, we reached home in seven days, settling all bills on the way. That year was a type of others until I was eighteen, at which age I could guess within twenty pounds of the weight of any beef on foot, and when I bought calves and yearling steers I knew just what kind of cattle they would make at maturity. In the mean time, one summer my father had gone west as far as the State of Missouri, traveling by boat to Jefferson City, and thence inland on horseback. Several of our neighbors had accompanied him, all of them buying land, my father securing four sections. I had younger brothers growing up, and the year my oldest brother attained his majority my father outfitted him with teams, wagons, and two trusty negro men, and we started for the nearest point on the Ohio River, our destination being the new lands in the West. We embarked on the first boat, drifting down the Ohio, and up the other rivers, reaching the Ultima Thule of our hopes within a month. The land was new; I liked it; we lived on venison and wild turkeys, and when once we had built a log house and opened a few fields, we were at peace with the earth.

But this happy existence was of short duration. Rumors of war reached us in our western elysium, and I turned my face homeward, as did many another son of Virginia. My brother was sensible enough to remain behind on the new farm; but with nothing to restrain me I soon found myself in St. Louis. There I met kindred spirits, eager for the coming fray, and before attaining my majority I was bearing arms and wearing the gray of the Confederacy. My regiment saw very little service during the first year of the war, as it was stationed in the western division, but early in 1862 it was engaged in numerous actions.

I shall never forget my first glimpse of the Texas cavalry. We had moved out from Corinth, under cover of darkness, to attack Grant at Pittsburg Landing. When day broke, orders were given to open out and allow the cavalry to pass ahead and reconnoitre our front. I had always felt proud of Virginian horsemanship, but those Texans were in a class by themselves. Centaur-like they sat their horses, and for our amusement, while passing at full gallop, swung from their saddles and picked up hats and handkerchiefs. There was something about the Texans that fascinated me, and that Sunday morning I resolved, if spared, to make Texas my future home. I have good cause to remember the battle of Shiloh, for during the second day I was twice wounded, yet saved from falling into the enemy's hands.

My recovery was due to youth and a splendid constitution. Within six weeks I was invalided home, and inside a few months I was assigned to the commissary department with the army in Virginia. It was while in the latter service that I made the acquaintance of many Texans, from whom I learned a great deal about the resources of their State, - its immense herds of cattle, the cheapness of its lands, and its perpetual summer. During the last year of the war, on account of their ability to handle cattle, a number of Texans were detailed to care for the army's beef supply. From these men I received much information and a pressing invitation to accompany them home, and after the parole at Appomattox I took their address, promising to join them in the near future. On my return to the old homestead I found the place desolate, with burnt barns and fields laid waste. The Shenandoah Valley had experienced war in its dread reality, for on every hand were the charred remains of once splendid homes. I had little hope that the country would ever recover, but my father, stout-hearted as ever, had already begun anew, and after helping him that summer and fall I again drifted west to my brother's farm.

The war had developed a restless, vagabond spirit in me. I had little heart to work, was unsettled as to my future, and, to add to my other troubles, after reaching Missouri one of my wounds reopened. In the mean time my brother had married, and had a fine farm opened up. He offered me every encouragement and assistance to settle down to the life of a farmer; but I was impatient, worthless, undergoing a formative period of early manhood, even spurning the advice of father, mother, and dearest friends. If to-day, across the lapse of years, the question were asked what led me from the bondage of my discontent, it would remain unanswered. Possibly it was the advantage of good birth; surely the prayers of a mother had always followed me, and my feet were finally led into the paths of industry. Since that day of uncertainty, grandsons have sat upon my knee, clamoring for a story about Indians, the war, or cattle trails. If I were to assign a motive for thus leaving a tangible record of my life, it would be that my posterity - not the present generation, absorbed in its greed of gain, but a more distant and a saner one - should be enabled to glean a faint idea of one of their forbears. A worthy and secondary motive is to give an idea of the old West and to preserve from oblivion a rapidly vanishing type of pioneers.

My personal appearance can be of little interest to coming generations, but rather what I felt, saw, and accomplished. It was always a matter of regret to me that I was such a poor shot with a pistol. The only two exceptions worthy of mention were mere accidents. In my boyhood's home, in Virginia, my father killed yearly a large number of hogs for the household needs as well as for supplying our slave families with bacon. The hogs usually ran in the woods, feeding and thriving on the mast, but before killing time we always baited them into the fields and finished their fattening with peas and corn. It was customary to wait until the beginning of winter, or about the second cold spell, to butcher, and at the time in question there were about fifty large hogs to kill. It was a gala event with us boys, the oldest of whom were allowed to shoot one or more with a rifle. The hogs had been tolled into a small field for the killing, and towards the close of the day a number of them, having been wounded and requiring a second or third shot, became cross. These subsequent shots were usually delivered from a six-shooter, and in order to have it at hand in case of a miss I was intrusted with carrying the pistol. There was one heavy-tusked five-year-old stag among the hogs that year who refused to present his head for a target, and took refuge in a brier thicket. He was left until the last, when we all sallied out to make the final kill. There were two rifles, and had the chance come to my father, I think he would have killed him easily; but the opportunity came to a neighbor, who overshot, merely causing a slight wound. The next instant the stag charged at me from the cover of the thickety fence corner. Not having sense enough to take to the nearest protection, I turned and ran like a scared wolf across the field, the hog following me like a hound. My father risked a running shot, which missed its target. The darkies were yelling, "Run, chile! Run, Mars' Reed! Shoot! Shoot!" when it occurred to me that I had a pistol; and pointing it backward as I ran, I blazed away, killing the big fellow in his tracks.

The other occasion was years afterward, when I was a trail foreman at Abilene, Kansas. My herd had arrived at that market in bad condition, gaunted from almost constant stampedes at night, and I had gone into camp some distance from town to quiet and recuperate them. That day I was sending home about half my men, had taken them to the depot with our wagon, and intended hauling back a load of supplies to my camp. After seeing the boys off I hastened about my other business, and near the middle of the afternoon started out of town. The distance to camp was nearly twenty miles, and with a heavy load, principally salt, I knew it would be after nightfall when I reached there. About five miles out of town there was a long, gradual slope to climb, and I had to give the through team their time in pulling to its summit. Near the divide was a small box house, the only one on the road if I remember rightly, and as I was nearing it, four or five dogs ran out and scared my team. I managed to hold them in the road, but they refused to quiet down, kicking, rearing, and plunging in spite of their load; and once as they jerked me forward, I noticed there was a dog or two under the wagon, nipping at their heels. There was a six-shooter lying on the seat beside me, and reaching forward I fired it downward over the end gate of the wagon. By the merest accident I hit a dog, who raised a cry, and the last I saw of him he was spinning like a top and howling like a wolf. I quieted the team as soon as possible, and as I looked back, there was a man and woman pursuing me, the latter in the lead. I had gumption enough to know that they were the owners of the dog, and whipped up the horses in the hope of getting away from them. But the grade and the load were against me, and the next thing I knew, a big, bony woman, with fire in her eye, was reaching for me. The wagon wheel warded her off, and I leaned out of her reach to the far side, yet she kept abreast of me, constantly calling for her husband to hurry up. I was pouring the whip into the horses, fearful lest she would climb into the wagon, when the hub of the front wheel struck her on the knee, knocking her down. I was then nearing the summit of the divide, and on reaching it, I looked back and saw the big woman giving her husband the pommeling that was intended for me. She was altogether too near me yet, and I shook the lines over the horses, firing a few shots to frighten them, and we tore down the farther slope like a fire engine.

There are two events in my life that this chronicle will not fully record. One of them is my courtship and marriage, and the other my connection with a government contract with the Indian department. Otherwise my life shall be as an open book, not only for my own posterity, but that he who runs may read. It has been a matter of observation with me that a plain man like myself scarcely ever refers to his love affairs. At my time of life, now nearing my allotted span, I have little sympathy with the great mass of fiction which exploits the world-old passion. In no sense of the word am I a well-read man, yet I am conscious of the fact that during my younger days the love story interested me; but when compared with the real thing, the transcript is usually a poor one. My wife and I have now walked up and down the paths of life for over thirty-five years, and, if memory serves me right, neither one of us has ever mentioned the idea of getting a divorce. In youth we shared our crust together; children soon blessed and brightened our humble home, and to-day, surrounded by every comfort that riches can bestow, no achievement in life has given me such great pleasure, I know no music so sweet, as the prattle of my own grandchildren. Therefore that feature of my life is sacred, and will not be disclosed in these pages.

I would omit entirely mention of the Indian contract, were it not that old friends may read this, my biography, and wonder at the omission. I have no apologies to offer for my connection with the transaction, as its true nature was concealed from me in the beginning, and a scandal would have resulted had I betrayed friends. Then again, before general amnesty was proclaimed I was debarred from bidding on the many rich government contracts for cattle because I had served in the Confederate army. Smarting under this injustice at the time the Indian contract was awarded, I question if I was thoroughly *reconstructed.* Before our disabilities were removed, we ex-Confederates could do all the work, run all the risk, turn in all the cattle in filling the outstanding contracts, but the middleman got the profits. The contract in question was a blanket one, requiring about fifty thousand cows for delivery at some twenty Indian agencies. The use of my name was all that was required of me, as I was the only cowman in the entire ring. My duty was to bid on the contract; the bonds would be furnished by my partners, of which I must have had a dozen. The proposals called for sealed bids, in the usual form, to be in the hands of the Department of the Interior before noon on a certain day, marked so and so, and to be opened at high noon a week later. The contract was a large one, the competition was ample. Several other Texas drovers besides myself had submitted bids; but they stood no show - *I had been furnished the figures of every competitor.* The ramifications of the ring of which I was the mere figure-head can be readily imagined. I sublet the contract to the next lowest bidder, who delivered the cattle, and we got a rake-off of a clean hundred thousand dollars. Even then there was little in the transaction for me, as it required too many people to handle it, and none of them stood behind the door at the final "divvy." In a single year I have since cleared twenty times what my interest amounted to in that contract and have done honorably by my fellowmen. That was my first, last, and only connection with a transaction that would need deodorizing if one described the details.

But I have seen life, have been witness to its poetry and pathos, have drunk from the cup of sorrow and rejoiced as a strong man to run a race. I have danced all night where wealth and beauty mingled, and again under the stars on a battlefield I have helped carry a stretcher when the wails of the wounded on every hand were like the despairing cries of lost souls. I have seen an old demented man walking the streets of a city, picking up every scrap of paper and scanning it carefully to see if a certain ship had arrived at port - a ship which had been lost at sea over forty years before, and aboard of which were his wife and children. I was once under the necessity of making a payment of twenty-five thousand dollars in silver at an Indian village. There were no means of transportation, and I was forced to carry the specie in on eight pack mules. The distance was nearly two hundred miles, and as we neared the encampment we were under the necessity of crossing a shallow river. It was summer-time, and as we halted the tired mules to loosen the lash ropes, in order to allow them to drink, a number of Indian children of both sexes, who were bathing in the river, gathered naked on either embankment in bewilderment at such strange intruders. In the innocence of these children of the wild there was no doubt inspiration for a poet; but our mission was a commercial one, and we relashed the mules and hurried into the village with the rent money.

I have never kept a diary. One might wonder that the human mind could contain such a mass of incident and experiences as has been my portion, yet I can remember the day and date of occurrences of fifty years ago. The scoldings of my father, the kind words of an indulgent mother, when not over five years of age, are vivid in my memory as I write to-day. It may seem presumptuous, but I can give the year and date of starting, arrival, and delivery of over one hundred herds of cattle which I drove over the trail as a common hand, foreman, or owner. Yet the warnings of years - the unsteady step, easily embarrassed, love of home and dread of leaving it - bid me hasten these memoirs. Even my old wounds act as a barometer in foretelling the coming of storms, as well as the change of season, from both of which I am comfortably sheltered. But as

Andy Adams

I look into the inquiring eyes of a circle of grandchildren, all anxious to know my life story, it seems to sweeten the task, and I am encouraged to go on with the work.

CHAPTER II

MY APPRENTICESHIP

During the winter of 1865-66 I corresponded with several of my old comrades in Texas. Beyond a welcome which could not be questioned, little encouragement was, with one exception, offered me among my old friends. It was a period of uncertainty throughout the South, yet a cheerful word reached me from an old soldier crony living some distance west of Fort Worth on the Brazos River. I had great confidence in my former comrade, and he held out a hope, assuring me that if I would come, in case nothing else offered, we could take his ox teams the next winter and bring in a cargo of buffalo robes. The plains to the westward of Fort Griffin, he wrote, were swarming with buffalo, and wages could be made in killing them for their hides. This caught my fancy and I was impatient to start at once; but the healing of my reopened wound was slow, and it was March before I started. My brother gave me a good horse and saddle, twenty-five dollars in gold, and I started through a country unknown to me personally. Southern Missouri had been in sympathy with the Confederacy, and whatever I needed while traveling through that section was mine for the asking. I avoided the Indian Territory until I reached Fort Smith, where I rested several days with an old comrade, who gave me instructions and routed me across the reservation of the Choctaw Indians, and I reached Paris, Texas, without mishap.

I remember the feeling that I experienced while being ferried across Red River. That watercourse was the northern boundary of Texas, and while crossing it I realized that I was leaving home and friends and entering a country the very name of which to the outside world was a synonym for crime and outlawry. Yet some of as good men as ever it was my pleasure to know came from that State, and undaunted I held a true course for my destination. I was disappointed on seeing Fort Worth, a straggling village on the Trinity River, and, merely halting to feed my mount, passed on. I had a splendid horse and averaged thirty to forty miles a day when traveling, and early in April reached the home of my friend in Paolo Pinto County. The primitive valley of the Brazos was enchanting, and the hospitality of the Edwards ranch was typical of my own Virginia. George Edwards, my crony, was a year my junior, a native of the State, his parents having moved west from Mississippi the year after Texas won her independence from Mexico. The elder Edwards had moved to his present home some fifteen years previous, carrying with him a stock of horses and cattle, which had increased until in 1866 he was regarded as one of the substantial ranchmen in the Brazos valley. The ranch house was a stanch one, built at a time when defense was to be considered as well as comfort, and was surrounded by fine cornfields. The only drawback I could see there was that there was no market for anything, nor was there any money in the country. The consumption of such a ranch made no impression on the increase of its herds, which grew to maturity with no demand for the surplus.

I soon became impatient to do something. George Edwards had likewise lost four years in the army, and was as restless as myself. He knew the country, but the only employment in sight for us was as teamsters with outfits, freighting government supplies to Fort Griffin. I should have jumped at the chance of driving oxen, for I was anxious to stay in the country, and suggested to George that we ride up to Griffin. But the family interposed, assuring us that there was no occasion for engaging in such menial work, and we folded our arms obediently, or rode the range under the pretense of looking after the cattle. I might as well admit right here that my anxiety to get away from the Edwards ranch was fostered by the presence of several sisters of my former comrade. Miss Gertrude was only four years my junior, a very dangerous age, and in spite of all resolutions to the contrary, I felt myself constantly slipping. Nothing but my poverty and the hopelessness of it kept me from falling desperately in love.

But a temporary relief came during the latter part of May. Reports came down the river that a firm of drovers were putting up a herd of cattle for delivery at Fort Sumner, New Mexico. Their headquarters were at Belknap, a long day's ride above, on the Brazos; and immediately, on receipt of the news, George and I saddled, and started up the river. The elder Edwards was very anxious to sell his beef-cattle and a surplus of cow-horses, and we were commissioned to offer them to the drovers at prevailing prices. On arriving at Belknap we met the pioneer drover of Texas, Oliver Loving, of the firm of Loving & Goodnight, but were disappointed to learn that the offerings in making up the herd were treble the drover's requirements; neither was there any chance to sell horses. But an application for work met with more favor. Mr. Loving warned us of the nature of the country, the dangers to be encountered, all of which we waived, and were accordingly employed at forty dollars a month in gold. The herd was to start early in June. George Edwards returned home to report, but I was immediately put to work, as the junior member of the firm was then out receiving cattle. They had established a camp, and at the time of our employment were gathering beef steers in Loving's brand and holding the herd as it arrived, so that I was initiated into my duties at once.

I was allowed to retain my horse, provided he did his share of the work. A mule and three range horses were also allotted to me, and I was cautioned about their care. There were a number of saddle mules in the remuda, and Mr. Loving explained that the route was through a dry country, and that experience had taught him that a mule could withstand thirst longer than a horse. I was a new man in the country, and absorbed every word and idea as a sponge does water. With the

Andy Adams

exception of roping, I made a hand from the start. The outfit treated me courteously, there was no concealment of my past occupation, and I soon had the friendship of every man in the camp. It was some little time before I met the junior partner, Charlie Goodnight, a strapping young fellow of about thirty, who had served all through the war in the frontier battalion of Texas Rangers. The Comanche Indians had been a constant menace on the western frontier of the State, and during the rebellion had allied themselves with the Federal side, and harassed the settlements along the border. It required a regiment of mounted men to patrol the frontier from Red River to the coast, as the Comanches claimed the whole western half of the State as their hunting grounds.

Early in June the herd began to assume its required numbers. George Edwards returned, and we naturally became bunkies, sharing our blankets and having the same guard on night-herd. The drovers encouraged all the men employed to bring along their firearms, and when we were ready to start the camp looked like an arsenal. I had a six-shooter, and my bunkie brought me a needle-gun from the ranch, so that I felt armed for any emergency. Each of the men had a rifle of some make or other, while a few of them had as many as four pistols, - two in their belts and two in saddle holsters. It looked to me as if this was to be a military expedition, and I began to wonder if I had not had enough war the past few years, but kept quiet. The start was made June 10, 1866, from the Brazos River, in what is now Young County, the herd numbering twenty-two hundred big beeves. A chuck-wagon, heavily loaded with supplies and drawn by six yoke of fine oxen, a remuda of eighty-five saddle horses and mules, together with seventeen men, constituted the outfit. Fort Sumner lay to the northwest, and I was mildly surprised when the herd bore off to the southwest. This was explained by young Goodnight, who was in charge of the herd, saying that the only route then open or known was on our present course to the Pecos River, and thence up that stream to our destination.

Indian sign was noticed a few days after starting. Goodnight and Loving both read it as easily as if it had been print, - the abandoned camps, the course of arrival and departure, the number of horses, indicating who and what they were, war or hunting parties - everything apparently simple and plain as an alphabet to these plainsmen. Around the camp-fire at night the chronicle of the Comanche tribe for the last thirty years was reviewed, and their overbearing and defiant attitude towards the people of Texas was discussed, not for my benefit, as it was common history. Then for the first time I learned that the Comanches had once mounted ten thousand warriors, had frequently raided the country to the coast, carrying off horses and white children, even dictating their own terms of peace to the republic of Texas. At the last council, called for the purpose of negotiating for the return of captive white children in possession of the Comanches, the assembly had witnessed a dramatic termination. The same indignity had been offered before, and borne by the whites, too weak to resist the numbers of the Comanche tribe. In this latter instance, one of the war chiefs, in spurning the remuneration offered for the return of a certain white girl, haughtily walked into the centre of the council, where an insult could be seen by all. His act, a disgusting one, was anticipated, as it was not the first time it had been witnessed, when one of the Texans present drew a six-shooter and killed the chief in the act. The hatchet of the Comanche was instantly dug up, and had not been buried at the time we were crossing a country claimed by him as his hunting ground.

Yet these drovers seemed to have no fear of an inferior race. We held our course without a halt, scarcely a day passing without seeing more or less fresh sign of Indians. After crossing the South Fork of the Brazos, we were attacked one morning just at dawn, the favorite hour of the Indian for a surprise. Four men were on herd with the cattle and one near by with the remuda, our night horses all securely tied to the wagon wheels. A feint attack was made on the commissary, but under the leadership of Goodnight a majority of us scrambled into our saddles and rode to the rescue of the remuda, the chief objective of the surprise. Two of the boys from the herd had joined the horse wrangler, and on our arrival all three were wickedly throwing lead at the circling Indians. The remuda was running at the time, and as we cut through between it and the savages we gave them the benefit of our rifles and six-shooter in passing. The shots turned the saddle stock back towards our camp and the mounted braves continued on their course, not willing to try issues with us, although they outnumbered us three to one. A few arrows had imbedded themselves in the ground around camp at the first assault, but once our rifles were able to distinguish an object clearly, the Indians kept well out of reach. The cattle made a few surges, but once the remuda was safe, there was an abundance of help in holding them, and they quieted down before sunrise. The Comanches had no use for cattle, except to kill and torture them, as they preferred the flesh of the buffalo, and once our saddle stock and the contents of the wagon were denied them, they faded into the dips of the plain.

The journey was resumed without the delay of an hour. Our first brush with the noble red man served a good purpose, as we were doubly vigilant thereafter whenever there was cause to expect an attack. There was an abundance of water, as we followed up the South Fork and its tributaries, passing through Buffalo Gap, which was afterward a well-known landmark on the Texas and Montana cattle trail. Passing over the divide between the waters of the Brazos and Concho, we struck the old Butterfield stage route, running by way of Fort Concho to El Paso, Texas, on the Rio Grande. This stage road was the original Staked Plain, surveyed and located by General John Pope in 1846. The route was originally marked by stakes, until it became a thoroughfare, from which the whole of northwest Texas afterward took its name. There was a ninety-six mile dry drive between the headwaters of the Concho and Horsehead Crossing on the Pecos, and before attempting it we rested a few days. Here Indians made a second attack on us, and although as futile as the first, one of the horse wranglers received an arrow in the shoulder. In attempting to remove it the shaft separated from the steel arrowhead, leaving the latter imbedded in the lad's shoulder. We were then one hundred and twelve miles distant from Fort Concho, the nearest point where medical relief might be expected. The drovers were alarmed for the man's welfare; it was impossible to hold the herd longer, so the young fellow volunteered to make the ride alone. He was given the best horse in the remuda, and with the falling of darkness started for Fort Concho. I had the pleasure of meeting him afterward, as happy as he was hale and hearty.

The start across the arid stretch was made at noon. Every hoof had been thoroughly watered in advance, and with the heat of summer on us it promised to be an ordeal to man and beast. But Loving had driven it before, and knew fully what was before him as we trailed out under a noonday sun. An evening halt was made for refreshing the inner man, and as soon as darkness settled over us the herd was again started. We were conscious of the presence of Indians, and deceived them by leaving our camp-fire burning, but holding our effects closely together throughout the night, the remuda even mixing with the cattle. When day broke we were fully thirty miles from our noon camp of the day before, yet with the exception of an hour's rest there was never a halt. A second day and night were spent in forging ahead, though it is doubtful if we averaged much over a mile an hour during that time. About fifteen miles out from the Pecos we were due to enter a cañon known as Castle Mountain Gap, some three or four miles long, the exit of which was in sight of the river. We were anxious to reach the entrance of this cañon before darkness on the third day, as we could then cut the cattle into bunches, the cliffs on either side forming a lane. Our horses were as good as worthless during the third day, but the saddle mules seemed to stand grief nobly, and by dint of ceaseless effort we reached the cañon and turned the cattle loose into it. This was the turning-point in the dry drive. That night two men took half the remuda and went through to Horsehead Crossing, returning with them early the next morning, and we once more had fresh mounts. The herd had been nursed through the cañon during the night, and although it was still twelve miles to the river, I have always believed that those beeves knew that water was at hand. They walked along briskly; instead of the constant

Andy Adams

moaning, their heads were erect, bawling loud and deep. The oxen drawing the wagon held their chains taut, and the commissary moved forward as if drawn by a fresh team. There was no attempt to hold the herd compactly, and within an hour after starting on our last lap the herd was strung out three miles. The rear was finally abandoned, and when half the distance was covered, the drag cattle to the number of fully five hundred turned out of the trail and struck direct for the river. They had scented the water over five miles, and as far as control was concerned the herd was as good as abandoned, except that the water would hold them.

Horsehead Crossing was named by General Pope. There is a difference of opinion as to the origin of the name, some contending that it was due to the meanderings of the river, forming a horse's head, and others that the surveying party was surprised by Indians and lost their stock. None of us had slept for three nights, and the feeling of relief on reaching the Pecos, shared alike by man and beast, is indescribable. Unless one has endured such a trial, only a faint idea of its hardships can be fully imagined - the long hours of patient travel at a snail's pace, enveloped by clouds of dust by day, and at night watching every shadow for a lurking savage. I have since slept many a time in the saddle, but in crossing that arid belt the one consuming desire to reach the water ahead benumbed every sense save watchfulness.

All the cattle reached the river before the middle of the afternoon, covering a front of five or six miles. The banks of the Pecos were abrupt, there being fully one hundred and twenty-five feet of deep water in the channel at the stage crossing. Entrance to the ford consisted of a wagon-way, cut through the banks, and the cattle crowded into the river above and below, there being but one exit on either side. Some miles above, the beeves had found several passageways down to the water, but in drifting up and down stream they missed these entrances on returning. A rally was made late that afternoon to rout the cattle out of the river-bed, one half the outfit going above, the remainder working around Horsehead, where the bulk of the herd had watered. I had gone upstream with Goodnight, but before we reached the upper end of the cattle fresh Indian sign was noticed. There was enough broken country along the river to shelter the redskins, but we kept in the open and cautiously examined every brake within gunshot of an entrance to the river. We succeeded in getting all the animals out of the water before dark, with the exception of one bunch, where the exit would require the use of a mattock before the cattle could climb it, and a few head that had bogged in the quicksand below Horsehead Crossing. There was little danger of a rise in the river, the loose contingent had a dry sand-bar on which to rest, and as the Indians had no use for them there was little danger of their being molested before morning.

We fell back about a mile from the river and camped for the night. Although we were all dead for sleep, extra caution was taken to prevent a surprise, either Goodnight or Loving remaining on guard over the outfit, seeing that the men kept awake on herd and that the guards changed promptly. Charlie Goodnight owned a horse that he contended could scent an Indian five hundred yards, and I have never questioned the statement. He had used him in the Ranger service. The horse by various means would show his uneasiness in the immediate presence of Indians, and once the following summer we moved camp at midnight on account of the warnings of that same horse. We had only a remuda with us at the time, but another outfit encamped with us refused to go, and they lost half their horses from an Indian surprise the next morning and never recovered them. I remember the ridicule which was expressed at our moving camp on the warnings of a horse. "Injun-bit," "Man-afraid-of-his-horses," were some of the terms applied to us, - yet the practical plainsman knew enough to take warning from his dumb beast. Fear, no doubt, gives horses an unusual sense of smell, and I have known them to detect the presence of a bear, on a favorable wind, at an incredible distance.

The night passed quietly, and early the next morning we rode to recover the remainder of the cattle. An effort was also made to rescue the bogged ones. On approaching the river, we found the beeves still resting quietly on the sand-bar. But we had approached them at an angle, for directly over head and across the river was a brake overgrown with thick brush, a splendid cover in which Indians might be lurking in the hope of ambushing any one who attempted to drive out the beeves. Two men were left with a single mattock to cut out and improve the exit, while the rest of us reconnoitered the thickety motte across the river. Goodnight was leery of the thicket, and suggested firing a few shots into it. We all had long-range guns, the distance from bank to bank was over two hundred yards, and a fusillade of shots was accordingly poured into the motte. To my surprise we were rewarded by seeing fully twenty Indians skulk out of the upper end of the cover. Every man raised his sights and gave them a parting volley, but a mesquite thicket, in which their horses were secreted, soon sheltered them and they fell back into the hills on the western side of the river. With the coast thus cleared, half a dozen of us rode down into the river-bed and drove out the last contingent of about three hundred cattle. Goodnight informed us that those Indians had no doubt been watching us for days, and cautioned us never to give a Comanche an advantage, advice which I never forgot.

On our return every one of the bogged cattle had been freed except two heavy beeves. These animals were mired above the ford, in rather deep water, and it was simply impossible to release them. The drovers were anxious to cross the river that afternoon, and a final effort was made to rescue the two steers. The oxen were accordingly yoked, and, with all the chain available, were driven into the river and fastened on to the nearest one. Three mounted drivers had charge of the team, and when the word was given six yoke of cattle bowed their necks and threw their weight against the yokes; but the quicksand held the steer in spite of all their efforts. The chain was freed from it, and the oxen were brought around and made fast again, at an angle and where the footing was better for the team. Again the word was given, and as the six yoke swung round, whips and ropes were plied amid a general shouting, and the team brought out the steer, but with a broken neck. There were no regrets, and our attention was at once given to the other steer. The team circled around, every available chain was brought into use, in order to afford the oxen good footing on a straight-away pull with the position in which the beef lay bogged. The word was given for an easy pull, the oxen barely stretched their chains, and were stopped. Goodnight cautioned the drivers that unless the pull was straight ahead another neck would be broken. A second trial was made; the oxen swung and weaved, the chains fairly cried, the beef's head went under water, but the team was again checked in time to keep the steer from drowning. After a breathing spell for oxen and victim, the call was made for a rush. A driver was placed over every yoke and the word given, and the oxen fell to their knees in the struggle, whips cracked over their backs, ropes were plied by every man in charge, and, amid a din of profanity applied to the struggling cattle, the team fell forward in a general collapse. At first it was thought the chain had parted, but as the latter came out of the water it held in its iron grasp the horns and a portion of the skull of the dying beef. Several of us rode out to the victim, whose brain lay bare, still throbbing and twitching with life. Rather than allow his remains to pollute the river, we made a last pull at an angle, and the dead beef was removed.

We bade Horsehead Crossing farewell that afternoon and camped for the night above Dagger Bend. Our route now lay to the northwest, or up the Pecos River. We were then out twenty-one days from Belknap, and although only half way to our destination, the worst of it was considered over. There was some travel up and down the Pecos valley, the route was even then known as the Chisum trail, and afterward extended as far north as Fort Logan in Colorado and other government posts in Wyoming. This cattle trace should never be confounded with the Chisholm trail, first opened by a half-breed named Jesse Chisholm, which ran from Red River Station on the northern boundary of Texas to various points in Kansas. In cutting across the bends of the Rio Pecos we secured water each day for the herd, although we were frequently under the necessity of sloping down the banks with mattocks to let the cattle into the river. By this method it often took us three or four hours to water the herd. Until we neared Fort Sumner precaution never relaxed against an Indian surprise. Their sign was seen almost daily, but as there were weaker outfits than ours passing through we escaped any further molestation.

The methods of handling such a herd were a constant surprise to me, as well as the schooling of these plainsmen drovers. Goodnight had come to the plains when a boy of ten, and was a thorough master of their secrets. On one occasion, about midway between Horsehead Crossing and our destination, difficulty was encountered in finding an entrance to the river on account of its abrupt banks. It was late in the day, and in order to insure a quiet night with the cattle water became an urgent necessity. Our young foreman rode ahead and found a dry, sandy creek, its bed fully fifty yards wide, but no water, though the sand was damp. The herd was held back until sunset, when the cattle were turned into the creek bed and held as compactly as possible. The heavy beeves naturally walked back and forth, up and down, the sand just moist enough to aggravate them after a day's travel under a July sun. But the tramping soon agitated the sands, and within half an hour after the herd had entered the dry creek the water arose in pools, and the cattle drank to their hearts' content. As dew falls at night, moisture likewise rises in the earth, and with the twilight hour, the agitation of the sands, and the weight of the cattle, a spring was produced in the desert waste.

Fort Sumner was a six-company post and the agency of the Apaches and Navajos. These two tribes numbered over nine thousand people, and our herd was intended to supply the needs of the military post and these Indians. The contract was held by Patterson & Roberts, eligible by virtue of having cast their fortunes with the victor in "the late unpleasantness," and otherwise fine men. We reached the post on the 20th of July. There was a delay of several days before the cattle were accepted, but all passed the inspection with the exception of about one hundred head. These were cattle which had not recuperated from the dry drive. Some few were footsore or thin in flesh, but taken as a whole the delivery had every earmark of an honest one. Fortunately this remnant was sold a few days later to some Colorado men, and we were foot-loose and free. Even the oxen had gone in on the main delivery, and harnesses were accordingly bought, a light tongue fitted to the wagon, and we were ready to start homeward. Mules were substituted for the oxen, and we averaged forty miles a day returning, almost itching for an Indian attack, as we had supplied ourselves with ammunition from the post sutler. The trip had been a financial success (the government was paying ten cents a pound for beef on foot), friendly relations had been established with the holders of the award, and we hastened home to gather and drive another herd.

CHAPTER III

A SECOND TRIP TO FORT SUMNER

On the return trip we traveled mainly by night. The proceeds from the sale of the herd were in the wagon, and had this fact been known it would have been a tempting prize for either bandits or Indians. After leaving Horsehead Crossing we had the advantage of the dark of the moon, as it was a well-known fact that the Comanches usually choose moonlight nights for their marauding expeditions. Another thing in our favor, both going and returning, was the lightness of travel westward, it having almost ceased during the civil war, though in '66 it showed a slight prospect of resumption. Small bands of Indians were still abroad on horse-stealing forays, but the rich prizes of wagon trains bound for El Paso or Santa Fé no longer tempted the noble red man in force. This was favorable wind to our sail, but these plainsmen drovers predicted that, once traffic westward was resumed, the Comanche and his ally would be about the first ones to know it. The redskins were constantly passing back and forth, to and from their reservation in the Indian Territory, and news travels fast even among savages.

We reached the Brazos River early in August. As the second start was not to be made until the latter part of the following month, a general settlement was made with the men and all reëngaged for the next trip. I received eighty dollars in gold as my portion, it being the first money I ever earned as a citizen. The past two months were a splendid experience for one going through a formative period, and I had returned feeling that I was once more a man among men. All the uncertainty as to my future had fallen from me, and I began to look forward to the day when I also might be the owner of lands and cattle. There was no good reason why I should not, as the range was as free as it was boundless. There were any quantity of wild cattle in the country awaiting an owner, and a good mount of horses, a rope, and a branding iron were all the capital required to start a brand. I knew the success which my father had made in Virginia before the war and had seen it repeated on a smaller scale by my elder brother in Missouri, but here was a country which discounted both of those in rearing cattle without expense. Under the best reasoning at my command, I had reached the promised land, and henceforth determined to cast my fortunes with Texas.

Rather than remain idle around the Loving headquarters for a month, I returned with George Edwards to his home. Altogether too cordial a welcome was extended us, but I repaid the hospitality of the ranch by relating our experiences of trail and Indian surprise. Miss Gertrude was as charming as ever, but the trip to Sumner and back had cooled my ardor and I behaved myself as an acceptable guest should. The time passed rapidly, and on the last day of the month we returned to Belknap. Active preparations were in progress for the driving of the second herd, oxen had been secured, and a number of extra fine horses were already added to the saddle stock. The remuda had enjoyed a good month's rest and were in strong working flesh, and within a few days all the boys reported for duty. The senior member of the firm was the owner of a large number of range cattle, and it was the intention to round up and gather as many of his beeves as possible for the coming drive. We should have ample time to do this; by waiting until the latter part of the month for starting, it was believed that few Indians would be encountered, as the time was nearing for their annual buffalo hunt for robes and a supply of winter meat. This was a gala occasion with the tribes which depended on the bison for food and clothing; and as the natural hunting grounds of the Comanches and Kiowas lay south of Red River, the drovers considered that that would be an opportune time to start. The Indians would no doubt confine their operations to the first few tiers of counties in Texas, as the robes and dried meat would tax the carrying capacity of their horses returning, making it an object to kill their supplies as near their winter encampment as possible.

Some twenty days were accordingly spent in gathering beeves along the main Brazos and Clear Fork. Our herd consisted of about a thousand in the straight ranch brand, and after receiving and road-branding five hundred outside cattle we were ready to start. Sixteen men constituted our numbers, the horses were culled down until but five were left to the man, and with the previous armament the start was made. Never before or since have I enjoyed such an outing as this was until we struck the dry drive on approaching the Pecos River. The absence of the Indians was correctly anticipated, and either their presence elsewhere, preying on the immense buffalo herds, or the drift of the seasons, had driven countless numbers of that animal across our pathway. There were days and days that we were never out of sight of the feeding myriads of these shaggy brutes, and at night they became a menace to our sleeping herd. During the day, when the cattle were strung out in trail formation, we had difficulty in keeping the two species separated, but we shelled the buffalo right and left and moved forward. Frequently, when they occupied the country ahead of us, several men rode forward and scattered them on either hand until a right of way was effected for the cattle to pass. While they remained with us we killed our daily meat from their numbers, and several of the boys secured fine robes. They were very gentle, but when occasion required could give a horse a good race, bouncing along, lacking grace in flight.

Our cook was a negro. One day as we were nearing Buffalo Gap, a number of big bulls, attracted by the covered wagon, approached the commissary, the canvas sheet of which shone like a white flag. The wagon was some distance in the rear, and as the buffalo began to approach it they would scare and circle around, but constantly coming nearer the object of their curiosity. The darky finally became alarmed for fear they would gore his oxen, and unearthed an old Creedmoor rifle which he carried in the wagon. The gun could be heard for miles, and when the cook opened on the playful denizens of the plain, a number of us hurried back, supposing it was an Indian attack. When within a quarter-mile of the wagon and the situation became clear, we took it more leisurely, but the fusillade never ceased until we rode up and it dawned on the darky's mind that rescue was at hand. He had halted his team, and from a secure position in the front end of the wagon had shot down a dozen buffalo bulls. Pure curiosity and the blood of their comrades had kept them within easy range of the murderous Creedmoor; and the frenzied negro, supposing that his team might be attacked any moment, had mown down a circle of the innocent animals. We charged and drove away the remainder, after which we formed a guard of honor in escorting the commissary until its timid driver overtook the herd.

The last of the buffalo passed out of sight before we reached the headwaters of the Concho. In crossing the dry drive approaching the Pecos we were unusually fortunate. As before, we rested in advance of starting, and on the evening of the second day out several showers fell, cooling the atmosphere until the night was fairly chilly. The rainfall continued all the following day in a gentle mist, and with little or no suffering to man or beast early in the afternoon we entered the cañon known as Castle Mountain Gap, and the dry drive was virtually over. Horsehead Crossing was reached early the next morning, the size of the herd making it possible to hold it compactly, and thus preventing any scattering along that stream. There had been no freshets in the river since June, and the sandy sediment had solidified, making a safe crossing for both herd and wagon. After the usual rest of a few days, the herd trailed up the Pecos with scarcely an incident worthy of mention. Early in November we halted some distance below Fort Sumner, where we were met by Mr. Loving, - who had gone on to the post in our advance, - with the report that other cattle had just been accepted, and that there was no prospect of an immediate delivery. In fact, the outlook was anything but encouraging, unless we wintered ours and had them ready for the first delivery in the spring.

The herd was accordingly turned back to Bosque Grande on the river, and we went into permanent quarters. There was a splendid winter range all along the Pecos, and we loose-herded the beeves or rode lines in holding them in the different bends of the river, some of which were natural inclosures. There was scarcely any danger of Indian molestation during the winter months, and with the exception of a few severe "northers" which swept down the valley, the cattle did comparatively well. Tents were secured at the post; corn was purchased for our saddle mules; and except during storms little or no privation was experienced during the winter in that southern climate. Wood was plentiful in the grove in which we were encamped, and a huge fireplace was built out of clay and sticks in the end of each tent, assuring us comfort against the elements.

The monotony of existence was frequently broken by the passing of trading caravans, both up and down the river. There was a fair trade with the interior of Mexico, as well as in various settlements along the Rio Grande and towns in northern New Mexico. When other means of diversion failed we had recourse to Sumner, where a sutler's bar and gambling games flourished. But the most romantic traveler to arrive or pass during the winter was Captain Burleson, late of the Confederacy. As a sportsman the captain was a gem of the first water, carrying with him, besides a herd of nearly a thousand cattle, three race-horses, several baskets of fighting chickens, and a pack of hounds. He had a large Mexican outfit in charge of his cattle, which were in bad condition on their arrival in March, he having drifted about all winter, gambling, racing his horses, and fighting his chickens. The herd represented his winnings. As we had nothing to match, all we could offer was our hospitality. Captain Burleson went into camp below us on the river and remained our neighbor until we rounded up and broke camp in the spring. He had been as far west as El Paso during the winter, and was then drifting north in the hope of finding a market for his herd. We indulged in many hunts, and I found him the true gentleman and sportsman in every sense of the word. As I recall him now, he was a lovable vagabond, and for years afterward stories were told around Fort Sumner of his wonderful nerve as a poker player.

Early in April an opportunity occurred for a delivery of cattle to the post. Ours were the only beeves in sight, those of Captain Burleson not qualifying, and a round-up was made and the herd tendered for inspection. Only eight hundred were received, which was quite a disappointment to the drovers, as at least ninety per cent of the tender filled every qualification. The motive in receiving the few soon became apparent, when a stranger appeared and offered to buy the remaining seven hundred at a ridiculously low figure. But the drovers had grown suspicious of the contractors and receiving agent, and, declining the offer, went back and bought the herd of Captain Burleson. Then, throwing the two contingents together, and boldly announcing their determination of driving to Colorado, they started the herd out past Fort Sumner with every field-glass in the post leveled on us. The military requirements of Sumner, for its own and Indian use, were well known to the drovers, and a scarcity of beef was certain to occur at that post before other cattle could be bargained for and arrive. My employers had evidently figured out the situation to a nicety, for during the forenoon of the second day out from the fort we were overtaken by the contractors. Of course they threw on the government inspector all the blame for the few cattle received, and offered to buy five or six hundred more out of the herd. But the shoe was on the other foot now, the drovers acting as independently as the proverbial hog on ice. The herd never halted, the contractors followed up, and when we went into camp that evening a trade was closed on one thousand steers at two dollars a head advance over those which were received but a few days before. The oxen were even reserved, and after delivering the beeves at Sumner we continued on northward with the remnant, nearly all of which were the Burleson cattle.

The latter part of April we arrived at the Colorado line. There we were halted by the authorities of that territory, under some act of quarantine against Texas cattle. We went into camp on the nearest water, expecting to prove that our little herd had wintered at Fort Sumner, and were therefore immune from quarantine, when buyers arrived from Trinidad, Colorado. The steers were a mixed lot, running from a yearling to big, rough four and five year olds, and when Goodnight returned from Sumner with a certificate, attested to by every officer of that post, showing that the cattle had wintered north of latitude 34, a trade was closed at once, even the oxen going in at the phenomenal figures of one hundred and fifty dollars a yoke. We delivered the herd near Trinidad, going into that town to outfit before returning. The necessary alterations were made to the wagon, mules were harnessed in, and we started home in gala spirits. In a little over thirty days my employers had more than doubled their money on the Burleson cattle and were naturally jubilant.

The proceeds of the Trinidad sale were carried in the wagon returning, though we had not as yet collected for the second delivery at Sumner. The songs of the birds mixed with our own as we traveled homeward, and the freshness of early summer on the primitive land, as it rolled away in dips and swells, made the trip a delightful outing. Fort Sumner was reached within a week, where we halted a day and then started on, having in the wagon a trifle over fifty thousand dollars in gold and silver. At Sumner two men made application to accompany us back to Texas, and as they were well armed and mounted, and numbers were an advantage, they were made welcome. Our winter camp at Bosque Grande was passed with but a single glance as we dropped down the Pecos valley at the rate of forty miles a day. Little or no travel was encountered en route, nor was there any sign of Indians until the afternoon of our reaching Horsehead Crossing. While passing Dagger Bend, four miles above the ford, Goodnight and a number of us boys were riding several hundred yards in advance of the wagon, telling stories of old sweethearts. The road made a sudden bend around some sand-hills, and the advance guard had passed out of sight of the rear, when a fresh Indian trail was cut; and as we reined in our mounts to examine the sign, we were fired on. The rifle-shots, followed by a flight of arrows, passed over us, and we took to shelter like flushed quail. I was riding a good saddle horse and bolted off on the opposite side of the road from the shooting; but in the scattering which ensued a number of mules took down the road. One of the two men picked up at the post was a German, whose mule stampeded after his mates, and who received a galling fire from the concealed Indians, the rest of us turning to the nearest shelter. With the exception of this one man, all of us circled back through the mesquite brush and reached the wagon, which had halted. Meanwhile the shooting had attracted the men behind, who charged through the sand-dunes, flanking the Indians, who immediately decamped. Security of the remuda and wagon was a first consideration, and danger of an ambush prevented our men from following up the redskins. Order was soon restored, when we proceeded, and shortly met the young German coming back up the road, who merely remarked on meeting us, "Dem Injuns shot at me."

The Indians had evidently not been expecting us. From where they turned out and where the attack was made we back-trailed them in the road for nearly a mile. They had simply heard us coming, and, supposing that the advance guard was all there was in the party, had made the attack and were in turn themselves surprised at our numbers. But the warning was henceforth heeded, and on reaching the crossing more Indian sign was detected. Several large parties had evidently crossed the river that morning, and were no doubt at that moment watching us from the surrounding hills. The cañon of Castle Mountain Gap was well adapted for an Indian ambush; and as it was only twelve miles from the ford to its mouth, we halted within a short distance of the entrance, as if encamping for the night. All the horses under saddle were picketed fully a quarter mile from the wagon, - easy marks for poor Lo, - and the remuda was allowed to wander at will, an air of perfect carelessness prevailing in the camp. From the sign which we had seen that day, there was little doubt but there were in the neighborhood of five hundred Indians in the immediate vicinity of Horsehead Crossing, and we did everything we could to create the impression that we were tender-feet. But with the falling of darkness every horse was brought in and we harnessed up and started, leaving the fire burning to identify our supposed camp. The drovers gave our darky cook instructions, in case of an attack while passing through the Gap, never to halt his team, but push ahead for the plain. About one third of us took the immediate lead of the wagon, the remuda following closely, and the remainder of the men bringing up the rear. The moon was on the wane and would not rise until nearly midnight, and for the first few miles, or until we entered the cañon, there was scarce a sound to disturb the stillness of the night. The sandy road even muffled the noise of the wagon and the tramping of horses; but once we entered that rocky cañon, the rattling of our commissary seemed to summon every Comanche and his ally to come and rob us. There was never a halt, the reverberations of our caravan seeming to reëcho through the Gap, resounding forward and back, until our progress must have been audible at Horsehead Crossing. But the expected never happens, and within an hour we reached the summit of the plain, where the country was open and clear and an attack could have been easily repelled. Four fresh mules had been harnessed in for the night, and striking a free gait, we put twenty miles of that arid stretch behind us before the moon rose. A short halt was made after midnight, for a change of teams and saddle horses, and then we continued our hurried travel until near dawn.

Some indistinct objects in our front caused us to halt. It looked like a caravan, and we hailed it without reply. Several of us dismounted and crept forward, but the only sign of life was a dull, buzzing sound which seemed to issue from an outfit of parked wagons. The report was laid before the two drovers, who advised that we await the dawn, which was then breaking, as it was possible that the caravan had been captured and robbed by Indians. A number of us circled around to the farther side, and as we again approached the wagons in the uncertain light we hailed again and received in reply a shot, which cut off the upper lobe of one of the boys' ears. We hugged the ground for some little time, until the presence of our outfit was discovered by the lone guardian of the caravan, who welcomed us. He apologized, saying that on awakening he supposed we were Indians, not having heard our previous challenge, and fired on us under the impulse of the moment. He was a well-known trader by the name of "Honey" Allen, and was then on his way to El Paso, having pulled out on the dry stretch about twenty-five miles and sent his oxen back to water. His present cargo consisted of pecans, honey, and a large number of colonies of live bees, the latter having done the buzzing on our first reconnoitre. At his destination, so he informed us, the pecans were worth fifty cents a quart, the honey a dollar a pound, and the bees one hundred dollars a hive. After repairing the damaged ear, we hurried on, finding Allen's oxen lying around the water on our arrival. I met him several years afterward in Denver, Colorado, dressed to kill, barbered, and highly perfumed. He had just sold eighteen hundred two-year-old steers and had twenty-five thousand dollars in the bank. "Son, let me tell you something," said he, as we were taking a drink together; "that Pecos country was a dangerous region to pick up an honest living in. I'm going back to God's country, - back where there ain't no Injuns."

Yet Allen died in Texas. There was a charm in the frontier that held men captive. I always promised myself to return to Virginia to spend the declining years of my life, but the fulfillment never came. I can now realize how idle was the expectation, having seen others make the attempt and fail. I recall the experience of an old cowman, laboring under a similar delusion, who, after nearly half a century in the Southwest, concluded to return to the scenes of his boyhood. He had made a substantial fortune in cattle, and had fought his way through the vicissitudes of the frontier until success crowned his efforts. A large family had in the mean time grown up around him, and under the pretense of giving his children the advantages of an older and established community he sold his holdings and moved back to his native borough. Within six months he returned to the straggling village which he had left on the plains, bringing the family with him. Shortly afterwards

I met him, and anxiously inquired the cause of his return. "Well, Reed," said he, "I can't make you understand near as well as though you had tried it yourself. You see I was a stranger in my native town. The people were all right, I reckon, but I found out that it was me who had changed. I tried to be sociable with them, but honest, Reed, I just couldn't stand it in a country where no one ever asked you to take a drink."

A week was spent in crossing the country between the Concho and Brazos rivers. Not a day passed but Indian trails were cut, all heading southward, and on a branch of the Clear Fork we nearly ran afoul of an encampment of forty teepees and lean-tos, with several hundred horses in sight. But we never varied our course a fraction, passing within a quarter mile of their camp, apparently indifferent as to whether they showed fight or allowed us to pass in peace. Our bluff had the desired effect; but we made it an object to reach Fort Griffin near midnight before camping. The Comanche and his ally were great respecters, not only of their own physical welfare, but of the Henri and Spencer rifle with which the white man killed the buffalo at the distance of twice the flight of an arrow. When every advantage was in his favor - ambush and surprise - Lo was a warrior bold; otherwise he used discretion.

CHAPTER IV

A FATAL TRIP

Before leaving Fort Sumner an agreement had been entered into between my employers and the contractors for a third herd. The delivery was set for the first week in September, and twenty-five hundred beeves were agreed upon, with a liberal leeway above and below that number in case of accident en route. Accordingly, on our return to Loving's ranch active preparations were begun for the next drive. Extra horses were purchased, several new guns of the most modern make were secured, and the gathering of cattle in Loving's brand began at once, continuing for six weeks. We combed the hills and valleys along the main Brazos, and then started west up the Clear Fork, carrying the beeves with us while gathering. The range was in prime condition, the cattle were fat and indolent, and with the exception of Indian rumors there was not a cloud in the sky.

Our last camp was made a few miles above Fort Griffin. Military protection was not expected, yet our proximity to that post was considered a security from Indian interference, as at times not over half the outfit were with the herd. We had nearly completed our numbers when, one morning early in July, the redskins struck our camp with the violence of a cyclone. The attack occurred, as usual, about half an hour before dawn, and, to add to the difficulty of the situation, the cattle stampeded with the first shot fired. I was on last guard at the time, and conscious that it was an Indian attack I unslung a new Sharp's rifle and tore away in the lead of the herd. With the rumbling of over two thousand running cattle in my ears, hearing was out of the question, while my sense of sight was rendered useless by the darkness of the morning hour. Yet I had some very distinct visions; not from the herd of frenzied beeves, thundering at my heels, but every shade and shadow in the darkness looked like a pursuing Comanche. Once I leveled my rifle at a shadow, but hesitated, when a flash from a six-shooter revealed the object to be one of our own men. I knew there were four of us with the herd when it stampeded, but if the rest were as badly bewildered as I was, it was dangerous even to approach them. But I had a king's horse under me and trusted my life to him, and he led the run until breaking dawn revealed our identity to each other.

The presence of two other men with the running herd was then discovered. We were fully five miles from camp, and giving our attention to the running cattle we soon turned the lead. The main body of the herd was strung back for a mile, but we fell on the leaders right and left, and soon had them headed back for camp. In the mean time, and with the breaking of day, our trail had been taken up by both drovers and half a dozen men, who overtook us shortly after sun-up. A count was made and we had every hoof. A determined fight had occurred over the remuda and commissary, and three of the Indians' ponies had been killed, while some thirty arrows had found lodgment in our wagon. There were no casualties in the cow outfit, and if any occurred among the redskins, the wounded or killed were carried away by their comrades before daybreak. All agreed that there were fully one hundred warriors in the attacking party, and as we slowly drifted the cattle back to camp doubt was expressed by the drovers whether it was advisable to drive the herd to its destination in midsummer with the Comanches out on their old hunting grounds.

A report of the attack was sent into Griffin that morning, and a company of cavalry took up the Indian trail, followed it until evening, and returned to the post during the night. Approaching a government station was generally looked upon as an audacious act of the redskins, but the contempt of the Comanche and his ally for citizen and soldier alike was well known on the Texas frontier and excited little comment. Several years later, in broad daylight, they raided the town of Weatherford, untied every horse from the hitching racks, and defiantly rode away with their spoil. But the prevailing spirits in our camp were not the kind to yield to an inferior race, and, true to their obligation to the contractors, they pushed forward preparations to start the herd. Within a week our numbers were completed, two extra men were secured, and on the morning of July 14, 1867, we trailed out up the Clear Fork with a few over twenty-six hundred big beeves. It was the same old route to the southwest, there was a decided lack of enthusiasm over the start, yet never a word of discouragement escaped the lips of men or employers. I have never been a superstitious man, have never had a premonition of impending danger, always rather felt an enthusiasm in my undertakings, yet that morning when the flag over Fort Griffin faded from our view, I believe there was not a man in the outfit but realized that our journey would be disputed by Indians.

Nor had we long to wait. Near the juncture of Elm Creek with the main Clear Fork we were again attacked at the usual hour in the morning. The camp was the best available, and yet not a good one for defense, as the ground was broken by shallow draws and dry washes. There were about one hundred yards of clear space on three sides of the camp, while on the exposed side, and thirty yards distant, was a slight depression of several feet. Fortunately we had a moment's warning, by several horses snorting and pawing the ground, which caused Goodnight to quietly awake the men sleeping near him, who in turn were arousing the others, when a flight of arrows buried themselves in the ground around us and the war-whoop of the Comanche sounded. Ever cautious, we had studied the situation on encamping, and had tied our horses, cavalry fashion, to a heavy rope stretched from the protected side of the wagon to a high stake driven for the purpose. With the attack the majority of the men flung themselves into their saddles and started to the rescue of the remuda, while three others and myself, detailed in anticipation, ran for the ravine and dropped into it about forty yards above the wagon. We could easily hear the exultations of the redskins just below us in the shallow gorge, and an enfilade fire was poured into them at short range. Two guns were cutting the grass from underneath the wagon, and, knowing the Indians had crept up the depression on foot, we began a rapid fire from our carbines and six-shooters, which created the impression of a dozen rifles on their flank, and they took to their heels in a headlong rout.

Once the firing ceased, we hailed our men under the wagon and returned to it. Three men were with the commissary, one of whom was a mere boy, who was wounded in the head from an arrow during the first moment of the attack, and was then raving piteously from his sufferings. The darky cook, who was one of the defenders of the wagon, was consoling the boy, so with a parting word of encouragement we swung into our saddles and rode in the direction of dim firing up the creek. The cattle were out of hearing, but the random shooting directed our course, and halting several times, we were finally piloted to the scene of activity. Our hail was met by a shout of welcome, and the next moment we dashed in among our own and reported the repulse of the Indians from the wagon. The remuda was dashing about, hither and yon, a mob of howling savages were circling about, barely within gunshot, while our men rode cautiously, checking and turning the frenzied saddle horses, and never missing a chance of judiciously throwing a little lead. There was no sign of daybreak, and, fearful for the safety of our commissary, we threw a cordon around the remuda and started for camp. Although there must have been over one hundred Indians in the general attack, we were still masters of the situation, though they followed us until the wagon was reached and the horses secured in a rope corral. A number of us again sought the protection of the ravine, and scattering above and below, we got in some telling shots at short range, when the redskins gave up the struggle and decamped. As they bore off westward on the main Clear Fork their hilarious shoutings could be distinctly heard for miles on the stillness of the morning air.

An inventory of the camp was taken at dawn. The wounded lad received the first attention. The arrowhead had buried itself below and behind the ear, but nippers were applied and the steel point was extracted. The cook washed the wound thoroughly and applied a poultice of meal, which afforded almost instant relief. While horses were being saddled to follow the cattle, I cast my eye over the camp and counted over two hundred arrows within a radius of fifty yards. Two had found lodgment in the bear-skin on which I slept. Dozens were imbedded in the running-gear and box of the wagon, while the stationary flashes from the muzzle of the cook's Creedmoor had concentrated an unusual number of arrows in and around his citadel. The darky had exercised caution and corded the six ox-yokes against the front wheel of the wagon in such a manner as to form a barrier, using the spaces between the spokes as port-holes. As he never varied his position under the wagon, the Indians had aimed at his flash, and during the rather brief fight twenty arrows had buried themselves in that barricade of ox-yokes.

The trail of the beeves was taken at dawn. This made the fifth stampede of the herd since we started, a very unfortunate thing, for stampeding easily becomes a mania with range cattle. The steers had left the bed-ground in an easterly direction, but finding that they were not pursued, the men had gradually turned them to the right, and at daybreak the herd was near Elm Creek, where it was checked. We rode the circle in a free gallop, the prairie being cut into dust and the trail as easy to follow as a highway. As the herd happened to land on our course, after the usual count the commissary was sent for, and it and the remuda were brought up. With the exception of wearing hobbles, the oxen were always given their freedom at night. This morning one of them was found in a dying condition from an arrow in his stomach. A humane shot had relieved the poor beast, and his mate trailed up to the herd, tied behind the wagon with a rope. There were several odd oxen among the cattle and the vacancy was easily filled. If I am lacking in compassion for my red brother, the lack has been heightened by his fiendish atrocities to dumb animals. I have been witness to the ruin of several wagon trains captured by Indians, have seen their ashes and irons, and even charred human remains, and was scarce moved to pity because of the completeness of the hellish work. Death is merciful and humane when compared to the hamstringing of oxen, gouging out their eyes, severing their ears, cutting deep slashes from shoulder to hip, and leaving the innocent victim to a lingering death. And when dumb animals are thus mutilated in every conceivable form of torment, as if for the amusement of the imps of the evil one, my compassion for poor Lo ceases.

It was impossible to send the wounded boy back to the settlements, so a comfortable bunk was made for him in the wagon. Late in the evening we resumed our journey, expecting to drive all night, as it was good starlight. Fair progress was made, but towards morning a rainstorm struck us, and the cattle again stampeded. In all my outdoor experience I never saw such pitchy darkness as accompanied that storm; although galloping across a prairie in a blustering rainfall, it required no strain of the imagination to see hills and mountains and forests on every hand. Fourteen men were with the herd, yet it was impossible to work in unison, and when day broke we had less than half the cattle. The lead had been maintained, but in drifting at random with the storm several contingents of beeves had cut off from the main body, supposedly from the rear. When the sun rose, men were dispatched in pairs and trios, the trail of the missing steers was picked up, and by ten o'clock every hoof was in hand or accounted for. I came in with the last contingent and found the camp in an uproar over the supposed desertion of one of the hands. Yankee Bill, a sixteen-year-old boy, and another man were left in charge of the herd when the rest of us struck out to hunt the missing cattle. An hour after sunrise the boy was seen to ride deliberately away from his charge, without cause or excuse, and had not returned. Desertion was the general supposition. Had he not been mounted on one of the firm's horses the offense might have been overlooked. But the delivery of the herd depended on the saddle stock, and two men were sent on his trail. The rain had freshened the ground, and after trailing the horse for fifteen miles the boy was overtaken while following cattle tracks towards the herd. He had simply fallen asleep in the saddle, and the horse had wandered away. Yankee Bill had made the trip to Sumner with us the fall before, and stood well with his employers, so the incident was forgiven and forgotten.

From Elm Creek to the beginning of the dry drive was one continual struggle with stampeding cattle or warding off Indians. In spite of careful handling, the herd became spoiled, and would run from the howl of a wolf or the snort of a horse. The dark hour before dawn was usually the crucial period, and until the arid belt was reached all hands were aroused at two o'clock in the morning. The start was timed so as to reach the dry drive during the full of the moon, and although it was a test of endurance for man and beast, there was relief in the desert waste - from the lurking savage - which recompensed for its severity. Three sleepless nights were borne without a murmur, and on our reaching Horsehead Crossing and watering the cattle they were turned back on the mesa and freed for the time being. The presence of Indian sign around the ford was the reason for turning loose, but at the round-up the next morning the experiment proved a costly one, as three hundred and sixty-three beeves were missing. The cattle were nervous and feverish through suffering from thirst, and had they been bedded closely, stampeding would have resulted, the foreman choosing the least of two alternatives in scattering the herd. That night we slept the sleep of exhausted men, and the next morning even awaited the sun on the cattle before throwing them together, giving the Indian thieves full ten hours the start. The stealing of cattle by the Comanches was something unusual, and there was just reason for believing that the present theft was instigated by renegade Mexicans, allies in the war of '36. Three distinct trails left the range around the Crossing, all heading south, each accompanied by fully fifty horsemen. One contingent crossed the Pecos at an Indian trail about twenty-five miles below Horsehead, another still below, while the third continued on down the left bank of the river. Yankee Bill and "Mocho" Wilson, a one-armed man, followed the latter trail, sighting them late in the evening, but keeping well in the open. When the Comanches had satisfied themselves that but two men were following them, small bands of warriors dropped out under cover of the broken country and attempted to gain the rear of our men. Wilson was an old plainsman, and once he saw the hopelessness of recovering the cattle, he and Yankee Bill began a cautious retreat. During the night and when opposite the ford where the first contingent of beeves crossed, they were waylaid, while returning, by the wily redskins. The nickering of a pony warned them of the presence of the enemy, and circling wide, they avoided an ambush, though pursued by the stealthy Comanches. Wilson was mounted on a good horse, while Yankee Bill rode a mule, and so closely were they pursued, that on reaching the first broken ground Bill turned into a coulee, while Mocho bore off on an angle, firing his six-shooter to attract the enemy after him. Yankee Bill told us afterward how he held the muzzle of his mule for an hour on dismounting, to keep the rascal from bawling after the departing horse. Wilson reached camp after midnight and reported the hopelessness of the situation; but morning came, and with it no Yankee Bill in camp. Half a dozen of us started in search of him, under the leadership of the one-armed plainsman, and an hour afterward Bill was met riding leisurely up the river. When rebuked by his comrade for not coming in under cover of darkness, he retorted, "Hell, man, I wasn't going to run my mule to death just because there were a few Comanches in the country!"

In trailing the missing cattle the day previous, I had accompanied Mr. Loving to the second Indian crossing. The country opposite the ford was broken and brushy, the trail was five or six hours old, and, fearing an ambush, the drover refused to follow them farther. With the return of Yankee Bill safe and sound to camp, all hope of recovering the beeves was abandoned, and we crossed the Pecos and turned up that river. An effort was now made to quiet the herd and bring it back to a normal condition, in order to fit it for delivery. With Indian raids, frenzy in stampeding, and an unavoidable dry drive, the cattle had gaunted like rails. But with an abundance of water and by merely grazing the remainder of the distance, it was believed that the beeves would recover their old form and be ready for inspection at the end of the month of August. Indian sign was still plentiful, but in smaller bands, and with an unceasing vigilance we wormed our way up the Pecos valley.

When within a day's ride of the post, Mr. Loving took Wilson with him and started in to Fort Sumner. The heat of August on the herd had made recovery slow, but if a two weeks' postponement could be agreed on, it was believed the beeves would qualify. The circumstances were unavoidable; the government had been lenient before; so, hopeful of accomplishing his mission, the senior member of the firm set out on his way. The two men left camp at daybreak, cautioned by Goodnight to cross the river by a well-known trail, keeping in the open, even though it was farther, as a matter of safety. They were well mounted for the trip, and no further concern was given to their welfare until the second morning, when Loving's horse came into camp, whinnying for his mates. There were blood-stains on the saddle, and the story of a man who was cautious for others and careless of himself was easily understood. Conjecture was rife. The presence of the horse admitted of several interpretations. An Indian ambush was the most probable, and a number of men were detailed to ferret out the mystery. We were then seventy miles below Sumner, and with orders to return to the herd at night six of us immediately started. The searching party was divided into squads, one on either side of the Pecos River, but no results were obtained from the first day's hunt. The herd had moved up fifteen miles during the day, and the next morning the search was resumed, the work beginning where it had ceased the evening before. Late that afternoon and from the east bank, as Goodnight and I were scanning the opposite side of the river, a lone man, almost naked, emerged from a cave across the channel and above us. Had it not been for his missing arm it is doubtful if we should have recognized him, for he seemed demented. We rode opposite and hailed, when he skulked back into his refuge; but we were satisfied that it was Wilson. The other searchers were signaled to, and finding an entrance into the river, we swam it and rode up to the cave.

A shout of welcome greeted us, and the next instant Wilson staggered out of the cavern, his eyes filled with tears.

He was in a horrible physical condition, and bewildered. We were an hour getting his story. They had been ambushed by Indians and ran for the brakes of the river, but were compelled to abandon their horses, one of which was captured, the other escaping. Loving was wounded twice, in the wrist and the side, but from the cover gained they had stood off the savages until darkness fell. During the night Loving, unable to walk, believed that he was going to die, and begged Wilson to make his escape, and if possible return to the herd. After making his employer as comfortable as possible, Wilson buried his own rifle, pistols, and knife, and started on his return to the herd. Being one-armed, he had discarded his boots and nearly all his clothing to assist him in swimming the river, which he had done any number of times, traveling by night and hiding during the day. When found in the cave, his feet were badly swollen, compelling him to travel in the river-bed to protect them from sandburs and thorns. He was taken up behind one of the boys on a horse, and we returned to camp.

Wilson firmly believed that Loving was dead, and described the scene of the fight so clearly that any one familiar with the river would have no difficulty in locating the exact spot. But the next morning as we were nearing the place we met an ambulance in the road, the driver of which reported that Loving had been brought into Sumner by a freight outfit. On receipt of this information Goodnight hurried on to the post, while the rest of us looked over the scene, recovered the buried guns of Wilson, and returned to the herd. Subsequently we learned that the next morning after Wilson left Loving had crawled to the river for a drink, and, looking upstream, saw some one a mile or more distant watering a team. By firing his pistol he attracted attention to himself and so was rescued, the Indians having decamped during the night. To his partner, Mr. Loving corroborated Wilson's story, and rejoiced to know that his comrade had also escaped. Everything that medical science could do was done by the post surgeons for the veteran cowman, but after lingering twenty-one days he died. Wilson and the wounded boy both recovered, the cattle were delivered in two installments, and early in October we started homeward, carrying the embalmed remains of the pioneer drover in a light conveyance. The trip was uneventful, the traveling was done principally by night, and on the arrival at Loving's frontier home, six hundred miles from Fort Sumner, his remains were laid at rest with Masonic honors.

Over thirty years afterward a claim was made against the government for the cattle lost at Horsehead Crossing. Wilson and I were witnesses before the commissioner sent to take evidence in the case. The hearing was held at a federal court, and after it was over, Wilson, while drinking, accused me of suspecting him of deserting his employer, - a suspicion I had, in fact, entertained at the time we discovered him at the cave. I had never breathed it to a living man, yet it was the truth, slumbering for a generation before finding expression.

CHAPTER V

SUMMER OF '68

The death of Mr. Loving ended my employment in driving cattle to Fort Sumner. The junior member of the firm was anxious to continue the trade then established, but the absence of any protection against the Indians, either state or federal, was hopeless. Texas was suffering from the internal troubles of Reconstruction, the paternal government had small concern for the welfare of a State recently in arms against the Union, and there was little or no hope for protection of life or property under existing conditions. The outfit was accordingly paid off, and I returned with George Edwards to his father's ranch. The past eighteen months had given me a strenuous schooling, but I had emerged on my feet, feeling that once more I was entitled to a place among men. The risk that had been incurred by the drovers acted like a physical stimulant, the outdoor life had hardened me like iron, and I came out of the crucible bright with the hope of youth and buoyant with health and strength.

Meanwhile there had sprung up a small trade in cattle with the North. Baxter Springs and Abilene, both in Kansas, were beginning to be mentioned as possible markets, light drives having gone to those points during the present and previous summers. The elder Edwards had been investigating the new outlet, and on the return of George and myself was rather enthusiastic over the prospects of a market. No Indian trouble had been experienced on the northern route, and although demand generally was unsatisfactory, the faith of drovers in the future was unshaken. A railroad had recently reached Abilene, stockyards had been built for the accommodation of shippers during the summer of 1861, while a firm of shrewd, far-seeing Yankees made great pretensions of having established a market and meeting-point for buyers and sellers of Texas cattle. The promoters of the scheme had a contract with the railroad, whereby they were to receive a bonus on all cattle shipped from that point, and the Texas drovers were offered every inducement to make Abilene their destination in the future. The unfriendliness of other States against Texas cattle, caused by the ravages of fever imparted by southern to domestic animals, had resulted in quarantine being enforced against all stock from the South. Matters were in an unsettled condition, and less than one per cent of the State's holdings of cattle had found an outside market during the year 1867, though ranchmen in general were hopeful.

I spent the remainder of the month of October at the Edwards ranch. We had returned in time for the fall branding, and George and I both made acceptable hands at the work. I had mastered the art of handling a rope, and while we usually corralled everything, scarcely a day passed but occasion occurred to rope wild cattle out of the brush. Anxiety to learn soon made me an expert, and before the month ended I had caught and branded for myself over one hundred mavericks. Cattle were so worthless that no one went to the trouble to brand completely; the crumbs were acceptable to me, and, since no one else cared for them and I did, the flotsam and jetsam of the range fell to my brand. Had I been ambitious, double that number could have been easily secured, but we never went off the home range in gathering calves to brand. All the hands on the Edwards ranch, darkies and Mexicans, were constantly throwing into the corrals and pointing out unclaimed cattle, while I threw and indelibly ran the figures "44" on their sides. I was partial to heifers, and when one was sighted there was no brush so thick or animal so wild that it was not "fish" to my rope. In many instances a cow of unknown brand was still followed by her two-year-old, yearling, and present calf. Under the customs of the country, any unbranded animal, one year old or over, was a maverick, and the property of any one who cared to brand the unclaimed stray. Thousands of cattle thus lived to old age, multiplied and increased, died and became food for worms, unowned.

The branding over, I soon grew impatient to be doing something. There would be no movement in cattle before the following spring, and a winter of idleness was not to my liking. Buffalo hunting had lost its charm with me, the contentious savages were jealous of any intrusion on their old hunting grounds, and, having met them on numerous occasions during the past eighteen months, I had no further desire to cultivate their acquaintance. I still owned my horse, now acclimated, and had money in my purse, and one morning I announced my intention of visiting my other comrades in Texas. Protests were made against my going, and as an incentive to have me remain, the elder Edwards offered to outfit George and me the following spring with a herd of cattle and start us to Kansas. I was anxious for employment, but assuring my host that he could count on my services, I still pleaded my anxiety to see other portions of the State and renew old acquaintances. The herd could not possibly start before the middle of April, so telling my friends that I would be on hand to help gather the cattle, I saddled my horse and took leave of the hospitable ranch.

After a week of hard riding I reached the home of a former comrade on the Colorado River below Austin. A hearty welcome awaited me, but the apparent poverty of the family made my visit rather a brief one. Continuing eastward, my next stop was in Washington County, one of the oldest settled communities in the State. The blight of Reconstruction seemed to have settled over the people like a pall, the frontier having escaped it. But having reached my destination, I was determined to make the best of it. At the house of my next comrade I felt a little more at home, he having married since his return and being naturally of a cheerful disposition. For a year previous to the surrender he and I had wrangled beef for the Confederacy and had been stanch cronies. We had also been in considerable mischief together; and his wife seemed to know me by reputation as well as I knew her husband. Before the wire edge wore off my visit I was as free with the couple as though they had been my own brother and sister. The fact was all too visible that they were struggling with poverty, though lightened by cheerfulness, and to remain long a guest would have been an imposition; accordingly I began to skirmish for something to do - anything, it mattered not what. The only work in sight was with a carpet-bag dredging company, improving the lower Brazos River, under a contract from the Reconstruction government of the State. My old crony pleaded with me to have nothing to do with the job, offering to share his last crust with me; but then he had not had all the animosities of the war roughed out of him, and I had. I would work for a Federal as soon as any one else, provided he paid me the promised wage, and, giving rein to my impulse, I made application at the dredging headquarters and was put in charge of a squad of negroes.

I was to have sixty dollars a month and board. The company operated a commissary store, a regular "pluck-me" concern, and I shortly understood the incentive in offering me such good wages. All employees were encouraged and expected to draw their pay in supplies, which were sold at treble their actual value from the commissary. I had been raised among negroes, knew how to humor and handle them, the work was easy, and I drifted along with all my faculties alert. Before long I saw that the improvement of the river was the least of the company's concern, the employment of a large number of men being the chief motive, so long as they drew their wages in supplies. True, we scattered a few lodgments of driftwood; with the aid of a flat-bottomed scow we windlassed up and cut out a number of old snags, felled trees into the river to prevent erosion of its banks, and we built a large number of wind-dams to straighten or change the channel. It seemed to be a blanket contract, - a reward to the faithful, - and permitted of any number of extras which might be charged for at any figures the contractors saw fit to make. At the end of the first month I naturally looked for my wages. Various excuses were made, but I was cordially invited to draw anything needed from the commissary.

A second month passed, during which time the only currency current was in the form of land certificates. The Commonwealth of Texas, on her admission into the Union, retained the control of her lands, over half the entire area of the State being unclaimed at the close of the civil war. The carpet-bag government, then in the saddle, was prodigal to its favorites in bonuses of land to any and all kinds of public improvement. Certificates were issued in the form of scrip calling for sections of the public domain of six hundred and forty acres each, and were current at from three to five cents an acre. The owner of one or more could locate on any of the unoccupied lands of the present State by merely surveying and recording his selection at the county seat. The scrip was bandied about, no one caring for it, and on the termination of my second month I was offered four sections for my services up to date, provided I would remain longer in the company's employ. I knew the value of land in the older States, in fact, already had my eye on some splendid valleys on the Clear Fork, and accepted the offered certificates. The idea found a firm lodgment in my mind, and I traded one of my six-shooters even for a section of scrip, and won several more in card games. I had learned to play poker in the army, - knew the rudiments of the game at least, - and before the middle of March I was the possessor of certificates calling for thirty sections of land. As the time was drawing near for my return to Palo Pinto County, I severed my connection with the dredging company and returned to the home of my old comrade. I had left my horse with him, and under the pretense of paying for feeding the animal well for the return trip, had slipped my crony a small gold piece several times during the winter. He ridiculed me over my land scrip, but I was satisfied, and after spending a day with the couple I started on my return.

Evidences of spring were to be seen on every hand. My ride northward was a race with the season, but I outrode the coming grass, the budding trees, the first flowers, and the mating birds, and reached the Edwards ranch on the last day of March. Any number of cattle had already been tendered in making up the herd, over half the saddle horses necessary were in hand or promised, and they were only awaiting my return. I had no idea what the requirements of the Kansas market were, and no one else seemed to know, but it was finally decided to drive a mixed herd of twenty-five hundred by way of experiment. The promoters of the Abilene market had flooded Texas with advertising matter during the winter, urging that only choice cattle should be driven, yet the information was of little value where local customs classified all live stock. A beef was a beef, whether he weighed eight or twelve hundred pounds, a cow was a cow when over three years old, and so on to the end of the chapter. From a purely selfish motive of wanting strong cattle for the trip, I suggested that nothing under three-year-olds should be used in making up the herd, a preference to be given matured beeves. George Edwards also favored the idea, and as our experience in trailing cattle carried some little weight, orders were given to gather nothing that had not age, flesh, and strength for the journey.

I was to have fifty dollars a month and furnish my own mount. Horses were cheap, but I wanted good ones, and after skirmishing about I secured four to my liking in return for one hundred dollars in gold. I still had some money left from my wages in driving cattle to Fort Sumner, and I began looking about for oxen in which to invest the remainder. Having little, I must be very careful and make my investment in something staple; and remembering the fine prices current in Colorado the spring before for work cattle, I offered to supply the oxen for the commissary. My proposal was accepted, and accordingly I began making inquiry for wagon stock. Finally I heard of a freight outfit in the adjoining county east, the owner of which had died the winter before, the administrator offering his effects for sale. I lost no time in seeing the oxen and hunting up their custodian, who proved to be a frontier surveyor at the county seat. There were two teams of six yoke each, fine cattle, and I had hopes of being able to buy six or eight oxen. But the surveyor insisted on selling both teams, offering to credit me on any balance if I could give him security. I had never mentioned my land scrip to any one, and wishing to see if it had any value, I produced and tendered the certificates to the surveyor. He looked them over, made a computation, and informed me that they were worth in his county about five cents an acre, or nearly one thousand dollars. He also offered to accept them as security, assuring me that he could use some of them in locating lands for settlers. But it was not my idea to sell the land scrip, and a trade was easily effected on the twenty-four oxen, yokes, and chains, I paying what money I could spare and leaving the certificates for security on the balance. As I look back over an eventful life, I remember no special time in which I felt quite as rich as the evening that I drove into the Edwards ranch with twelve yoke of oxen chained together in one team. The darkies and Mexicans gathered about, even the family, to admire the big fellows, and I remember a thrill which shivered through me as Miss Gertrude passed down the column, kindly patting each near ox as though she felt a personal interest in my possessions.

We waited for good grass before beginning the gathering. Half a dozen round-ups on the home range would be all that was necessary in completing the numbers allotted to the Edwards ranch. Three other cowmen were going to turn in a thousand head and furnish and mount a man each, there being no occasion to road-brand, as every one knew the ranch, brands which would go to make up the herd. An outfit of twelve men was considered sufficient, as it was an open prairie country and through civilized tribes between Texas and Kansas. All the darkies and Mexicans from the home ranch who could be spared were to be taken along, making it necessary to hire only three outside men. The drive was looked upon as an experiment, there being no outlay of money, even the meal and bacon which went into the commissary being supplied from the Edwards household. The country contributed the horses and cattle, and if the project paid out, well and good; if not there was small loss, as they were worth nothing at home. The 20th of April was set for starting. Three days' work on the home range and we had two thousand cattle under herd, consisting of dry or barren cows and steers three years old or over, fully half the latter being heavy beeves. We culled back and trimmed our allotment down to sixteen hundred, and when the outside contingents were thrown in we had a few over twenty-eight hundred cattle in the herd. A Mexican was placed in charge of the remuda, a darky, with three yoke of oxen, looked after the commissary, and with ten mounted men around the herd we started.

Five and six horses were allotted to the man, each one had one or two six-shooters, while half a dozen rifles of different makes were carried in the wagon. The herd moved northward by easy marches, open country being followed until we reached Red River, where we had the misfortune to lose George Edwards from sickness. He was the foreman from whom all took orders. While crossing into the Chickasaw Nation it was necessary to swim the cattle. We cut them into small bunches, and in fording and refording a whole afternoon was spent in the water. Towards evening our foreman was rendered useless from a chill, followed by fever during the night. The next morning he was worse, and as it was necessary to move the herd out to open country, Edwards took an old negro with him and went back to a ranch on the Texas side. Several days afterward the darky overtook us with the word that his master would be unable to accompany the cattle, and that I was to take the herd through to Abilene. The negro remained with us, and at the first opportunity I picked up another man. Within a week we encountered a country trail, bearing slightly northwest, over which herds had recently passed. This trace led us into another, which followed up the south side of the Washita River, and two weeks after reaching the Nation we entered what afterward became famous as the Chisholm trail. The Chickasaw was one of the civilized tribes; its members had intermarried with the whites until their identity as Indians was almost lost. They owned fine homes and farms in the Washita valley, were hospitable to strangers, and where the aboriginal blood was properly diluted the women were strikingly beautiful. In this same valley, fifteen years afterward, I saw a herd of one thousand and seven head of corn-fed cattle. The grain was delivered at feed-lots at ten cents a bushel, and the beeves had then been on full feed for nine months. There were no railroads in the country and the only outlet for the surplus corn was to feed it to cattle and drive them to some shipping-point in Kansas.

Compared with the route to Fort Sumner, the northern one was a paradise. No day passed but there was an abundance of water, while the grass simply carpeted the country. We merely soldiered along, crossing what was then one of the No-man's lands and the Cherokee Outlet, never sighting another herd until after entering Kansas. We amused ourselves like urchins out for a holiday, the country was full of all kinds of game, and our darky cook was kept busy frying venison and roasting turkeys. A calf was born on the trail, the mother of which was quite gentle, and we broke her for a milk cow, while "Bull," the youngster, became a great pet. A cow-skin was slung under the wagon for carrying wood and heavy cooking utensils, and the calf was given a berth in the hammock until he was able to follow. But when Bull became older he hung around the wagon like a dog, preferring the company of the outfit to that of his own mother. He soon learned to eat cold biscuit and corn-pone, and would hang around at meal-time, ready for the scraps. We always had to notice where the calf lay down to sleep, as he was a black rascal, and the men were liable to stumble over him while changing guards during the night. He never could be prevailed on to walk with his mother, but followed the wagon or rode in his hammock, and was always happy as a lark when the recipient of the outfit's attentions. We sometimes secured as much as two gallons of milk a day from the cow, but it was pitiful to watch her futile efforts at coaxing her offspring away from the wagon.

We passed to the west of the town of Wichita and reached our destination early in June. There I found several letters awaiting me, with instructions to dispose of the herd or to report what was the prospect of effecting a sale. We camped about five miles from Abilene, and before I could post myself on cattle values half a dozen buyers had looked the herd over. Men were in the market anxious for beef cattle with which to fill army and Indian contracts, feeders from Eastern States, shippers and speculators galore, cowmen looking for she stuff with which to start new ranches, while scarcely a day passed but inquiry was made by settlers for oxen with which to break prairie. A dozen herds had arrived ahead of us, the market had fairly opened, and, once I got the drift of current prices, I was as busy as a farmer getting ready to cut his buckwheat. Every yoke of oxen was sold within a week, one ranchman took all the cows, an army contractor took one thousand of the largest beeves, feeders from Iowa took the younger steers, and within six weeks after arriving I did not have a hoof left. In the mean time I kept an account of each sale, brands and numbers, in order to render a statement to the owners of the cattle. As fast as the money was received I sent it home by drafts, except the proceeds from the oxen, which was a private matter. I bought and sold two whole remudas of horses on speculation, clearing fifteen of the best ones and three hundred dollars on the transactions.

The facilities for handling cattle at Abilene were not completed until late in the season of '67, yet twenty-five thousand cattle found a market there that summer and fall. The drive of the present year would triple that number, and every one seemed pleased with future prospects. The town took on an air of frontier prosperity; saloons and gambling and dance halls multiplied, and every legitimate line of business flourished like a green bay tree. I made the acquaintance of every drover and was generally looked upon as an extra good salesman, the secret being in our cattle, which were choice. For instance, Northern buyers could see three dollars a head difference in three-year-old steers, but with the average Texan the age classified them all alike. My boyhood knowledge of cattle had taught me the difference, but in range dealing it was impossible to apply the principle. I made many warm friends among both buyers and drovers, bringing them together and effecting sales, and it was really a matter of regret that I had to leave before the season was over. I loved the atmosphere of dicker and traffic, had made one of the largest sales of the season with our beeves, and was leaving, firm in the conviction that I had overlooked no feature of the market of future value.

After selling the oxen we broke some of our saddle stock to harness, altered the wagon tongue for horses, and started across the country for home, taking our full remuda with us. Where I had gone up the trail with five horses, I was going back with twenty; some of the oxen I had sold at treble their original cost, while none of them failed to double my money - on credit. Taking it all in all, I had never seen such good times and made money as easily. On the back track we followed the trail, but instead of going down the Washita as we had come, we followed the Chisholm trail to the Texas boundary, crossing at what was afterward known as Red River Station. From there home was an easy matter, and after an absence of four months and five days the outfit rode into the Edwards ranch with a flourish.

CHAPTER VI

SOWING WILD OATS

The results from driving cattle north were a surprise to every one. My employers were delighted with their experiment, the general expense of handling the herd not exceeding fifty cents a head. The enterprise had netted over fifty-two thousand dollars, the saddle horses had returned in good condition, while due credit was given me in the general management. From my sale accounts I made out a statement, and once my expenses were approved it was an easy matter to apportion each owner his just dues in the season's drive. This over I was free to go my way. The only incident of moment in the final settlement was the waggish contention of one of the owners, who expressed amazement that I ever remitted any funds or returned, roguishly admitting that no one expected it. Then suddenly, pretending to have discovered the governing motive, he summoned Miss Gertrude, and embarrassed her with a profusion of thanks, averring that she alone had saved him from a loss of four hundred beeves.

The next move was to redeem my land scrip. The surveyor was anxious to buy a portion of it, but I was too rich to part with even a single section. During our conversation, however, it developed that he held his commission from the State, and when I mentioned my intention of locating land, he made application to do the surveying. The fact that I expected to make my locations in another county made no difference to a free-lance official, and accordingly we came to an agreement.

Andy Adams

The apple of my eye was a valley on the Clear Fork, above its juncture with the main Brazos, and from maps in the surveyor's office I was able to point out the locality where I expected to make my locations. He proved an obliging official and gave me all the routine details, and an appointment was made with him to report a week later at the Edwards ranch. A wagon and cook would be necessary, chain carriers and flagmen must be taken along, and I began skirmishing about for an outfit. The three hired men who had been up the trail with me were still in the country, and I engaged them and secured a cook. George Edwards loaned me a wagon and two yoke of oxen, even going along himself for company. The commissary was outfitted for a month's stay, and a day in advance of the expected arrival of the surveyor the outfit was started up the Brazos. Each of the men had one or more private horses, and taking all of mine along, we had a remuda of thirty odd saddle horses. George and I remained behind, and on the arrival of the surveyor we rode by way of Palo Pinto, the county seat, to which all unorganized territory to the west was attached for legal purposes. Our chief motive in passing the town was to see if there were any lands located near the juncture of the Clear Fork with the mother stream, and thus secure an established corner from which to begin our survey. But the records showed no land taken up around the confluence of these watercourses, making it necessary to establish a corner.

Under the old customs, handed down from the Spanish to the Texans, corners were always established from natural landmarks. The union of creeks arid rivers, mounds, lagoons, outcropping of rock, in fact anything unchangeable and established by nature, were used as a point of commencement. In the locating of Spanish land grants a century and a half previous, sand-dunes were frequently used, and when these old concessions became of value and were surveyed, some of the corners had shifted a mile or more by the action of the wind and seasons on the sand-hills. Accordingly, on overtaking our outfit we headed for the juncture of the Brazos and Clear Fork, reaching our destination the second day. The first thing was to establish a corner or commencement point. Some heavy timber grew around the confluence, so, selecting an old patriarch pin oak between the two streams, we notched the tree and ran a line to low water at the juncture of the two rivers. Other witness trees were established and notched, lines were run at angles to the banks of either stream, and a hole was dug two feet deep between the roots of the pin oak, a stake set therein, and the excavation filled with charcoal and covered. A legal corner or commencement point was thus established; but as the land that I coveted lay some distance up the Clear Fork, it was necessary first to run due south six miles and establish a corner, and thence run west the same distance and locate another one.

The thirty sections of land scrip would entitle me to a block of ground five by six miles in extent, and I concluded to locate the bulk of it on the south side of the Clear Fork. A permanent camp was now established, the actual work of locating the land requiring about ten days, when the surveyor and Edwards set out on their return. They were to touch at the county seat, record the established corners and file my locations, leaving the other boys and me behind. It was my intention to build a corral and possibly a cabin on the land, having no idea that we would remain more than a few weeks longer. Timber was plentiful, and, selecting a site well out on the prairie, we began the corral. It was no easy task; palisades were cut twelve feet long and out of durable woods, and the gate-posts were fourteen inches in diameter at the small end, requiring both yoke of oxen to draw them to the chosen site. The latter were cut two feet longer than the palisades, the extra length being inserted in the ground, giving them a stability to carry the bars with which the gateway was closed. Ten days were spent in cutting and drawing timber, some of the larger palisades being split in two so as to enable five men to load them on the wagon. The digging of the narrow trench, five feet deep, in which the palisades were set upright, was a sore trial; but the ground was sandy, and by dint of perseverance it was accomplished. Instead of a few weeks, over a month was spent on the corral, but when it was finished it would hold a thousand stampeding cattle through the stormiest night that ever blew.

After finishing the corral we hunted a week. The country was alive with game of all kinds, even an occasional buffalo, while wild and unbranded cattle were seen daily. None of the men seemed anxious to leave the valley, but the commissary had to be replenished, so two of us made the trip to Belknap with a pack horse, returning the next day with meal, sugar, and coffee. A cabin was begun and completed in ten days, a crude but stable affair, with clapboard roof, clay floor, and ample fireplace. It was now late in September, and as the usual branding season was at hand, cow-hunting outfits might be expected to pass down the valley. The advantage of corrals would naturally make my place headquarters for cowmen, and we accordingly settled down until the branding season was over. But the abundance of mavericks and wild cattle was so tempting that we had three hundred under herd when the first cow-hunting outfits arrived. At one lake on what is now known as South Prairie, in a single moonlight night, we roped and tied down forty head, the next morning finding thirty of them unbranded and therefore unowned. All tame cattle would naturally water in the daytime, and anything coming in at night fell a victim to our ropes. A wooden toggle was fastened with rawhide to its neck, so it would trail between its forelegs, to prevent running, when the wild maverick was freed and allowed to enter the herd. After a week or ten days, if an animal showed any disposition to quiet down, it was again thrown, branded, and the toggle removed. We corralled the little herd every night, adding to it daily, scouting far and wide for unowned or wild cattle. But when other outfits came up or down the valley of the Clear Fork we joined forces with them, tendering our corrals for branding purposes, our rake-off being the mavericks and eligible strays. Many a fine quarter of beef was left at our cabin by passing ranchmen, and when the gathering ended we had a few over five hundred cattle for our time and trouble.

Fine weather favored us and we held the mavericks under herd until late in December. The wild ones gradually became gentle, and with constant handling these wild animals were located until they would come in of their own accord for the privilege of sleeping in a corral. But when winter approached the herd was turned free, that the cattle might protect themselves from storms, and we gathered our few effects together and started for the settlements. It was with reluctance that I left that primitive valley. Somehow or other, primal conditions possessed a charm for me which, coupled with an innate love of the land and the animals that inhabit it, seemed to influence and outline my future course of life. The pride of possession was mine; with my own hands and abilities had I earned the land, while the overflow from a thousand hills stocked my new ranch. I was now the owner of lands and cattle; my father in his palmiest days never dreamed of such possessions as were mine, while youth and opportunity encouraged me to greater exertions.

We reached the Edwards ranch a few days before Christmas. The boys were settled with and returned to their homes, and I was once more adrift. Forty odd calves had been branded as the increase of my mavericking of the year before, and, still basking in the smile of fortune, I found a letter awaiting me from Major Seth Mabry of Austin, anxious to engage my services as a trail foreman for the coming summer. I had met Major Seth the spring before at Abilene, and was instrumental in finding him a buyer for his herd, and otherwise we became fast friends. There were no outstanding obligations to my former employers, so when a protest was finally raised against my going, I had the satisfaction of vouching for George Edwards, to the manner born, and a better range cowman than I was. The same group of ranchmen expected to drive another herd the coming spring, and I made it a point to see each one personally, urging that nothing but choice cattle should be sent up the trail. My long acquaintance with the junior Edwards enabled me to speak emphatically and to the point, and I lectured him thoroughly as to the requirements of the Abilene market.

Andy Adams

I notified Major Mabry that I would be on hand within a month. The holiday season soon passed, and leaving my horses at the Edwards ranch, I saddled the most worthless one and started south. The trip was uneventful, except that I traded horses twice, reaching my destination within a week, having seen no country en route that could compare with the valley of the Clear Fork. The capital city was a straggling village on the banks of the Colorado River, inert through political usurpation, yet the home of many fine people. Quite a number of cowmen resided there, owning ranches in outlying and adjoining counties, among them being my acquaintance of the year before and present employer. It was too early by nearly a month to begin active operations, and I contented myself about town, making the acquaintance of other cowmen and their foremen who expected to drive that year. New Orleans had previously been the only outlet for beef cattle in southern Texas, and even in the spring of '69 very few had any confidence of a market in the north. Major Mabry, however, was going to drive two herds to Abilene, one of beeves and the other of younger steers, dry cows, and thrifty two-year-old heifers, and I was to have charge of the heavy cattle. Both herds would be put up in Llano County, it being the intention to start with the grass. Mules were to be worked to the wagons, oxen being considered too slow, while both outfits were to be mounted seven horses to the man.

During my stay at Austin I frequently made inquiry for land scrip. Nearly all the merchants had more or less, the current prices being about five cents an acre. There was a clear distinction, however, in case one was a buyer or seller, the former being shown every attention. I allowed the impression to circulate that I would buy, which brought me numerous offers, and before leaving the town I secured twenty sections for five hundred dollars. I needed just that amount to cover a four-mile bend of the Clear Fork on the west end of my new ranch, - a possession which gave me ten miles of that virgin valley. My employer congratulated me on my investment, and assured me that if the people ever overthrew the Reconstruction usurpers the public domain would no longer be bartered away for chips and whetstones. I was too busy to take much interest in the political situation, and, so long as I was prosperous and employed, gave little heed to politics.

Major Mabry owned a ranch and extensive cattle interests northwest in Llano County. As we expected to start the herds as early as possible, the latter part of February found us at the ranch actively engaged in arranging for the summer's work. There were horses to buy, wagons to outfit, and hands to secure, and a busy fortnight was spent in getting ready for the drive. The spring before I had started out in debt; now, on permission being given me, I bought ten horses for my own use and invested the balance of my money in four yoke of oxen. Had I remained in Palo Pinto County the chances were that I might have enlarged my holdings in the coming drive, as in order to have me remain several offered to sell me cattle on credit. But so long as I was enlarging my experience I was content, while the wages offered me were double what I received the summer before.

We went into camp and began rounding up near the middle of March. All classes of cattle were first gathered into one herd, after which the beeves were cut separate and taken charge of by my outfit. We gathered a few over fifteen hundred of the latter, all prairie-raised cattle, four years old or over, and in the single ranch brand of my employer. Major Seth had also contracted for one thousand other beeves, and it became our duty to receive them. These outside contingents would have to be road-branded before starting, as they were in a dozen or more brands, the work being done in a chute built for that purpose. My employer and I fully agreed on the quality of cattle to be received, and when possible we both passed on each tender of beeves before accepting them. The two herds were being held separate, and a friendly rivalry existed between the outfits as to which herd would be ready to start first. It only required a few days extra to receive and road-brand the outside cattle, when all were ready to start. As Major Seth knew the most practical route, in deference to his years and experience I insisted that he should take the lead until after

Red River was crossed. I had been urging the Chisholm trail in preference to more eastern ones, and with the compromise that I should take the lead after passing Fort Worth, the two herds started on the last day of March.

There was no particular trail to follow. The country was all open, and the grass was coming rapidly, while the horses and cattle were shedding their winter coats with the change of the season. Fine weather favored us, no rains at night and few storms, and within two weeks we passed Fort Worth, after which I took the lead. I remember that at the latter point I wrote a letter to the elder Edwards, inclosing my land scrip, and asking him to send a man out to my new ranch occasionally to see that the improvements were not destroyed. Several herds had already passed the fort, their destination being the same as ours, and from thence onward we had the advantage of following a trail. As we neared Red River, nearly all the herds bore off to the eastward, but we held our course, crossing into the Chickasaw Nation at the regular Chisholm ford. A few beggarly Indians, renegades from the Kiowas and Comanches on the west, annoyed us for the first week, but were easily appeased with a lame or stray beef. The two herds held rather close together as a matter of mutual protection, as in some of the encampments were fully fifty lodges with possibly as many able-bodied warriors. But after crossing the Washita River no further trouble was encountered from the natives, and we swept northward at the steady pace of an advancing army. Other herds were seen in our rear and front, and as we neared the Kansas line several long columns of cattle were sighted coming in over the safer eastern routes.

The last lap of the drive was reached. A fortnight later we went into camp within twelve miles of Abilene, having been on the trail two months and eleven days. The same week we moved north of the railroad, finding ample range within seven miles of town. Herds were coming in rapidly, and it was important to secure good grazing grounds for our cattle. Buyers were arriving from every territory in the Northwest, including California, while the usual contingent of Eastern dealers, shippers, and market-scalpers was on hand. It could hardly be said that prices had yet opened, though several contracted herds had already been delivered, while every purchaser was bearing the market and prophesying a drive of a quarter million cattle. The drovers, on the other hand, were combating every report in circulation, even offering to wager that the arrivals of stock for the entire summer would not exceed one hundred thousand head. Cowmen reported en route with ten thousand beeves came in with one fifth the number, and sellers held the whip hand, the market actually opening at better figures than the summer before. Once prices were established, I was in the thick of the fight, selling my oxen the first week to a freighter, constantly on the skirmish for a buyer, and never failing to recognize one with whom I had done business the summer before. In case Major Mabry had nothing to suit, the herd in charge of George Edwards was always shown, and I easily effected two sales, aggregating fifteen hundred head, from the latter cattle, with customers of the year previous.

But my zeal for bartering in cattle came to a sudden end near the close of June. A conservative estimate of the arrivals then in sight or known to be en route for Abilene was placed at one hundred and fifty thousand cattle. Yet instead of any weakening in prices, they seemed to strengthen with the influx of buyers from the corn regions, as the prospects of the season assured a bountiful new crop. Where States had quarantined against Texas cattle the law was easily circumvented by a statement that the cattle were immune from having wintered in the north, which satisfied the statutes - as there was no doubt but they had wintered somewhere. Steer cattle of acceptable age and smoothness of build were in demand by feeders; all classes in fact felt a stimulus. My beeves were sold for delivery north of Cheyenne, Wyoming, the buyers, who were ranchmen as well as army contractors, taking the herd complete, including the remuda and wagon. Under the terms, the cattle were to start immediately and be grazed through. I was given until the middle of September to reach my destination, and at once moved out on a northwest course. On reaching the Republican River, we followed it to the Colorado line, and then tacked north for Cheyenne. Reporting our progress to the buyers, we were met and directed to pass to the eastward of that village, where we halted a week, and seven hundred of the fattest beeves were cut out for delivery at Fort Russell. By various excuses we were detained until frost fell before we reached the ranch, and a second and a third contingent of beeves were cut out for other deliveries, making it nearly the middle of October before I was finally relieved.

With the exception of myself, a new outfit of men had been secured at Abilene. Some of them were retained at the ranch of the contractors, the remainder being discharged, all of us returning to Cheyenne together, whence we scattered to the four winds. I spent a week in Denver, meeting Charlie Good-night, who had again fought his way up the Pecos route and delivered his cattle to the contractors at Fort Logan. Continuing homeward, I took the train for Abilene, hesitating whether to stop there or visit my brother in Missouri before returning to Texas. I had twelve hundred dollars with me, as the proceeds of my wages, horses, and oxen, and, feeling rather affluent, I decided to stop over a day at the new trail town. I knew the market was virtually over, and what evil influence ever suggested my stopping at Abilene is unexplainable. But I did stop, and found things just as I expected, - everybody sold out and gone home. A few trail foremen were still hanging around the town under the pretense of attending to unsettled business, and these welcomed me with a fraternal greeting. Two of them who had served in the Confederate army came to me and frankly admitted that they were broke, and begged me to help them out of town by redeeming their horses and saddles. Feed bills had accumulated and hotel accounts were unpaid; the appeals of the rascals would have moved a stone to pity.

The upshot of the whole matter was that I bought a span of mules and wagon and invited seven of the boys to accompany me overland to Texas. My friends insisted that we could sell the outfit in the lower country for more than cost, but before I got out of town my philanthropic venture had absorbed over half my savings. As long as I had money the purse seemed a public one, and all the boys borrowed just as freely as if they expected to repay it. I am sure they felt grateful, and had I been one of the needy no doubt any of my friends would have shared his purse with me.

It was a delightful trip across the Indian Territory, and we reached Sherman, Texas, just before the holidays. Every one had become tired of the wagon, and I was fortunate enough to sell it without loss. Those who had saddle horses excused themselves and hurried home for the Christmas festivities, leaving a quartette of us behind. But before the remainder of us proceeded to our destinations two of the boys discovered a splendid opening for a monte game, in which we could easily recoup all our expenses for the trip. I was the only dissenter to the programme, not even knowing the game; but under the pressure which was brought to bear I finally yielded, and became banker for my friends. The results are easily told. The second night there was heavy play, and before ten o'clock the monte bank closed for want of funds, it having been tapped for its last dollar. The next morning I took stage for Dallas, where I arrived with less than twenty dollars, and spent the most miserable Christmas day of my life. I had written George Edwards from Denver that I expected to go to Missouri, and asked him to take my horses and go out to the little ranch and brand my calves. There was no occasion now to contradict my advice of that letter, neither would I go near the Edwards ranch, yet I hungered for that land scrip and roundly cursed myself for being a fool. It would be two months and a half before spring work opened, and what to do in the mean time was the one absorbing question. My needs were too urgent to allow me to remain idle long, and, drifting south, working when work was to be had, at last I reached the home of my soldier crony in Washington County, walking and riding in country wagons the last hundred miles of the distance. No experience in my life ever humiliated me as that one did, yet I have laughed about it since. I may have previously heard of riches taking wings, but in this instance, now mellowed by time, no injustice will be done by simply recording it as the parting of a fool and his money.

CHAPTER VII

"THE ANGEL"

The winds of adversity were tempered by the welcome extended me by my old comrade and his wife. There was no concealment as to my financial condition, but when I explained the causes my former crony laughed at me until the tears stood in his eyes. Nor did I protest, because I so richly deserved it. Fortunately the circumstances of my friends had bettered since my previous visit, and I was accordingly relieved from any feeling of intrusion. In two short years the wheel had gone round, and I was walking heavily on my uppers and continually felt like a pauper or poor relation. To make matters more embarrassing, I could appeal to no one, and, fortified by pride from birth, I ground my teeth over resolutions that will last me till death. Any one of half a dozen friends, had they known my true condition, would have gladly come to my aid, but circumstances prevented me from making any appeal. To my brother in Missouri I had previously written of my affluence; as for friends in Palo Pinto County, - well, for the very best of reasons my condition would remain a sealed book in that quarter; and to appeal to Major Mabry might arouse his suspicions. I had handled a great deal of money for him, accounting for every cent, but had he known of my inability to take care of my own frugal earnings it might have aroused his distrust. I was sure of a position with him again as trail foreman, and not for the world would I have had him know that I could be such a fool as to squander my savings thoughtlessly.

What little correspondence I conducted that winter was by roundabout methods. I occasionally wrote my brother that I was wallowing in wealth, always inclosing a letter to Gertrude Edwards with instructions to remail, conveying the idea to her family that I was spending the winter with relatives in Missouri. As yet there was no tacit understanding between Miss Gertrude and me, but I conveyed that impression to my brother, and as I knew he had run away with his wife, I had confidence he would do my bidding. In writing my employer I reported myself as busy dealing in land scrip, and begged him not to insist on my appearance until it was absolutely necessary. He replied that I might have until the 15th of March in which to report at Austin, as my herd had been contracted for north in Williamson County. Major Mabry expected to drive three herds that spring, the one already mentioned and two from Llano County, where he had recently acquired another ranch with an extensive stock of cattle. It therefore behooved me to keep my reputation unsullied, a rather difficult thing to do when our escapade at Sherman was known to three other trail foremen. They might look upon it as a good joke, while to me it was a serious matter.

Had there been anything to do in Washington County, it was my intention to go to work. The dredging company had departed for newer fields, there was no other work in sight, and I was compelled to fold my hands and bide my time. My crony and I blotted out the days by hunting deer and turkeys, using hounds for the former and shooting the animals at game crossings. By using a turkey-call we could entice the gobblers within rifle-shot, and in several instances we were able to locate their roosts. The wild turkey of Texas was a wary bird, and although I have seen flocks of hundreds, it takes a crafty hunter to bag one. I have always loved a gun and been fond of hunting, yet the time hung heavy on my hands, and I counted the days like a prisoner until I could go to work. But my sentence finally expired, and preparations were made for my start to Austin. My friends offered their best wishes, - about all they had, - and my old comrade went so far as to take me one day on horseback to where he had an acquaintance living.

There we stayed over night, which was more than half way to my destination, and the next morning we parted, he to his home with the horses, while I traveled on foot or trusted to country wagons. I arrived in Austin on the appointed day, with less than five dollars in my pocket, and registered at the best hotel in the capital. I needed a saddle, having sold mine in Wyoming the fall before, and at once reported to my employer. Fortunately my arrival was being awaited to start a remuda and wagon to Williamson County, and when I assured Major Mabry that all I lacked was a saddle, he gave me an order on a local dealer, and we started that same evening.

At last I was saved. With the opening of work my troubles lifted like a night fog before the rising sun. Even the first view of the remuda revived my spirits, as I had been allotted one hundred fine cow-horses. They had been brought up during the winter, had run in a good pasture for some time, and with the opening of spring were in fine condition. Many trail men were short-sighted in regard to mounting their outfits, and although we had our differences, I want to say that Major Mabry and his later associates never expected a man to render an honest day's work unless he was properly supplied with horses. My allowance for the spring of 1870 was again seven horses to the man, with two extra for the foreman, which at that early day in trailing cattle was considered the maximum where Kansas was the destination. Many drovers allowed only five horses to the man, but their men were frequently seen walking with the herd, their mounts mingling with the cattle, unable to carry their riders longer.

The receiving of the herd in Williamson County was an easy matter. Four prominent ranchmen were to supply the beeves to the number of three thousand. Nearly every hoof was in the straight ranch brand of the sellers, only some two hundred being mixed brands and requiring the usual road-branding. In spite of every effort to hold the herd down to the contracted number, we received one hundred and fifty extra; but then they were cattle that no justifiable excuse could be offered in refusing. The last beeves were received on the 22d of the month, and after cutting separate all cattle of outside brands, they were sent to the chute to receive the road-mark. Major Mabry was present, and a controversy arose between the sellers and himself over our refusal to road-brand, or at least vent the ranch brands, on the great bulk of the herd. Too many brands on an animal was an objection to the shippers and feeders of the North, and we were anxious to cater to their wishes as far as possible. The sellers protested against the cattle leaving their range without some mark to indicate their change of ownership. The country was all open; in case of a stampede and loss of cattle within a few hundred miles they were certain to drift back to their home range, with nothing to distinguish them from their brothers of the same age. Flesh marks are not a good title by which to identify one's property, where those possessions consist of range cattle, and the law recognized the holding brand as the hall-mark of ownership. But a compromise was finally agreed upon, whereby we were to run the beeves through the chute and cut the brush from their tails. In a four or five year old animal this tally-mark would hold for a year, and in no wise work any hardship to the animal in warding off insect life. In case of any loss on the trail my employer agreed to pay one dollar a head for regathering any stragglers that returned within a year. The proposition was a fair one, the ranchmen yielded, and we ran the whole herd through the chute, cutting the brush within a few inches of the end of the tail-bone. By tightly wrapping the brush once around the blade of a sharp knife, it was quick work to thus vent a chuteful of cattle, both the road-branding and tally-marking being done in two days.

The herd started on the morning of the 25th. I had a good outfit of men, only four of whom were with me the year before. The spring could not be considered an early one, and therefore we traveled slow for the first few weeks, meeting with two bad runs, three days apart, but without the loss of a hoof. These panics among the cattle were unexplainable, as they were always gorged with grass and water at bedding time, the weather was favorable, no unseemly noises were heard by the men on guard, and both runs occurred within two hours of daybreak. There was a half-breed Mexican in the outfit, a very quiet man, and when the causes of the stampedes were being discussed around the camp-fire, I noticed that he shrugged his shoulders in derision of the reasons advanced. The half-breed was my horse wrangler, old in years and experience, and the idea struck me to sound him as to his version of the existing trouble among the cattle. He was inclined to be distant, but I approached him cautiously, complimented him on his handling of the remuda, rode with him several hours, and adroitly drew out his opinion of what caused our two stampedes. As he had never worked with the herd, his first question was, did we receive any blind cattle or had any gone blind since we started? He then informed me that the old Spanish rancheros would never leave a sightless animal in a corral with sound ones during the night for fear of a stampede. He cautioned me to look the herd over carefully, and if there was a blind animal found to cut it out or the trouble would he repeated in spite of all precaution. I rode back and met the herd, accosting every swing man on one side with the inquiry if any blind animal had been seen, without results until the drag end of the cattle was reached. Two men were at the rear, and when approached with the question, both admitted noticing, for the past week, a beef which acted as if he might be crazy. I had them point out the steer, and before I had watched him ten minutes was satisfied that he was stone blind. He was a fine, big fellow, in splendid flesh, but it was impossible to keep him in the column; he was always straggling out and constantly shying from imaginary objects. I had the steer roped for three or four nights and tied to a tree, and as the stampeding ceased we cut him out every evening when bedding down the herd, and allowed him to sleep alone. The poor fellow followed us, never venturing to leave either day or night, but finally fell into a deep ravine and broke his neck. His affliction had befallen him on the trail, affecting his nervous system to such an extent that he would jump from imaginary objects and thus stampede his brethren. I remember it occurred to me, then, how little I knew about cattle, and that my wrangler and I ought to exchange places. Since that day I have always been an attentive listener to the humblest of my fellowmen when interpreting the secrets of animal life.

Another incident occurred on this trip which showed the observation and insight of my half-breed wrangler. We were passing through some cross-timbers one morning in northern Texas, the remuda and wagon far in the lead. We were holding the herd as compactly as possible to prevent any straying of cattle, when our saddle horses were noticed abandoned in thick timber. It was impossible to leave the herd at the time, but on reaching the nearest opening, about two miles ahead, I turned and galloped back for fear of losing horses. I counted the remuda and found them all there, but the wrangler was missing. Thoughts of desertion flashed through my mind, the situation was unexplainable, and after calling, shooting, and circling around for over an hour, I took the remuda in hand and started after the herd, mentally preparing a lecture in case my wrangler returned. While nooning that day some six or seven miles distant, the half-breed jauntily rode into camp, leading a fine horse, saddled and bridled, with a man's coat tied to the cantle-strings. He explained to us that he had noticed the trail of a horse crossing our course at right angles. The freshness of the sign attracted his attention, and trailing it a short distance in the dewy morning he had noticed that something attached to the animal was trailing. A closer examination was made, and he decided that it was a bridle rein and not a rope that was attached to the wandering horse. From the freshness of the trail, he felt positive that he would overtake the animal shortly, but after finding him some difficulty was encountered before the horse would allow himself to be caught. He apologized for his neglect of duty, considering the incident as nothing unusual, and I had not the heart even to scold him. There were letters in the pocket of the coat, from which the owner was identified, and on arriving at Abilene the pleasure was mine of returning the horse and accoutrements and receiving a twenty-dollar gold piece for my wrangler. A stampede of trail cattle had occurred some forty miles to the northwest but a few nights before our finding the horse, during which the herd ran into some timber, and a low-hanging limb unhorsed the foreman, the animal escaping until captured by my man.

On approaching Fort Worth, still traveling slowly on account of the lateness of the spring, I decided to pay a flying visit to Palo Pinto County. It was fully eighty miles from the Fort across to the Edwards ranch, and appointing one of my old men as segundo, I saddled my best horse and set out an hour before sunset. I had made the same ride four years previously on coming to the country, a cool night favored my mount, and at daybreak I struck the Brazos River within two miles of the ranch. An eventful day followed; I reeled off innocent white-faced lies by the yard, in explaining the delightful winter I had spent with my brother in Missouri. Fortunately the elder Edwards was not driving any cattle that year, and George was absent buying oxen for a Fort Griffin freighter. Good reports of my new ranch awaited me, my cattle were increasing, and the smile of prosperity again shed its benediction over me. No one had located any lands near my little ranch, and the coveted addition on the west was still vacant and unoccupied. The silent monitor within my breast was my only accuser, but as I rode away from the Edwards ranch in the shade of evening, even it was silenced, for I held the promise of a splendid girl to become my wife. A second sleepless night passed like a pleasant dream, and early the next morning, firmly anchored in resolutions that no vagabond friends could ever shake, I overtook my herd.

After crossing Red River, the sweep across the Indian country was but a repetition of other years, with its varying monotony. Once we were waterbound for three days, severe drifts from storms at night were experienced, delaying our progress, and we did not reach Abilene until June 15. We were aware, however, of an increased drive of cattle to the north; evidences were to be seen on every hand; owners were hanging around the different fords and junctions of trails, inquiring if herds in such and such brands had been seen or spoken. While we were crossing the Nations, men were daily met hunting for lost horses or inquiring for stampeded cattle, while the regular trails were being cut into established thoroughfares from increasing use. Neither of the other Mabry herds had reached their destination on our arrival, though Major Seth put in an appearance within a week and reported the other two about one hundred miles to the rear. Cattle were arriving by the thousands, buyers from the north, east, and west were congregating, and the prospect of good prices was flattering. I was fortunate in securing my old camp-ground north of the town; a dry season had set in nearly a month before, maturing the grass, and our cattle took on flesh rapidly. Buyers looked them over daily, our prices being firm. Wintered cattle were up in the pictures, a rate war was on between all railroad lines east of the Mississippi River, cutting to the bone to secure the Western live-stock traffic. Three-year-old steers bought the fall before at twenty dollars and wintered on the Kansas prairies were netting their owners as high as sixty dollars on the Chicago market. The man with good cattle for sale could afford to be firm.

At this juncture a regrettable incident occurred, which, however, proved a boon to me. Some busybody went to the trouble of telling Major Mabry about my return to Abilene the fall before and my subsequent escapade in Texas, embellishing the details and even intimating that I had squandered funds not my own. I was thirty years old and as touchy as gunpowder, and felt the injustice of the charge like a knife-blade in my heart. There was nothing to do but ask for my release, place the facts in the hands of my employer, and court a thorough investigation. I had always entertained the highest regard for Major Mabry, and before the season ended I was fully vindicated and we were once more fast friends.

In the mean time I was not idle. By the first of July it was known that three hundred thousand cattle would be the minimum of the summer's drive to Abilene. My extensive acquaintance among buyers made my services of value to new drovers. A commission of twenty-five cents a head was offered me for effecting sales. The first week after severing my connection with Major Seth my earnings from a single trade amounted to seven hundred and fifty dollars. Thenceforth I was launched on a business of my own. Fortune smiled on me, acquaintances nicknamed me "The Angel," and instead of my foolishness reflecting on me, it made me a host of friends. Cowmen insisted on my selling their cattle, shippers consulted me, and I was constantly in demand with buyers, who wished my opinion on young steers before closing trades. I was chosen referee in a dozen disputes in classifying cattle, my decisions always giving satisfaction. Frequently, on an order, I turned buyer. Northern men seemed timid in relying on their own judgment of Texas cattle. Often, after a trade was made, the buyer paid me the regular commission for cutting and receiving, not willing to risk his judgment on range cattle. During the second week in August I sold five thousand head and bought fifteen hundred. Every man who had purchased cattle the year before had made money and was back in the market for more. Prices were easily advanced as the season wore on, whole herds were taken by three or four farmers from the corn regions, and the year closed with a flourish. In the space of four months I was instrumental in selling, buying, cutting, or receiving a few over thirty thousand head, on all of which I received a commission.

I established a camp of my own during the latter part of August. In order to avoid night-herding his cattle the summer before, some one had built a corral about ten miles northeast of Abilene. It was a temporary affair, the abrupt, bluff banks of a creek making a perfect horseshoe, requiring only four hundred feet of fence across the neck to inclose a corral of fully eight acres. The inclosure was not in use, so I hired three men and took possession of it for the time being. I had noticed in previous years that when a drover had sold all his herd but a remnant, he usually sacrificed his culls in order to reduce the expense of an outfit and return home. I had an idea that there was money in buying up these remnants and doing a small jobbing business. Frequently I had as many as seven hundred cull cattle on hand. Besides, I was constantly buying and selling whole remudas of saddle horses. So when a drover had sold all but a few hundred cattle he would come to me, and I would afford him the relief he wanted. Cripples and sore-footed animals were usually thrown in for good measure, or accepted at the price of their hides. Some buyers demanded quality and some cared only for numbers. I remember effecting a sale of one hundred culls to a settler, southeast on the Smoky River, at seven dollars a head. The terms were that I was to cut out the cattle, and as many were cripples and cost me little or nothing, they afforded a nice profit besides cleaning up my herd. When selling my own, I always priced a choice of my cattle at a reasonable figure, or offered to cull out the same number at half the price. By this method my herd was kept trimmed from both ends and the happy medium preserved.

I love to think of those good old days. Without either foresight or effort I made all kinds of money during the summer of 1870. Our best patrons that fall were small ranchmen from Kansas and Nebraska, every one of whom had coined money on their purchases of the summer before. One hundred per cent for wintering a steer and carrying him less than a year had brought every cattleman and his cousin back to Abilene to duplicate their former ventures. The little ranchman who bought five hundred steers in the fall of 1869 was in the market the present summer for a thousand head. Demand always seemed to meet supply a little over half-way. The market closed firm, with every hoof taken and at prices that were entirely satisfactory to drovers. It would seem an impossibility were I to admit my profits for that year, yet at the close of the season I started overland to Texas with fifty choice saddle horses and a snug bank account. Surely those were the golden days of the old West.

My last act before leaving Abilene that fall was to meet my enemy and force a personal settlement. Major Mabry washed his hands by firmly refusing to name my accuser, but from other sources I traced my defamer to a liveryman of the town. The fall before, on four horses and saddles, I paid a lien, in the form of a feed bill, of one hundred and twenty dollars for my stranded friends. The following day the same man presented me another bill for nearly an equal amount, claiming it had been assigned to him in a settlement with other parties. I investigated the matter, found it to be a disputed gambling account, and refused payment. An attempt was made, only for a moment, to hold the horses, resulting in my incurring the stableman's displeasure. The outcome was that on our return the next spring our patronage went to another *bran*, and the story, born in malice and falsehood, was started between employer and employee. I had made arrangements to return to Texas with the last one of Major Mabry's outfits, and the wagon and remuda had already started, when I located my traducer in a well-known saloon. I invited him to a seat at a table, determined to bring matters to an issue. He reluctantly complied, when I branded him with every vile epithet that my tongue could command, concluding by arraigning him as a coward. I was hungering for him to show some resistance, expecting to kill him, and when he refused to notice my insults, I called the barkeeper and asked for two glasses of whiskey and a pair of six-shooters. Not a word passed between us until the bartender brought the drinks and guns on a tray. "Now take your choice," said I. He replied, "I believe a little whiskey will do me good."

CHAPTER VIII

THE "LAZY L"

The homeward trip was a picnic. Counting mine, we had one hundred and fifty saddle horses. All surplus men in the employ of Major Mabry had been previously sent home until there remained at the close of the season only the drover, seven men, and myself. We averaged forty miles a day returning, sweeping down the plains like a north wind until Red River Station was reached. There our ways parted, and cutting separate my horses, we bade each other farewell, the main outfit heading for Fort Worth, while I bore to the westward for Palo Pinto. Major Seth was anxious to secure my services for another year, but I made no definite promises. We parted the best of friends. There were scattering ranches on my route, but driving fifty loose horses made traveling slow, and it was nearly a week before I reached the Edwards ranch.

The branding season was nearly over. After a few days' rest, an outfit of men was secured, and we started for my little ranch on the Clear Fork. Word was sent to the county seat, appointing a date with the surveyor, and on arriving at the new ranch I found that the corrals had been in active use by branding parties. We were soon in the thick of the fray, easily holding our own, branding every maverick on the range as well as catching wild cattle. My weakness for a good horse was the secret of much of my success in ranching during the early days, for with a remuda of seventy picked horses it was impossible for any unowned animal to escape us. Our drag-net scoured

Andy Adams

the hills and valleys, and before the arrival of the surveyor we had run the "44" on over five hundred calves, mavericks, and wild cattle. Different outfits came down the Brazos and passed up the Clear Fork, always using my corrals when working in the latter valley. We usually joined in with these cow-hunting parties, extending to them every possible courtesy, and in return many a thrifty yearling was added to my brand. Except some wild-cattle hunting which we had in view, every hoof was branded up by the time the surveyor arrived at the ranch.

The locating of twenty sections of land was an easy matter. We had established corners from which to work, and commencing on the west end of my original location, we ran off an area of country, four miles west by five south. New outside corners were established with buried charcoal and stakes, while the inner ones were indicated by half-buried rock, nothing divisional being done except to locate the land in sections. It was a beautiful tract, embracing a large bend of the Clear Fork, heavily timbered in several places, the soil being of a rich, sandy loam and covered with grass. I was proud of my landed interest, though small compared to modern ranches; and after the surveying ended, we spent a few weeks hunting out several rendezvous of wild cattle before returning to the Edwards ranch.

I married during the holidays. The new ranch was abandoned during the winter months, as the cattle readily cared for themselves, requiring no attention. I now had a good working capital, and having established myself by marriage into a respectable family of the country, I found several avenues open before me. Among the different openings for attractive investment was a brand of cattle belonging to an estate south in Comanche County. If the cattle were as good as represented they were certainly a bargain, as the brand was offered straight through at four dollars and a half a head. It was represented that nothing had been sold from the brand in a number of years, the estate was insolvent, and the trustee was anxious to sell the entire stock outright. I was impressed with the opportunity, and early in the winter George Edwards and I rode down to look the situation over. By riding around the range a few days we were able to get a good idea of the stock, and on inquiry among neighbors and men familiar with the brand, I was satisfied that the cattle were a bargain. A lawyer at the county seat was the trustee, and on opening negotiations with him it was readily to be seen that all he knew about the stock was that shown by the books and accounts. According to the branding for the past few years, it would indicate a brand of five or six thousand cattle. The only trouble in trading was to arrange the terms, my offer being half cash and the balance in six months, the cattle to be gathered early the coming spring. A bewildering list of references was given and we returned home. Within a fortnight a letter came from the trustee, accepting my offer and asking me to set a date for the gathering. I felt positive that the brand ought to run forty per cent steer cattle, and unless there was some deception, there would be in the neighborhood of two thousand head fit for the trail. I at once bought thirty more saddle horses, outfitted a wagon with oxen to draw it, besides hiring fifteen cow-hands. Early in March we started for Comanche County, having in the mean time made arrangements with the elder Edwards to supply one thousand head of trail cattle, intended for the Kansas market.

An early spring favored the work. By the 10th of the month we were actively engaged in gathering the stock. It was understood that we were to have the assistance of the ranch outfit in holding the cattle, but as they numbered only half a dozen and were miserably mounted, they were of little use except as herders. All the neighboring ranches gave us round-ups, and by the time we reached the home range of the brand I was beginning to get uneasy on account of the numbers under herd. My capital was limited, and if we gathered six thousand head it would absorb my money. I needed a little for expenses on the trail, and too many cattle would be embarrassing. There was no intention on my part to act dishonestly in the premises, even if we did drop out any number of yearlings during the last few days of the gathering. It was absolutely necessary to hold the numbers down to five thousand head, or as near that number as possible, and by keeping the ranch outfit on herd and my men out on round-ups, it was managed quietly, though we let no steer cattle two years old or over escape. When the gathering was finished, to the surprise of every one the herd counted out fifty-six hundred and odd cattle. But the numbers were still within the limits of my capital, and at the final settlement I asked the privilege of cutting out and leaving on the range one hundred head of weak, thin stock and cows heavy in calf. I offered to tally-mark and send after them during the fall branding, when the trustee begged me to make him an offer on any remnant of cattle, making me full owner of the brand. I hesitated to involve myself deeper in debt, but when he finally offered me the "Lazy L" brand outright for the sum of one thousand dollars, and on a credit, I never stuttered in accepting his proposal.

I culled back one hundred before starting, there being no occasion now to tally-mark, as I was in full possession of the brand. This amount of cattle in one herd was unwieldy to handle. The first day's drive we scarcely made ten miles, it being nearly impossible to water such an unmanageable body of animals, even from a running stream. The second noon we cut separate all the steers two years old and upward, finding a few under twenty-three hundred in the latter class. This left three thousand and odd hundred in the mixed herd, running from yearlings to old range bulls. A few extra men were secured, and some progress was made for the next few days, the steers keeping well in the lead, the two herds using the same wagon, and camping within half a mile of each other at night. It was fully ninety miles to the Edwards ranch; and when about two thirds the distance was covered, a messenger met us and reported the home cattle under herd and ready to start. It still lacked two days of the appointed time for our return, but rather than disappoint any one, I took seven men and sixty horses with the lead herd and started in to the ranch, leaving the mixed cattle to follow with the wagon. We took a day's rations on a pack horse, touched at a ranch, and on the second evening reached home. My contingent to the trail herd would have classified approximately seven hundred twos, six hundred threes, and one thousand four years old or over.

The next morning the herd started up the trail under George Edwards as foreman. It numbered a few over thirty-three hundred head and had fourteen men, all told, and ninety-odd horses, with four good mules to a new wagon. I promised to overtake them within a week, and the same evening rejoined the mixed herd some ten miles back down the country. Calves were dropping at an alarming rate, fully twenty of them were in the wagon, their advent delaying the progress of the herd. By dint of great exertion we managed to reach the ranch the next evening, where we lay over a day and rigged up a second wagon, purposely for calves. It was the intention to send the stock cattle to my new ranch on the Clear Fork, and releasing all but four men, the idle help about the home ranch were substituted. In moving cattle from one range to another, it should always be done with the coming of grass, as it gives them a full summer to locate and become attached to their new range. When possible, the coming calf crop should be born where the mothers are to be located, as it strengthens the ties between an animal and its range by making sacred the birthplace of its young. From instinctive warnings of maternity, cows will frequently return to the same retreat annually to give birth to their calves.

It was about fifty miles between the home and the new ranch. As it was important to get the cattle located as soon as possible, they were accordingly started with but the loss of a single day. Two wagons accompanied them, every calf was saved, and by nursing the herd early and late we managed to average ten miles between sunrise and sunset. The elder Edwards, anxious to see the new ranch, accompanied us, his patience with a cow being something remarkable. When we lacked but a day's drive of the Clear Fork it was considered advisable for me to return. Once the cattle reached the new range, four men would loose-herd them for a month, after which they would continue to ride the range and turn back all stragglers. The veteran cowman assumed control, and I returned to the home ranch, where a horse had been left on which to overtake the trail herd.

My wife caught several glimpses of me that spring; with stocking a new ranch and starting a herd on the trail I was as busy as the proverbial cranberry-merchant. Where a year before I was moneyless, now my obligations were accepted for nearly fourteen thousand dollars.

I overtook the herd within one day's drive of Red River. Everything was moving nicely, the cattle were well trail-broken, not a run had occurred, and all was serene and lovely. We crossed into the Nations at the regular ford, nothing of importance occurring until we reached the Washita River. The Indians had been bothering us more or less, but we brushed them aside or appeased their begging with a stray beef. At the crossing of the Washita quite an encampment had congregated, demanding six cattle and threatening to dispute our entrance to the ford. Several of the boys with us pretended to understand the sign language, and this resulted in an animosity being engendered between two of the outfit over interpreting a sign made by a chief. After we had given the Indians two strays, quite a band of bucks gathered on foot at the crossing, refusing to let us pass until their demand had been fulfilled. We had a few carbines, every lad had a six-shooter or two, and, summoning every mounted man, we rode up to the ford. The braves outnumbered us about three to one, and it was easy to be seen that they had bows and arrows concealed under their blankets. I was determined to give up no more cattle, and in the powwow that followed the chief of the band became very defiant. I accused him and his band of being armed, and when he denied it one of the boys jumped a horse against the chief, knocking him down. In the mêlée, the leader's blanket was thrown from him, exposing a strung bow and quiver of arrows, and at the same instant every man brought his carbine or six-shooter to bear on the astonished braves. Not a shot was fired, nor was there any further resistance offered on the part of the Indians; but as they turned to leave the humiliated chief pointed to the sun and made a circle around his head as if to indicate a threat of scalping.

It was in interpreting this latter sign that the dispute arose between two of the outfit. One of the boys contended that I was to be scalped before the sun set, while the other interpreted the threat that we would all he scalped before the sun rose again. Neither version troubled me, but the two fellows quarreled over the matter while returning to the herd, until the lie was passed and their six-shooters began talking. Fortunately they were both mounted on horses that were gun-shy, and with the rearing and plunging the shots went wild. Every man in the outfit interfered, the two fellows were disarmed, and we started on with the cattle. No interference was offered by the Indians at the ford, the guards were doubled that night, and the incident was forgotten within a week. I simply mention this to give some idea of the men of that day, willing to back their opinions, even on trivial matters, with their lives. "I'm the quickest man on the trigger that ever came over the trail," said a cowpuncher to me one night in a saloon in Abilene. "You're a blankety blank liar," said a quiet little man, a perfect stranger to both of us, not even casting a glance our way. I wrested a six-shooter from the hand of my acquaintance and hustled him out of the house, getting roundly cursed for my interference, though no doubt I saved human life.

On reaching Stone's Store, on the Kansas line, I left the herd to follow, and arrived at Abilene in two days and a half. Only some twenty-five herds were ahead of ours, though I must have passed a dozen or more in my brief ride, staying over night with them and scarcely ever missing a meal on the road. My motive in reaching Abilene in advance of our cattle was to get in touch with the market, secure my trading-corrals again, and perfect my arrangements to do a commission business. But on arriving, instead of having the field to myself, I found the old corrals occupied by a trio of jobbers, while two new ones had been built within ten miles of town, and half a dozen firms were offering their services as salesmen. There was a lack of actual buyers, at least among my acquaintances, and the railroads had adjusted their rates, while a largely increased drive was predicted. The spring had been a wet one, the grass was washy and devoid of nutriment, and there was nothing in

Andy Adams

the outlook of an encouraging nature. Yet the majority of the drovers were very optimistic of the future, freely predicting better prices than ever before, while many declared their intention of wintering in case their hopes were not realized. By the time our herd arrived, I had grown timid of the market in general and was willing to sell out and go home. I make no pretension to having any extra foresight, probably it was my outstanding obligations in Texas that fostered my anxiety, but I was prepared to sell to the first man who talked business.

Our cattle arrived in good condition. The weather continued wet and stormy, the rank grass harbored myriads of flies and mosquitoes, and the through cattle failed to take on flesh as in former years. Rival towns were competing for the trail business, wintered cattle were lower, and a perfect chaos existed as to future prices, drovers bolstering and pretended buyers depressing them. Within a week after their arrival I sold fifteen hundred of our heaviest beeves to an army contractor from Fort Russell in Dakota. He had brought his own outfit down to receive the cattle, and as his contract called for a million and a half pounds on foot, I assisted him in buying sixteen hundred more. The contractor was a shrewd Yankee, and although I admitted having served in the Confederate army, he offered to form a partnership with me for supplying beef to the army posts along the upper Missouri River. He gave me an insight into the profits in that particular trade, and even urged the partnership, but while the opportunity was a golden one, I was distrustful of a Northern man and declined the alliance. Within a year I regretted not forming the partnership, as the government was a stable patron, and my adopted State had any quantity of beef cattle.

My brother paid me a visit during the latter part of June. We had not seen each other in five years, during which time he had developed into a prosperous stockman, feeding cattle every winter on his Missouri farm. He was anxious to interest me in corn-feeding steers, but I had my hands full at home, and within a week he went on west and bought two hundred Colorado natives, shipping them home to feed the coming winter. Meanwhile a perfect glut of cattle was arriving at Abilene, fully six hundred thousand having registered at Stone's Store on passing into Kansas, yet prices remained firm, considering the condition of the stock. Many drovers halted only a day or two, and turned westward looking for ranges on which to winter their herds. Barely half the arrivals were even offered, which afforded fair prices to those who wished to sell. Before the middle of July the last of ours was closed out at satisfactory prices, and the next day the outfit started home, leaving me behind. I was anxious to secure an extra remuda of horses, and, finding no opposition in that particular field, had traded extensively in saddle stock ever since my arrival at Abilene. Gentle horses were in good demand among shippers and ranchmen, and during my brief stay I must have handled a thousand head, buying whole remudas and retailing in quantities to suit, not failing to keep the choice ones for my own use. Within two weeks after George Edwards started home, I closed up my business, fell in with a returning outfit, and started back with one hundred and ten picked saddle horses. After crossing Red River, I hired a boy to assist me in driving the remuda, and I reached home only ten days behind the others.

I was now the proud possessor of over two hundred saddle horses which had actually cost me nothing. To use a borrowed term, they were the "velvet" of my trading operations. I hardly feel able to convey an idea of the important rôle that the horses play in the operations of a cowman. Whether on the trail or on the ranch, there is a complete helplessness when the men are not properly mounted and able to cope with any emergency that may arise. On the contrary, and especially in trail work, when men are well mounted, there is no excuse for not riding in the lead of any stampede, drifting with the herd on the stormiest night, or trailing lost cattle until overtaken. Owing to the nature of the occupation, a man may be frequently wet, cold, and hungry, and entitled to little sympathy; but once he feels that he is no longer mounted, his grievance becomes a real one. The cow-horse subsisted on the range, and if ever used to exhaustion was worthless for weeks afterward. Hence the value of a good mount in numbers, and the importance of frequent changes when the duties were arduous. The importance of good horses was first impressed on me during my trips to Fort Sumner, and I then resolved that if fortune ever favored me to reach the prominence of a cowman, the saddle stock would have my first consideration.

On my return it was too early for the fall branding. I made a trip out to the new ranch, taking along ample winter supplies, two extra lads, and the old remuda of sixty horses. The men had located the new cattle fairly well, the calf crop was abundant, and after spending a week I returned home. I had previously settled my indebtedness in Comanche County by remittances from Abilene, and early in the fall I made up an outfit to go down and gather the remnant of "Lazy L" cattle. Taking along the entire new remuda, we dropped down in advance of the branding season, visited among the neighboring ranches, and offered a dollar a head for solitary animals that had drifted any great distance from the range of the brand. A camp was established at some corrals on the original range, extra men were employed with the opening of the branding season, and after twenty days' constant riding we started home with a few over nine hundred head, not counting two hundred and odd calves. Little wonder the trustee threatened to sue me; but then it was his own proposition.

On arriving at the Edwards ranch, we halted a few days in order to gather the fruits of my first mavericking. The fall work was nearly finished, and having previously made arrangements to put my brand under herd, we received two hundred and fifty more, with seventy-five thrifty calves, before proceeding on to the new ranch on the Clear Fork. On arriving there we branded the calves, put the two brands under herd, corralling them at night and familiarizing them with their new home, and turning them loose at the end of two weeks. Moving cattle in the fall was contrary to the best results, but it was an idle time, and they were all young stuff and easily located. During the interim of loose-herding this second contingent of stock cattle, the branding had been finished on the ranch, and I was able to take an account of my year's work. The "Lazy L" was continued, and from that brand alone there was an increase of over seventeen hundred calves. With all the expenses of the trail deducted, the steer cattle alone had paid for the entire brand, besides adding over five thousand dollars to my cash capital. Who will gainsay my statement that Texas was a good country in the year 1871?

CHAPTER IX

THE SCHOOL OF EXPERIENCE

Success had made me daring. And yet I must have been wandering aimlessly, for had my ambition been well directed, there is no telling to what extent I might have amassed a fortune. Opportunity was knocking at my gate, a giant young commonwealth was struggling in the throes of political revolution, while I wandered through it all like a blind man led by a child. Precedent was of little value, as present environment controlled my actions. The best people in Texas were doubtful of ever ridding themselves of the baneful incubus of Reconstruction. Men on whose judgment I relied laughed at me for acquiring more land than a mere homestead. Stock cattle were in such disrepute that they had no cash value. Many a section of deeded land changed owners for a milk cow, while surveyors would no longer locate new lands for the customary third, but insisted on a half interest. Ranchmen were so indifferent that many never went off their home range in branding the calf crop, not considering a ten or twenty per cent loss of any importance. Yet through it all - from my Virginia rearing - there lurked a wavering belief that some day, in some manner, these lands and cattle would have a value. But my faith was neither the bold nor the assertive kind, and I drifted along, clinging to any passing straw of opinion.

The Indians were still giving trouble along the Texas frontier. A line of government posts, extending from Red River on the north to the Rio Grande on the south, made a pretense of holding the Comanches and their allies in check, while this arm of the service was ably seconded by the Texas Rangers. Yet in spite of all precaution, the redskins raided the settlements at their pleasure, stealing horses and adding rapine and murder to their category of crimes. Hence for a number of years after my marriage we lived at the Edwards ranch as a matter of precaution against Indian raids. I was absent from home so much that this arrangement suited me, and as the new ranch was distant but a day's ride, any inconvenience was more than recompensed in security. It was my intention to follow the trail and trading, at the same time running a ranch where anything unfit for market might be sent to mature or increase. As long as I could add to my working capital, I was content, while the remnants of my speculations found a refuge on the Clear Fork.

During the winter of 1871-72 very little of importance transpired. Several social letters passed between Major Mabry and myself, in one of which he casually mentioned the fact that land scrip had declined until it was offered on the streets of the capital as low as twenty dollars a section. He knew I had been dabbling in land certificates, and in a friendly spirit wanted to post me on their decline, and had incidentally mentioned the fact for my information. Some inkling of horse sense told me that I ought to secure more land, and after thinking the matter over, I wrote to a merchant in Austin, and had him buy me one hundred sections. He was very anxious to purchase a second hundred at the same figure, but it would make too serious an inroad into my trading capital, and I declined his friendly assistance. My wife was the only person whom I took into confidence in buying the scrip, and I even had her secrete it in the bottom of a trunk, with strict admonitions never to mention it unless it became of value. It was not taxable, the public domain was bountiful, and I was young enough man those days to bide my time.

The winter proved a severe one in Kansas. Nearly every drover who wintered his cattle in the north met with almost complete loss. The previous summer had been too wet for cattle to do well, and they had gone into winter thin in flesh. Instead of curing like hay, the buffalo grass had rotted from excessive rains, losing its nutritive qualities, and this resulted in serious loss among all range cattle. The result was financial ruin to many drovers, and even augured a lighter drive north the coming spring. Early in the winter I bought two brands of cattle in Erath County, paying half cash and getting six months' time on the remainder. Both brands occupied the same range, and when we gathered them in the early spring, they counted out a few over six thousand animals. These two contingents were extra good cattle, costing me five dollars a head, counting yearlings up, and from them I selected two thousand steer cattle for the trail. The mixed stuff was again sent to my Clear Fork ranch, and the steers went into a neighborhood herd intended for the Kansas market. But when the latter was all ready to start, such discouraging reports came down from the north that my friends weakened, and I bought their cattle outright.

My reputation as a good trader was my capital. I had the necessary horses, and, straining my credit, the herd started thirty-one hundred strong. The usual incidents of flood and storm, of begging Indians and caravans like ourselves, formed the chronicle of the trip. Before arriving at the Kansas line we were met by solicitors of rival towns, each urging the advantages of their respective markets for our cattle. The summer before a small business had sprung up at Newton, Kansas, it being then the terminal of the Santa Fé Railway. And although Newton lasted as a trail town but a single summer, its reputation for bloodshed and riotous disorder stands notoriously alone among its rivals. In the mean time the Santa Fé had been extended to Wichita on the Arkansas River, and its representatives were now bidding for our patronage. Abilene was abandoned, yet a rival to Wichita had sprung up at Ellsworth, some sixty-five miles west of the former market, on the Kansas Pacific Railway. The railroads were competing for the cattle traffic, each one advertising its superior advantages to drovers, shippers, and feeders. I was impartial, but as Wichita was fully one hundred miles the nearest, my cattle were turned for that point.

Wichita was a frontier village of about two thousand inhabitants. We found a convenient camp northwest of town, and went into permanent quarters to await the opening of the market. Within a few weeks a light drive was assured, and prices opened firm. Fully a quarter-million less cattle would reach the markets within the State that year, and buyers became active in securing their needed supply. Early in July I sold the last of my herd and started my outfit home, remaining behind to await the arrival of my brother. The trip was successful; the purchased cattle had afforded me a nice profit, while the steers from the two brands had more than paid for the mixed stuff left at home on the ranch. Meanwhile I renewed old acquaintances among drovers and dealers, Major Mabry among the former. In a confidential mood I confessed to him that I had bought, on the recent decline, one hundred certificates of land scrip, when he surprised me by saying that there had been a later decline to sixteen dollars a section. I was unnerved for an instant, but Major Mabry agreed with me that to a man who wanted the land the price was certainly cheap enough, - two and a half cents an acre. I pondered over the matter, and as my nerve returned I sent my merchant friend at Austin a draft and authorized him to buy me two hundred sections more of land scrip. I was actually nettled to think that my judgment was so short-sighted as to buy anything that would depreciate in value.

My brother arrived and reported splendid success in feeding Colorado cattle. He was anxious to have me join forces with him and corn-feed an increased number of beeves the coming winter on his Missouri farm. My judgment hardly approved of the venture, but when he urged a promised visit of our parents to his home, I consented and agreed to furnish the cattle. He also encouraged me to bring as many as my capital would admit of, assuring me that I would find a ready sale for any surplus among his neighbors. My brother returned to Missouri, and I took the train for Ellsworth, where I bought a carload of picked cow-horses, shipping them to Kit Carson, Colorado. From there I drifted into the Fountain valley at the base of the mountains, where I made a trade for seven hundred native steers, three and four years old. They were fine cattle, nearly all reds and roans. While I was gathering them a number of amusing incidents occurred. The round-ups carried us down on to the main Arkansas River, and in passing Pueblo we discovered a number of range cattle impounded in the town. I cannot give it as a fact, but the supposition among the cowmen was that the object of the officials was to raise some revenue by distressing the cattle. The result was that an outfit of men rode into the village during the night, tore down the pound, and turned the cattle back on the prairie. The prime movers in the raid were suspected, and the next evening when a number of us rode into town an attempt was made to arrest us, resulting in a fight, in which an officer was killed and two cowboys wounded. The citizens rallied to the support of the officers, and about thirty range men, including myself, were arrested and thrown into jail. We sent for a lawyer, and the following morning the majority of us were acquitted. Some three or four of the boys were held for trial, bonds being furnished by the best men in the town, and that night a party of cowboys reëntered the village, carried away the two wounded men and spirited them out of the country.

Pueblo at that time was a unique town. Live-stock interests were its main support, and I distinctly remember Gann's outfitting store. At night one could find anywhere from ten to thirty cowboys sleeping on the counters, the proprietor turning the keys over to them at closing time, not knowing one in ten, and sleeping at his own residence. The same custom prevailed at Gallup the saddler's, never an article being missed from either establishment, and both men amassing fortunes out of the cattle trade in subsequent years. The range man's patronage had its peculiarities; the firm of Wright, Beverly & Co. of Dodge City, Kansas, accumulated seven thousand odd vests during the trail days. When a cow-puncher bought a new suit he had no use for an unnecessary garment like a vest and left it behind. It was restored to the stock, where it can yet be found.

Early in August the herd was completed. I accepted seven hundred and twenty steers, investing every cent of spare money, reserving only sufficient to pay my expenses en route. It was my intention to drive the cattle through to Missouri, the distance being a trifle less than six hundred miles or a matter of six weeks' travel. Four men were secured, a horse was packed with provisions and blankets, and we started down the Arkansas River. For the first few days I did very little but build air castles. I pictured myself driving herds from Texas in the spring, reinvesting the proceeds in better grades of cattle and feeding them corn in the older States, selling in time to again buy and come up the trail. I even planned to send for my wife and baby, and looked forward to a happy reunion with my parents during the coming winter, with not a cloud in my roseate sky. But there were breakers ahead.

An old military trail ran southeast from Fort Larned to other posts in the Indian Territory. Over this government road had come a number of herds of Texas cattle, all of them under contract, which, in reaching their destination, had avoided the markets of Wichita and Ellsworth. I crossed their trail with my Colorado natives, - the through cattle having passed a month or more before, - never dreaming of any danger. Ten days afterward I noticed a number of my steers were ailing; their ears drooped, they refused to eat, and fell to the rear as we grazed forward. The next morning there were forty head unable to leave the bed-ground, and by noon a number of them had died. I had heard of Texas fever, but always treated it as more or less a myth, and now it held my little herd of natives in its toils. By this time we had reached some settlement on the Cottonwood, and the pioneer settlers in Kansas arose in arms and quarantined me. No one knew what the trouble was, yet the cattle began dying like sheep; I was perfectly helpless, not knowing which way to turn or what to do. Quarantine was unnecessary, as within a few days half the cattle were sick, and it was all we could do to move away from the stench of the dead ones.

A veterinary was sent for, who pronounced it Texas fever. I had previously cut open a number of dead animals, and found the contents of their stomachs and manifolds so dry that they would flash and burn like powder. The fever had dried up their very internals. In the hope of administering a purgative, I bought whole fields of green corn, and turned the sick and dying cattle into them. I bought oils by the barrel, my men and myself worked night and day, inwardly drenching affected animals, yet we were unable to stay the ravages of death. Once the cause of the trouble was located, - crossing ground over which Texas cattle had passed, - the neighbors became friendly, and sympathized with me. I gave them permission to take the fallen hides, and in return received many kindnesses where a few days before I had been confronted by shotguns. This was my first experience with Texas fever, and the lessons that I learned then and afterward make me skeptical of all theories regarding the transmission of the germ.

The story of the loss of my Colorado herd is a ghastly one. This fever is sometimes called splenic, and in the present case, where animals lingered a week or ten days, while yet alive, their skins frequently cracked along the spine until one could have laid two fingers in the opening. The whole herd was stricken, less than half a dozen animals escaping attack, scores dying within three days, the majority lingering a week or more. In spite of our every effort to save them, as many as one hundred died in a single day. I stayed with them for six weeks, or until the fever had run through the herd, spent my last available dollar in an effort to save the dumb beasts, and, having my hopes frustrated, sold the remnant of twenty-six head for five dollars apiece. I question if they were worth the money, as three fourths of them were fever-burnt and would barely survive a winter, the only animals of value being some half dozen which had escaped the general plague. I gave each of my men two horses apiece, and divided my money with them, and they started back to Colorado, while I turned homeward a wiser but poorer man. Whereas I had left Wichita three months before with over sixteen thousand dollars clear cash, I returned with eighteen saddle horses and not as many dollars in money.

My air-castles had fallen. Troubles never come singly, and for the last two weeks, while working with the dying cattle, I had suffered with chills and fever. The summer had been an unusually wet one, vegetation had grown up rankly in the valley of the Arkansas, and after the first few frosts the very atmosphere reeked with malaria. I had been sleeping on the ground along the river for over a month, drinking impure water from the creeks, and I fell an easy victim to the prevailing miasma. Nearly all the Texas drovers had gone home, but, luckily for me, Jim Daugherty had an outfit yet at Wichita and invited me to his wagon. It might be a week or ten days before he would start homeward, as he was holding a herd of cows, sold to an Indian contractor, who was to receive the same within two weeks. In the interim of waiting, still suffering from fever and ague, I visited around among the few other cow-camps scattered up and down the river. At one of these I met a stranger, a quiet little man, who also had been under the weather from malaria, but was then recovering. He took an interest in my case and gave me some medicine to break the chills, and we visited back and forth. I soon learned that he had come down with some of his neighbors from Council Grove; that they expected to buy cattle, and that he was banker for the party. He was much interested in everything pertaining to Texas; and when I had given him an idea of the cheapness of lands and live stock in my adopted State, he expressed himself as anxious to engage in trailing cattle north. A great many Texas cattle had been matured in his home county, and he thoroughly understood the advantages of developing southern steers in a northern climate. Many of his neighbors had made small fortunes in buying young stock at Abilene, holding them a year or two, and shipping them to market as fat cattle.

The party bought six hundred two-year-old steers, and my new-found friend, the banker, invited me to assist in the receiving. My knowledge of range cattle was a decided advantage to the buyers, who no doubt were good farmers, yet were sadly handicapped when given pick and choice from a Texas herd and confined to ages. I cut, counted, and received the steers, my work giving such satisfaction that the party offered to pay me for my services. It was but a neighborly act, unworthy of recompense, yet I won the lasting regard of the banker in protecting the interests of his customers. The upshot of the acquaintance was that we met in town that evening and had a few drinks together. Neither one ever made any inquiry of the other's past or antecedents, both seeming to be satisfied with a soldier's acquaintance. At the final parting, I gave him my name and address and invited him to visit me, promising that we would buy a herd of cattle together and drive them up the trail the following spring. He accepted the invitation with a hearty grasp of the hand, and the simple promise "I'll come." Those words were the beginning of a partnership which lasted eighteen years, and a friendship that death alone will terminate.

The Indian contractor returned on time, and the next day I started home with Daugherty's outfit. And on the way, as if I were pursued by some unrelenting Nemesis, two of my horses, with others, were stolen by the Indians one night when we were encamped near Red River. We trailed them westward nearly fifty miles, but, on being satisfied they were traveling night and day, turned back and continued our journey. I reached home with sixteen horses, which for years afterwards, among my hands and neighbors, were pointed out as Anthony's thousand-dollar cow-ponies. There is no denying the fact that I keenly felt the loss of my money, as it crippled me in my business, while my ranch expenses, amounting to over one thousand dollars, were unpaid. I was rich in unsalable cattle, owned a thirty-two-thousand-acre ranch, saddle horses galore, and was in debt. My wife's trunk was half full of land scrip, and to have admitted the fact would only have invited ridicule. But my tuition was paid, and all I asked was a chance, for I knew the ropes in handling range cattle. Yet this was the second time that I had lost my money and I began to doubt myself. "You stick to cows," said Charlie Goodnight to me that winter, "and they'll bring you out on top some day. I thought I saw something in you when you first went to work for Loving and me. Reed, if you'll just imbibe a little caution with your energy, you'll make a fortune out of cattle yet."

CHAPTER X

THE PANIC OF '73

I have never forgotten those encouraging words of my first employer. Friends tided my finances over, and letters passed between my banker friend and myself, resulting in an appointment to meet him at Fort Worth early in February. There was no direct railroad at the time, the route being by St. Louis and Texarkana, with a long trip by stage to the meeting point. No definite agreement existed between us; he was simply paying me a visit, with the view of looking into the cattle trade then existing between our respective States. There was no obligation whatever, yet I had hopes of interesting him sufficiently to join issues with me in driving a herd of cattle. I wish I could describe the actual feelings of a man who has had money and lost it. Never in my life did such opportunities present themselves for investment as were tendered to me that winter. No less than half a dozen brands of cattle were offered to me at the former terms of half cash and the balance to suit my own convenience. But I lacked the means to even provision a wagon for a month's work, and I was compelled to turn my back on all bargains, many of which were duplicates of my former successes. I was humbled to the very dust; I bowed my neck to the heel of circumstances, and looked forward to the coming of my casual acquaintance.

I have read a few essays on the relation of money to a community. None of our family were ever given to theorizing, yet I know how it feels to be moneyless, my experience with

Texas fever affording me a post-graduate course. Born with a restless energy, I have lived in the pit of despair for the want of money, and again, with the use of it, have bent a legislature to my will and wish. All of which is foreign to my tale, and I hasten on. During the first week in February I drove in to Fort Worth to await the arrival of my friend, Calvin Hunter, banker and stockman of Council Grove, Kansas. Several letters were awaiting me in the town, notifying me of his progress, and in due time he arrived and was welcomed. The next morning we started, driving a good span of mules to a buckboard, expecting to cover the distance to the Brazos in two days. There were several ranches at which we could touch, en route, but we loitered along, making wide detours in order to drive through cattle, not a feature of the country escaping the attention of my quiet little companion. The soil, the native grasses, the natural waters, the general topography of the country, rich in its primal beauty, furnished a panorama to the eye both pleasing and exhilarating. But the main interest centred in the cattle, thousands of which were always in sight, lingering along the watercourses or grazing at random.

We reached the Edwards ranch early the second evening. In the two days' travel, possibly twenty thousand cattle came under our immediate observation. All the country was an open range, brands intermingling, all ages and conditions, running from a sullen bull to seven-year-old beeves, or from a yearling heifer to the grandmother of younger generations. My anxiety to show the country and its cattle met a hearty second in Mr. Hunter, and abandoning the buckboard, we took horses and rode up the Brazos River as far as old Fort Belknap. All cattle were wintering strong. Turning south, we struck the Clear Fork above my range and spent a night at the ranch, where my men had built a second cabin, connecting the two by a hallway. After riding through my stock for two days, we turned back for the Brazos. My ranch hands had branded thirty-one hundred calves the fall before, and while riding over the range I was delighted to see so many young steers in my different brands. But our jaunt had only whetted the appetite of my guest to see more of the country, and without any waste of time we started south with the buckboard, going as far as Comanche County. Every day's travel brought us in contact with cattle for sale; the prices were an incentive, but we turned east and came back up the valley of the Brazos. I offered to continue our sightseeing, but my guest pleaded for a few days' time until he could hear from his banking associates. I needed a partner and needed one badly, and was determined to interest Mr. Hunter if it took a whole month. And thereby hangs a tale.

The native Texan is not distinguished for energy or ambition. His success in cattle is largely due to the fact that nearly all the work can be done on horseback. Yet in that particular field he stands at the head of his class; for whether in Montana or his own sunny Texas, when it comes to handling cattle, from reading brands to cutting a trainload of beeves, he is without a peer. During the palmy days of the Cherokee Strip, a Texan invited Captain Stone, a Kansas City man, to visit his ranch in Tom Green County and put up a herd of steers to be driven to Stone's beef ranch in the Cherokee Outlet. The invitation was accepted, and on the arrival of the Kansas City man at the Texan's ranch, host and guest indulged in a friendly visit of several days' duration. It was the northern cowman's first visit to the Lone Star State, and he naturally felt impatient to see the cattle which he expected to buy. But the host made no movement to show the stock until patience ceased to be a virtue, when Captain Stone moved an adjournment of the social session and politely asked to be shown a sample of the country's cattle. The two cowmen were fast friends, and no offense was intended or taken; but the host assured his guest there was no hurry, offering to get up horses and show the stock the following day. Captain Stone yielded, and the next morning they started, but within a few miles met a neighbor, when all three dismounted in the shade of a tree. Commonplace chat of the country occupied the attention of the two Texans until hunger or some other warning caused one of them to look at his watch, when it was discovered to be three o'clock in the afternoon. It was then too late in the day to make an extensive ride, and the ranchman invited his neighbor and guest to return to the ranch for the night. Another day was wasted in entertaining the neighbor, the northern cowman, in the meantime, impatient and walking on nettles until a second start was made to see the cattle. It was a foggy morning, and they started on a different route from that previously taken, the visiting ranchman going along. Unnoticed, a pack of hounds followed the trio of horsemen, and before the fog lifted a cougar trail was struck and the dogs opened in a brilliant chorus. The two Texans put spurs to their horses in following the pack, the cattle buyer of necessity joining in, the chase leading into some hills, from which they returned after darkness, having never seen a cow during the day. One trivial incident after another interfered with seeing the cattle for ten days, when the guest took his host aside and kindly told him that he must be shown the cattle or he would go home.

"You're not in a hurry, are you, captain?" innocently asked the Texan. "All right, then; no trouble to show the cattle. Yes, they run right around home here within twenty-five miles of the ranch. Show you a sample of the stock within an hour's ride. You can just bet that old Tom Green County has got the steers! Sugar, if I'd a-known that you was in a hurry, I could have shown you the cattle the next morning after you come. Captain, you ought to know me well enough by this time to speak your little piece without any prelude. You Yankees are so restless and impatient that I seriously doubt if you get all the comfort and enjoyment out of life that's coming to you. Make haste, some of you boys, and bring in a remuda; Captain Stone and I are going to ride over on the Middle Fork this morning. Make haste, now; we're in a hurry."

In due time I suppose I drifted into the languorous ways of the Texan; but on the occasion of Mr. Hunter's first visit I was in the need of a moneyed partner, and accordingly danced attendance. Once communication was opened with his Northern associates, we made several short rides into adjoining counties, never being gone over two or three days. When we had looked at cattle to his satisfaction, he surprised me by offering to put fifty thousand dollars into young steers for the Kansas trade. I never fainted in my life, but his proposition stunned me for an instant, or until I could get my bearings. The upshot of the proposal was that we entered into an agreement whereby I was to purchase and handle the cattle, and he was to make himself useful in selling and placing the stock in his State. A silent partner was furnishing an equal portion of the means, and I was to have a third of the net profits. Within a week after this agreement was perfected, things were moving. I had the horses and wagons, men were plentiful, and two outfits were engaged. Early in March a contract was let in Parker County for thirty-one hundred two-year-old steers, and another in Young for fourteen hundred threes, the latter to be delivered at my ranch. George Edwards was to have the younger cattle, and he and Mr. Hunter received the same, after which the latter hurried west, fully ninety miles, to settle for those bought for delivery on the Clear Fork. In the mean time my ranch outfit had gathered all our steer cattle two years old and over, having nearly twenty-five hundred head under herd on my arrival to receive the three-year-olds. This amount would make an unwieldy herd, and I culled back all short-aged twos and thin steers until my individual contingent numbered even two thousand. The contracted steers came in on time, fully up to the specifi-cations, and my herd was ready to start on the appointed day.

Every dollar of the fifty thousand was invested in cattle, save enough to provision the wagons en route. My ranch outfit, with the exception of two men and ten horses, was pressed into trail work as a matter of economy, for I was determined to make some money for my partners. Both herds were to meet and cross at Red River Station. The season was favorable, and everything augured for a prosperous summer. At the very last moment a cloud arose between Mr. Hunter and me, but happily passed without a storm. The night before the second herd started, he and I sat up until a late hour, arranging our affairs, as it was not his intention to accompany the herds overland. After all business matters were settled, lounging around a camp-fire, we grew reminiscent, when the fact developed that my quiet little partner had served in the Union army, and with the rank of major. I always enjoy a joke, even on myself, but I flashed hot and cold on this confession. What! Reed Anthony forming a partnership with a Yankee major? It seemed as though I had. Fortunately I controlled myself, and under the excuse of starting the herd at daybreak, I excused myself and sought my blankets. But not to sleep. On the one hand, in the stillness of the night and across the years, came the accusing voices of old comrades. My very wounds seemed to reopen and curse me. Did my sufferings after Pittsburg Landing mean nothing? A vision of my dear old mother in Virginia, welcoming me, the only one of her three sons who returned from the war, arraigned me sorely. And yet, on the other hand, this man was my guest. On my invitation he had eaten my salt. For mutual benefit we had entered into a partnership, and I expected to profit from the investment of his money. More important, he had not deceived me nor concealed anything; neither did he know that I had served in the Confederate army. The man was honest. I was anxious to do right. Soldiers are generous to a foe. While he lay asleep in my camp, I reviewed the situation carefully, and judged him blameless. The next morning, and ever afterward, I addressed him by his military title. Nearly a year passed before Major Hunter knew that he and his Texas partner had served in the civil war under different flags.

My partner returned to the Edwards ranch and was sent in to Fort Worth, where he took stage and train for home. The straight two-year-old herd needed road-branding, as they were accepted in a score or more brands, which delayed them in starting. Major Hunter expected to sell to farmers, to whom brands were offensive, and was therefore opposed to more branding than was absolutely necessary. In order to overcome this objection, I tally-marked all outside cattle which went into my herd by sawing from each steer about two inches from the right horn. As fast as the cattle were received this work was easily done in a chute, while in case of any loss by stampede the mark would last for years. The grass was well forward when both herds started, but on arriving at Red River no less than half a dozen herds were waterbound, one of which was George Edwards's. A delay of three days occurred, during which two other herds arrived, when the river fell, permitting us to cross. I took the lead thereafter, the second herd half a day to the rear, with the almost weekly incident of being waterbound by intervening rivers. But as we moved northward the floods seemed lighter, and on our arrival at Wichita the weather settled into well-ordered summer.

I secured my camp of the year before. Major Hunter came down by train, and within a week after our arrival my outfit was settled with and sent home. It was customary to allow a man half wages returning, my partner approving and paying the men, also taking charge of all the expense accounts. Everything was kept as straight as a bank, and with one outfit holding both herds separate, expenses were reduced to a minimum. Major Hunter was back and forth, between his home town and Wichita, and on nearly every occasion brought along buyers, effecting sales at extra good prices. Cattle paper was considered gilt-edge security among financial men, and we sold to worthy parties a great many cattle on credit, the home bank with which my partners were associated taking the notes at their face. Matters rocked along, we sold when we had an opportunity, and early in August the remnant of each herd was thrown together and half the remaining outfit sent home. A drive of fully half a million cattle had reached Kansas that year, the greater portion of which had centred at Wichita. We were persistent in selling, and, having strong local connections, had sold out all our cattle long before the financial panic of '73 even started. There was a profitable business, however, in buying herds and selling again in small quantities to farmers and stockmen. My partners were anxious to have me remain to the end of the season, doing the buying, maintaining the camp, and holding any stock on hand. In rummaging through the old musty account-books, I find that we handled nearly seven thousand head besides our own drive, fifteen hundred being the most we ever had on hand at any one time.

My active partner proved a shrewd man in business, and in

spite of the past our friendship broadened and strengthened. Weeks before the financial crash reached us he knew of its coming, and our house was set in order. When the panic struck the West we did not own a hoof of cattle, while the horses on hand were mine and not for sale; and the firm of Hunter, Anthony & Co. rode the gale like a seaworthy ship. The panic reached Wichita with over half the drive of that year unsold. The local banks began calling in money advanced to drovers, buyers deserted the market, and prices went down with a crash. Shipments of the best through cattle failed to realize more than sufficient to pay commission charges and freight. Ruin stared in the face every Texan drover whose cattle were unsold. Only a few herds were under contract for fall delivery to Indian and army contractors. We had run from the approaching storm in the nick of time, even settling with and sending my outfit home before the financial cyclone reached the prairies of Kansas. My last trade before the panic struck was an individual account, my innate weakness for an abundance of saddle horses asserting itself in buying ninety head and sending them home with my men.

I now began to see the advantages of shrewd and far-seeing business associates. When the crash came, scarce a dozen drovers had sold out, while of those holding cattle at Wichita nearly every one had locally borrowed money or owed at home for their herds. When the banks, panic-stricken themselves, began calling in short-time loans, their frenzy paralyzed the market, many cattle being sacrificed at forced sale and with scarce a buyer. In the depreciation of values from the prices which prevailed in the early summer, the losses to the Texas drovers, caused by the panic, would amount to several million dollars. I came out of the general wreck and ruin untouched, though personally claiming no credit, as that must be given my partners. The year before, when every other drover went home prosperous and happy, I returned "broke," while now the situation was reversed.

I spent a week at Council Grove, visiting with my business associates. After a settlement of the year's business, I was anxious to return home, having agreed to drive cattle the next year on the same terms and conditions. My partners gave me a cash settlement, and outside of my individual cattle, I cleared over ten thousand dollars on my summer's work. Major Hunter, however, had an idea of reëntering the market, - with the first symptom of improvement in the financial horizon in the East, - and I was detained. The proposition of buying a herd of cattle and wintering them on the range had been fully discussed between us, and prices were certainly an incentive to make the venture. In an ordinary open winter, stock subsisted on the range all over western Kansas, especially when a dry fall had matured and cured the buffalo-grass like hay. The range was all one could wish, and Major Hunter and I accordingly dropped down to Wichita to look the situation over. We arrived in the midst of the panic and found matters in a deplorable condition. Drovers besought and even begged us to make an offer on their herds, while the prevailing prices of a month before had declined over half. Major Hunter and I agreed that at present figures, even if half the cattle were lost by a severe winter, there would still be money in the venture. Through financial connections East my partners knew of the first signs of improvement in the money-centres of the country. As I recall the circumstances, the panic began in the East about the middle of September, and it was the latter part of October before confidence was restored, or there was any noticeable change for the better in the monetary situation. But when this came, it found us busy buying saddle horses and cattle. The great bulk of the unsold stock consisted of cows, heifers, and young steers unfit for beef. My partners contended that a three-year-old steer ought to winter anywhere a buffalo could, provided he had the flesh and strength to withstand the rigors of the climate. I had no opinions, except what other cowmen had told me, but was willing to take the chances where there was a reasonable hope of success.

The first move was to buy an outfit of good horses. This was done by selecting from half a dozen remudas, a trail wagon was picked up, and a complement of men secured. Once it was known that we were in the market for cattle, competition was brisk, the sellers bidding against each other and fixing the prices at which we accepted the stock. None but three-year-old steers were taken, and in a single day we closed trades on five thousand head. I received the cattle, confining my selections to five road and ten single-ranch brands, as it was not our intention to rebrand so late in the season. There was nothing to do but cut, count, and accept, and on the evening of the third day the herd was all ready to start for its winter range. The wagon had been well provisioned, and we started southwest, expecting to go into winter quarters on the first good range encountered. I had taken a third interest in the herd, paying one sixth of its purchase price, the balance being carried for me by my partners. Major Hunter accompanied us, the herd being altogether too large and unwieldy to handle well, but we grazed it forward with a front a mile wide. Delightful fall weather favored the cattle, and on the tenth day we reached the Medicine River, where, by the unwritten law of squatter's rights, we preëmpted ten miles of its virgin valley. The country was fairly carpeted with well-cured buffalo-grass; on the north and west was a range of sand-dunes, while on the south the country was broken by deep coulees, affording splendid shelter in case of blizzards or wintry storms.

A dugout was built on either end of the range. Major Hunter took the wagon and team and went to the nearest settlement, returning with a load of corn, having contracted for the delivery of five hundred bushels more. Meanwhile I was busy locating the cattle, scattering them sparsely over the surrounding country, cutting them into bunches of not more than ten to twenty head. Corrals and cosy shelters were built for a few horses, comfortable quarters for the men, and we settled down for the winter with everything snug and secure. By the first of December the force was reduced to four men at each camp, all of whom were experienced in holding cattle in the winter. Lines giving ample room to our cattle were established, which were to be ridden both evening and morning in any and all weather. Two Texans, both experts as trailers, were detailed to trail down any cattle which left the boundaries of the range. The weather continued fine, and with the camps well provisioned, the major and I returned to the railroad and took train for Council Grove. I was impatient to go home, and took the most direct route then available. Railroads were just beginning to enter the West, and one had recently been completed across the eastern portion of the Indian Territory, its destination being south of Red River. With nothing but the clothes on my back and a saddle, I started home, and within twenty-four hours arrived at Denison, Texas. Connecting stages carried me to Fort Worth, where I bought a saddle horse, and the next evening I was playing with the babies at the home ranch. It had been an active summer with me, but success had amply rewarded my labors, while every cloud had disappeared and the future was rich in promise.

CHAPTER XI

A PROSPEROUS YEAR

An open winter favored the cattle on the Medicine River. My
partners in Kansas wrote me encouragingly, and plans were
outlined for increasing our business for the coming summer.
There was no activity in live stock during the winter in Texas,
and there would be no trouble in putting up herds at
prevailing prices of the spring before. I spent an inactive
winter, riding back and forth to my ranch, hunting with
hounds, and killing an occasional deer. While visiting at
Council Grove the fall before, Major Hunter explained to our
silent partner the cheapness of Texas lands. Neither one of my
associates cared to scatter their interests beyond the boundaries
of their own State, yet both urged me to acquire every acre of
cheap land that my means would permit. They both recited
the history and growth in value of the lands surrounding The
Grove, telling me how cheaply they could have bought the
same ten years before, - at the government price of a dollar and
a quarter an acre, - and that already there had been an advance
of four to five hundred per cent. They urged me to buy scrip
and locate land, assuring me that it was only a question of time
until the people of Texas would arise in their might and throw
off the yoke of Reconstruction.

At home general opinion was just the reverse. No one cared for
more land than a homestead or for immediate use. No
locations had been made adjoining my ranch on the Clear
Fork, and it began to look as if I had more land than I needed.

Yet I had confidence enough in the advice of my partners to reopen negotiations with my merchant friend at Austin for the purchase of more land scrip. The panic of the fall before had scarcely affected the frontier of Texas, and was felt in only a few towns of any prominence in the State. There had been no oney in circulation since the war, and a financial stringency elsewhere made little difference among the local people. True, the Kansas cattle market had sent a little money home, but a bad winter with drovers holding cattle in the North, followed by a panic, had bankrupted nearly every cowman, many of them with heavy liabilities in Texas. There were very few banks in the State, and what little money there was among the people was generally hoarded to await the dawn of a brighter day.

My wife tells a story about her father, which shows similar conditions prevailing during the civil war. The only outlet for cotton in Texas during the rebellion was by way of Mexico. Matamoros, near the mouth of the Rio Grande, waxed opulent in its trade of contrabrand cotton, the Texas product crossing the river anywhere for hundreds of miles above and being freighted down on the Mexican side to tide-water. The town did an immense business during the blockade of coast seaports, twenty-dollar gold pieces being more plentiful then than nickels are to-day, the cotton finding a ready market at war prices and safe shipment under foreign flags. My wife's father was engaged in the trade of buying cotton at interior points, freighting it by ox trains over the Mexican frontier, and thence down the river to Matamoros. Once the staple reached neutral soil, it was palmed off as a local product, and the Federal government dared not touch it, even though they knew it to be contrabrand of war. The business was transacted in gold, and it was Mr. Edwards's custom to bury the coin on his return from each trading trip. My wife, then a mere girl and the oldest of the children at home, was taken into her father's confidence in secreting the money. The country was full of bandits, either government would have confiscated the gold had they known its whereabouts, and the only way to insure its safety was to bury it. After several years trading in cotton, Mr. Edwards accumulated considerable money, and on one occasion buried the treasure at night between two trees in an adjoining wood. Unexpectedly one day he had occasion to use some money in buying a cargo of cotton, the children were at a distant neighbor's, and he went into the woods alone to unearth the gold. But hogs, running in the timber, had rooted up the ground in search of edible roots, and Edwards was unable to locate the spot where his treasure lay buried. Fearful that possibly the money had been uprooted and stolen, he sent for the girl, who hastily returned. As my wife tells the story, great beads of perspiration were dripping from her father's brow as the two entered the woods. And although the ground was rooted up, the girl pointed out the spot, midway between two trees, and the treasure was recovered without a coin missing. Mr. Edwards lost confidence in himself, and thereafter, until peace was restored, my wife and a younger sister always buried the family treasure by night, keeping the secret to themselves, and producing the money on demand.

The merchant at Austin reported land scrip plentiful at fifteen to sixteen dollars a section. I gave him an order for two hundred certificates, and he filled the bill so promptly that I ordered another hundred, bringing my unlocated holdings up to six hundred sections. My land scrip was a standing joke between my wife and me, and I often promised her that when we built a house and moved to the Clear Fork, if the scrip was still worthless she might have the certificates to paper a room with. They were nicely lithographed, the paper was of the very best quality, and they went into my wife's trunk to await their destiny. Had it been known outside that I held such an amount of scrip, I would have been subjected to ridicule, and no doubt would have given it to some surveyor to locate on shares. Still I had a vague idea that land at two and a half cents an acre would never hurt me. Several times in the past I had needed the money tied up in scrip, and then I would regret having bought it. After the loss of my entire working capital by Texas fever, I was glad I had foresight enough to buy a quantity that summer. And thus I swung like a pendulum between personal necessities and public opinion; but when those long-headed Yankee partners of mine urged me to buy land, I felt once more that I was on the right track and recovered my grasp. I might have located fifty miles of the valley of the Clear Fork that winter, but it would have entailed some little expense, the land would then have been taxable, and I had the use of it without outlay or trouble.

An event of great importance to the people of Texas occurred during the winter of 1873-74. The election the fall before ended in dispute, both great parties claiming the victory. On the meeting of the legislature to canvass the vote, all the negro militia of the State were concentrated in and around the capitol building. The Reconstruction régime refused to vacate, and were fighting to retain control; the best element of the people were asserting in no unmistakable terms their rights and bloodshed seemed inevitable. The federal government was appealed to, but refused to interfere. The legislature was with the people, and when the latter refused to be intimidated by a display of force, those in possession yielded the reins, and Governor Coke was inaugurated January 15, 1874; and thus the prediction of my partners, uttered but a few mouths before, became history.

Major Hunter came down again about the last of February. Still unshaken in his confidence in the future of Texas, he complimented me on securing more land scrip. He had just returned from our camps on the Medicine River, and reported the cattle coming through in splendid condition. Gray wolves had harassed the herd during the early winter; but long-range rifles and poison were furnished, and our men waged a relentless war on these pirates along the Medicine. Cattle in Texas had wintered strong, which would permit of active operations beginning earlier than usual, and after riding the range for a week we were ready for business. It was well known in all the surrounding country that we would again be in the market for trail cattle, and offerings were plentiful. These tenders ran anywhere from stock cattle to heavy beeves; but the market which we were building up with farmers at Council Grove required young two and three year old steers. It again fell to my province to do the buying, and with the number of brands for sale in the country I expected, with the consent of my partners, to make a new departure. I was beginning to understand the advantages of growing cattle. My holdings of mixed stock on the Clear Fork had virtually cost me nothing, and while they may have been unsalable, yet there was a steady growth and they were a promising source of income. From the results of my mavericking and my trading operations I had been enabled to send two thousand young steers up the trail the spring before, and the proceeds from their sale had lifted me from the slough of despond and set me on a financial rock. Therefore my regard for the eternal cow was enhancing.

Home prices were again ten dollars for two-year-old steers and twelve for threes. Instead of buying outright at these figures, my proposition was to buy individually brands of stock cattle, and turn over all steers of acceptable ages at prevailing prices to the firm of Hunter, Anthony & Co. in making up trail herds. We had already agreed to drive ten thousand head that spring, and my active partner readily saw the advantages that would accrue where one had the range and outfit to take care of the remnants of mixed stock. My partners were both straining their credit at home, and since it was immaterial to them, I was given permission to go ahead. This method of buying might slightly delay the starting of herds, and rather than do so I contracted for three thousand straight threes in Erath County. This herd would start ten days in advance of any other, which would give us cattle on the market at Wichita with the opening of the season. My next purchase was two brands whose range was around the juncture of the main Brazos and Clear Fork, adjoining my ranch. These cattle were to be delivered at our corrals, as, having received the three-year-olds from both brands the spring before, I had a good idea how the stock ought to classify. A third brand was secured up the Clear Fork, adjacent to my range, supposed to number about three thousand, from which nothing had been sold in four years. This latter contingent cost me five dollars a head, but my boys knew the brand well enough to know that they would run forty per cent steer cattle. In all three cases I bought all right and title to the brand, giving them until the last day of March to gather, and anything not tendered for count on receiving, the tail went with the hide.

From these three brands I expected to make up the second herd easily. With no market for cattle, it was safe to count on a brand running one third steers or better, from which I ought to get twenty-five per cent of age for trail purposes. Long before any receiving began I bought four more brands outright in adjoining counties, setting the day for receiving on the 5th of April, everything to be delivered on my ranch on the Clear Fork. There were fully twenty-five thousand cattle in these seven brands, and as I had bought them all half cash and the balance on six months' time, it behooved me to be on the alert and protect my interests. A trusty man was accordingly sent from my ranch to assist in the gathering of each of the four outside brands, to be present at all round-ups, to see that no steer cattle were held back, and that the dropping calves were cared for and saved. This precaution was not taken around my ranch, for any animal which failed to be counted my own men would look out for by virtue of ownership of the brand. My saddle horses were all in fine condition, and were cut into remudas of ninety head each, two new wagons were fitted up, and all was ready to move.

The Erath County herd was to be delivered to us on the 20th of March. George Edwards was to have charge, and he and Major Hunter started in ample time to receive the cattle, the latter proving an apt scholar, while the former was a thorough cowman. In the mean time I had made up a second outfit, putting a man who had made a number of trips with me as foreman in charge, and we moved out to the Clear Fork. The first herd started on the 22d, Major Hunter accompanying it past the Edwards ranch and then joining us on my range. We had kept in close touch with the work then in progress along the Brazos and Clear Fork, and it was probable that we might be able to receive in advance of the appointed day. Fortunately this happened in two cases, both brands overrunning all expectations in general numbers and the quantity of steer cattle. These contingents were met, counted, and received ten miles from the ranch, nothing but the steers two years old and upward being brought in to the corrals. The third brand, from west on the Clear Fork, came in on the dot, and this also surprised me in its numbers of heavy steer cattle. From the three contingents I received over thirteen thousand head, nearly four thousand of which were steers of trail age. On the first day of April we started the second herd of thirty-five hundred twos and threes, the latter being slightly in the majority, but we classified them equally. Major Hunter was pleased with the quality of the cattle, and I was more than satisfied with results, as I had nearly five hundred heavy steers left which would easily qualify as beeves. Estimating the latter at what they ought to net me at Wichita, the remnants of stock cattle cost me about a dollar and a half a head, while I had received more cash than the amount of the half payment.

The beef steers were held under herd to await the arrival of the other contingents. If they fell short in twos and threes, I had hopes of finding an outlet for my beeves with the last herd. The young stuff and stock cattle were allowed to drift back on their own ranges, and we rested on our oars. We had warning of the approach of outside brands, several arriving in advance of appointment, and they were received at once. As before, every brand overran expectations, with no shortage in steers. My men had been wide awake, any number of mature beeves coming in with the mixed stock. As fast as they arrived we cut all steers of desirable age into our herd of beeves, sending the remnant up the river about ten miles to be put under loose herd for the first month. Fifteen-thousand cattle were tendered in the four brands, from which we cut out forty-six hundred steers of trail age. The numbers were actually embarrassing, not in stock cattle, but in steers, as our trail herd numbered now over five thousand. The outside outfits were all detained a few days for a settlement, lending their assistance, as we tally-marked all the stock cattle before sending them up the river to be put under herd. This work was done in a chute with branding irons, running a short bar over the holding-brand, the object being to distinguish animals received then from what might be gathered afterward. There were nearly one hundred men present, and with the amount of help available the third herd was ready to start on the morning of the 6th. It numbered thirty-five hundred, again nearly equal in twos and threes, my ranch foreman having charge. With the third herd started, the question arose what to do with the remnant of a few over sixteen hundred beeves. To turn them loose meant that with the first norther that blew they would go back to their own range. Major Hunter suggested that I drive an individual herd. I tried to sell him an interest in the cattle, but as their ages were unsuited to his market, he pleaded bankruptcy, yet encouraged me to fill up the herd and drive them on my own account.

Something had to be done. I bought sixty horses from the different outfits then waiting for a settlement, adding thirty of my own to the remuda, made up an outfit from the men present, rigged a wagon, and called for a general round-up of my range. Two days afterward we had fifteen hundred younger steers of my own raising in the herd, and on the 10th of the month the fourth one moved out. A day was lost in making a general settlement, after which Major Hunter and I rode through the mixed cattle under herd, finding them contentedly occupying nearly ten miles of the valley of the Clear Fork. Calves were dropping at the rate of one hundred a day, two camps of five men each held them on an ample range, riding lines well back from the valley. The next morning we turned homeward, passing my ranch and corrals, which but a few days before were scenes of activity, but now deserted even by the dogs. From the Edwards ranch we were driven in to Fort Worth, and by the middle of the month reached Wichita.

No herds were due to arrive for a month. My active partner continued on to his home at The Grove, and I started for our camps on the Medicine River. The grass was coming with a rush, the cattle were beginning to shed their winter coats, and our men assured me that the known loss amounted to less than twenty head. The boys had spent an active winter, only a few storms ever bunching the cattle, with less than half a dozen contingents crossing the established lines. Even these were

Andy Adams

followed by our trailers and brought back to their own range; and together with wolfing the time had passed pleasantly. An incident occurred at the upper camp that winter which clearly shows the difference between the cow-hand of that day and the modern bronco-buster. In baiting for wolves, many miles above our range, a supposed trail of cattle was cut by one of the boys, who immediately reported the matter to our Texas trailer at camp. They were not our cattle to a certainty, yet it was but a neighborly act to catch them, so the two men took up the trail. From appearances there were not over fifteen head in the bunch, and before following them many miles, the trailer became suspicious that they were buffalo and not cattle. He trailed them until they bedded down, when he dismounted and examined every bed. No cow ever lay down without leaving hair on its bed, so when the Texan had examined the ground where half a dozen had slept, his suspicions were confirmed. Declaring them buffalo, the two men took up the trail in a gallop, overtaking the band within ten miles and securing four fine robes. There is little or no difference in the tracks of the two animals. I simply mention this, as my patience has been sorely tried with the modern picturesque cowboy, who is merely an amateur when compared with the men of earlier days.

I spent three weeks riding the range on the Medicine. The cattle had been carefully selected, now four and five years old, and if the season was favorable they would be ready for shipment early in the fall. The lower camp was abandoned in order to enlarge the range nearly one third, and after providing for the wants of the men, I rode away to the southeast to intercept the Chisholm trail where it crossed the Kansas line south of Wichita. The town of Caldwell afterward sprang up on the border, but at this time among drovers it was known as Stone's Store, a trading-post conducted by Captain Stone, afterward a cowman, and already mentioned in these memoirs. Several herds had already passed on my arrival; I watched the trail, meeting every outfit for nearly a week, and finally George Edwards came snailing along. He reported our other cattle from seven to ten days behind, but was not aware that I had an individual herd on the trail. Edwards moved on to Wichita, and I awaited the arrival of our second outfit. A brisk rivalry existed between the solicitors for Ellsworth and Wichita, every man working faithfully for his railroad or town, and at night they generally met in social session over a poker game. I never played a card for money now, not that my morals were any too good, but I was married and had partners, and business generally absorbed me to such an extent that I neglected the game.

I met the second herd at Pond Creek, south in the Cherokee Outlet, and after spending a night with them rode through to Wichita in a day and night. We went into camp that year well up the Arkansas River, as two outfits would again hold the four herds. Our second outfit arrived at the chosen grazing grounds on time, the men were instantly relieved, and after a good carouse in town they started home. The two other herds came in without delay, the beeves arriving on the last of the month. Barely half as many cattle would arrive from Texas that summer, as many former drovers from that section were bankrupt on account of the panic of the year before. Yet the market was fairly well supplied with offerings of wintered Texans, the two classes being so distinct that there was very little competition between them. My active partner was on hand early, reporting a healthy inquiry among former customers, all of whom were more than pleased with the cattle supplied them the year before. By being in a position to extend a credit to reliable men, we were enabled to effect sales where other drovers dared not venture.

Business opened early with us. I sold fifteen hundred of my heaviest beeves to an army contractor from Wyoming. My active partner sold the straight three-year-old herd from Erath County to an ex-governor from Nebraska, and we delivered it on the Republican River in that State. Small bunches of from three to five hundred were sold to farmers, and by the first of August we had our holdings reduced to two herds in charge of one outfit. When the hipping season began with our customers at The Grove, trade became active with us at Wichita. Scarcely a week passed but Major Hunter sold a thousand or more to his neighbors, while I skirmished around in the general market. When the outfit returned from the Republican River, I took it in charge, went down on the Medicine, and cut out a thousand beeves, bringing them to the railroad and shipping them to St. Louis. I never saw fatter cattle in my life. When we got the returns from the first consignment, we shipped two trainloads every fortnight until our holding's on the Medicine were reduced to a remnant. A competent bookkeeper was employed early in the year, and in keeping our accounts at Wichita, looking after our shipments, keeping individual interests, by brands, separate from the firm's, he was about the busiest man connected with the summer's business. Aside from our drive of over thirteen thousand head, we bought three whole herds, retailing them in small quantities to our customers, all of which was profitable. I bought four whole remudas on personal account, culled out one hundred and fifty head and sold them at a sacrifice, sending home the remaining two hundred saddle horses. I found it much cheaper and more convenient to buy my supply of saddle stock at trail terminals than at home. Once railroad connections were in operation direct between Kansas and Texas, every outfit preferred to go home by rail, but I adhered to former methods for many years.

In summing up the year's business, never were three partners more surprised. With a remnant of nearly one hundred beeves unfit for shipment, the Medicine River venture had cleared us over two hundred per cent, while the horses on hand were worth ten dollars a head more than what they had cost, owing to their having wintered in the North. The ten thousand trail cattle paid splendidly, while my individual herd had sold out in a manner, leaving the stock cattle at home clear velvet. A programme was outlined for enlarging our business for the coming year, and every dollar of our profits was to be reinvested in wintering and trailing cattle from Texas. Next to the last shipment, the through outfit went home, taking the extra two hundred saddle horses with it, the final consignment being brought in to Wichita for loading out by our ranch help. The shipping ended in October. My last work of the year was the purchase of seven thousand three-year-old steers, intended for our Medicine River range. We had intentionally held George Edwards and his outfit for this purpose, and cutting the numbers into two herds, the Medicine River lads led off for winter quarters. We had bought the cattle worth the money, but not at a sacrifice like the year before, neither would we expect such profits. It takes a good nerve, but experience has taught me that in land and cattle the time of the worst depression is the time to buy. Major Hunter accompanied the herds to their winter quarters, sending Edwards with his outfit, after their arrival on the Medicine, back to Texas, while I took the train and reached home during the first week in November.

CHAPTER XII

CLEAR FORK AND SHENANDOAH

I arrived home in good time for the fall work. The first outfit relieved at Wichita had instructions to begin, immediately on reaching the ranch, a general cow-hunt for outside brands. It was possible that a few head might have escaped from the Clear Fork range and returned to their old haunts, but these would bear a tally-mark distinguishing them from any not gathered at the spring delivery. My regular ranch hands looked after the three purchased brands adjoining our home range, but an independent outfit had been working the past four months gathering strays and remnants in localities where I had previously bought brands. They went as far south as Comanche County and picked up nearly one hundred "Lazy L's," scoured the country where I had purchased the two brands in the spring of 1872, and afterward confined themselves to ranges from which the outside cattle were received that spring. They had made one delivery on the Clear Fork of seven hundred head before my return, and were then away on a second cow-hunt.

On my reaching the ranch the first contingent of gathered cattle were under herd. They were a rag-tag lot, many of them big steers, while much of the younger stuff was clear of earmark or brand until after their arrival at the home corrals. The ranch help herded them by day and penned them at night, but on the arrival of the independent outfit with another contingent of fifteen hundred the first were freed and the second put under herd. Counting both bunches, the strays numbered nearly a thousand head, and cattle bearing no tally-mark fully as many more, while the remainder were mavericks and would have paid the expenses of the outfit for the past four months. I now had over thirty thousand cattle on the Clear Fork, holding them in eleven brands, but decided thereafter to run all the increase in the original "44." This rule had gone into effect the fall previous, and I now proposed to run it on all calves branded. Never before had I felt the necessity of increasing my holdings in land, but with the number of cattle on hand it behooved me to possess a larger acreage of the Clear Fork valley. A surveyor was accordingly sent for, and while the double outfit was branding the home calf crop, I located on the west end of my range a strip of land ten miles long by five wide. At the east end of my ranch another tract was located, five by ten miles, running north and taking in all that country around the junction of the Clear Fork with the mother Brazos. This gave me one hundred and fifty sections of land, lying in the form of an immense Lazy L, and I felt that the expense was justified in securing an ample range for my stock cattle.

My calf crop that fall ran a few over seven thousand head. They were good northern Texas calves, and it would cost but a trifle to run them until they were two-year-olds; and if demand continued in the upper country, some day a trail herd of steers could easily be made up from their numbers. I was beginning to feel rather proud of my land and cattle; the former had cost me but a small outlay, while the latter were clear velvet, as I had sold thirty-five hundred from their increase during the past two years. Once the surveying and branding was over, I returned to the Edwards ranch for the winter. The general outlook in Texas was for the better; quite a mileage of railroad had been built within the State during the past year, and new and prosperous towns had sprung up along their lines. The political situation had quieted down, and it was generally admitted that a Reconstruction government could never again rear its head on Texas soil. The result was that confidence was slowly being restored among the local people, and the press of the State was making a fight for recognition, all of which augured for a brighter future. Living on the frontier and absent the greater portion of the time, I took little interest in local politics, yet could not help but feel that the restoration of self-government to the best elements of our people would in time reflect on the welfare of the State. Since my advent in Texas I had been witness to the growth of Fort Worth from a straggling village in the spring of 1866 to quite a pretentious town in the fall of 1874.

Ever since the partnership was formed I had been aware of and had fostered the political ambitions of the firm's silent member. He had been prominently identified with the State of Kansas since it was a territory, had held positions of trust, and had been a representative in Congress, and all three of us secretly hoped to see him advanced to the United States Senate. We had fully discussed the matter on various occasions, and as the fall elections had gone favorably, the present was considered the opportune time to strike. The firm mutually agreed to stand the expense of the canvass, which was estimated on a reasonable basis, and the campaign opened with a blare of trumpets. Assuming the rôle of a silent partner, I had reports furnished me regularly, and it soon developed that our estimate on the probable expense was too low. We had boldly entered the canvass, our man was worthy, and I wrote back instructing my partners to spare no expense in winning the fight. There were a number of candidates in the race and the legislature was in session, when an urgent letter reached me, urging my presence at the capital of Kansas. The race was narrowing to a close, a personal consultation was urged, and I hastened north as fast as a relay of horses and railroad trains could carry me. On my arrival at Topeka the fight had almost narrowed to a financial one, and we questioned if the game were worth the candle. Yet we were already involved in a considerable outlay, and the consultation resulted in our determination to win, which we did, but at an expense of a little over four times the original estimate, which, however, afterward proved a splendid investment.

I now had hopes that we might enlarge our operations in handling government contracts. Major Hunter saw possibilities along the same line, and our silent partner was awakened to the importance of maintaining friendly relations with the Interior and War departments, gathering all the details in contracting beef with the government for its Indian agencies and army posts in the West. Up to date this had been a lucrative field which only a few Texas drovers had ventured into, most of the contractors being Northern and Eastern men, and usually buying the cattle with which to fill the contracts near the point of delivery. I was impatient to get into this trade, as the Indian deliveries generally took cows, and the army heavy beef, two grades of cattle that at present our firm had no certain demand for. Also the market was gradually moving west from Wichita, and it was only a question of a few years until the settlements of eastern Kansas would cut us off from our established trade around The Grove. I had seen Abilene pass away as a market, Wichita was doomed by the encroachments of agriculture, and it behooved us to be alert for a new outlet.

I made up my mind to buy more land scrip. Not that there had been any perceptible improvement in wild lands, but the general outlook justified its purchase. My agent at Austin reported scrip to be had in ordinary quantities at former prices, and suggested that I supply myself fully, as the new administration was an economical one, and once the great flood of certificates issued by the last Reconstruction régime were absorbed, an advance in land scrip was anticipated. I accordingly bought three hundred sections more, hardly knowing what to do with it, yet I knew there was an empire of fine grazing country between my present home and the Pecos River. If ever the Comanches were brought under subjection there would be ranches and room for all; and our babies were principally boys.

Major Hunter came down earlier than usual. He reported a clear, cold winter on the Medicine and no serious drift of cattle, and expressed the belief that we would come through with a loss not exceeding one per cent. This was encouraging, as it meant fat cattle next fall, fit for any market in the country. It was yet too early to make any move towards putting up herds for the trail, and we took train and went down the country as far as Austin. There was always a difference in cattle prices, running from one to two dollars a head, between the northern and southern parts of the State. Both of us were anxious to acquaint ourselves with the different grades, and made stops in several intervening counties, looking at cattle on the range and pricing them. We spent a week at the capital city and met all the trail drovers living there, many of whom expected to put up herds for that year southeast on the Colorado River. "Shanghai" Pierce had for some time been a prominent figure in the markets of Abilene and Wichita, driving herds of his own from the extreme coast country. But our market required a better quality than coasters and Mexican cattle, and we turned back up the country. Before leaving the capital, Major Hunter and I had a long talk with my merchant friend over the land scrip market, and the latter urged its purchase at once, if wanted, as the issue afloat was being gradually absorbed. Already there had been a noticeable advance in the price, and my partner gave me no peace until I bought, at eighteen dollars a section, two hundred certificates more. Its purchase was making an inroad on my working capital, but the major frowned on my every protest, and I yielded out of deference to his superior judgment.

Returning, we stopped in Bell County, where we contracted for fifteen thousand two and three year old steers. They were good prairie-raised cattle, and we secured them at a dollar a head less than the prices prevailing in the first few counties south of Red River. Major Hunter remained behind, arranging his banking facilities, and I returned home after my outfits. Before leaving Bell County, I left word that we could use fifty good men for the trail, but they would have to come recommended by the ranchmen with whom we were dealing. We expected to make up five herds, and the cattle were to be ready for delivery to us between the 15th and 30th of March. I hastened home and out to the ranch, gathered our saddle stock, outfitted wagons, and engaged all my old foremen and twenty trusty men, and we started with a remuda of five hundred horses to begin the operations of the coming summer. Receiving cattle with me was an old story by this time, and frequently matters came to a standstill between the sellers and ourselves. We paid no attention to former customs of the country; all cattle had to come up full-aged or go into the younger class, while inferior or knotty stags were turned back as not wanted. Scarcely a day passed but there was more or less dispute; but we proposed paying for them, and insisted that all cattle tendered must come up to the specifications of the contract. We stood firm, and after the first two herds were received, all trouble on that score passed, and in making up the last three herds there was actually a surplus of cattle tendered. We used a road brand that year on all steers purchased, and the herds moved out from two to three days apart, the last two being made up in Coryell, the adjoining county north.

George Edwards had charge of the rear herd. There were fourteen days between the first and the last starts, a fortnight of hard work, and we frequently received from ten to thirty miles distant from the branding pens. I rode almost night and day, and Edwards likewise, while Major Hunter kept all the accounts and settled with the sellers. As fast as one herd was ready, it moved out under a foreman and fourteen men, one hundred saddle horses, and a well-stocked commissary. We did our banking at Belton, the county seat, and after the last herd started we returned to town and received quite an ovation from the business men of the village. We had invested a little over one hundred and fifty thousand dollars in cattle in that community, and a banquet was even suggested in our honor by some of the leading citizens. Most of the contracts were made with merchants, many of whom did not own a hoof of cattle, but depended on their customers to deliver the steers. The business interests of the town were anxious to have us return next year. We declined the proposed dinner, as neither Major Hunter nor myself would have made a presentable guest. A month or more had passed since I had left the ranch on the Clear Fork, the only clothes I had were on my back, and they were torn in a dozen places from running cattle in the brush. My partner had been living in cow-camps for the past three weeks, and preferred to be excused from receiving any social attentions. So we thanked our friends and started for the railroad.

Major Hunter went through to The Grove, while I stopped at Fort Worth. A buckboard from home was awaiting me, and the next morning I was at the Edwards ranch. A relay team was harnessed in, and after counting the babies I started for the Clear Fork. By early evening I was in consultation with my ranch foreman, as it was my intention to drive an individual herd if everything justified the venture. I never saw the range on the Clear Fork look better, and the books showed that we could easily gather two thousand twos and threes, while the balance of the herd could be made up of dry and barren cows. All we lacked was about thirty horses, and my ranch hands were anxious to go up the trail; but after riding the range one day I decided that it would be a pity to disturb the pastoral serenity of the valley. It was fairly dotted with my own cattle; month-old calves were playing in groups, while my horse frequently shied at new-born ones, lying like fawns in the tall grass. A round-up at that time meant the separation of mothers from their offspring and injury to cows approaching maternity, and I decided that no commercial necessity demanded the sacrifice. Then again it seemed a short-sighted policy to send half-matured steers to market, when no man could bring the same animals to a full development as cheaply as I could. Barring contagious diseases, cattle are the healthiest creatures that walk the earth, and even on an open range seldom if ever does one voluntarily forsake its birthplace.

I spent two weeks on the ranch and could have stayed the summer through, for I love cattle. Our lead herd was due on the Kansas state line early in May, so remaining at the Edwards ranch until the last possible hour, I took train and reached Wichita, where my active partner was awaiting me. He had just returned from the Medicine River, and reported everything serene. He had made arrangements to have the men attend all the country round-ups within one hundred miles of our range. Several herds had already reached Wichita, and the next day I started south on horseback to meet our cattle at Caldwell on the line, or at Pond Creek in the Cherokee Outlet. It was going to be difficult to secure range for herds within fifteen miles of Wichita, and the opinion seemed general that this would be the last year that town could hope to hold any portion of the Texas cattle trade. On arriving at Pond Creek I found that fully half the herds were turning up that stream, heading for Great Bend, Ellsworth, Ellis, and Nickerson, all markets within the State of Kansas. The year before nearly one third the drive had gone to the two first-named points, and now other towns were offering inducements and bidding for a share of the present cattle exodus.

Our lead herd arrived without an incident en route. The second one came in promptly, both passing on and picking their way through the border settlements to Wichita. I waited until the third one put in an appearance, leaving orders for it and the two rear ones to camp on some convenient creek in the Outlet near Caldwell. Arrangements were made with Captain Stone for supplying the outfits, and I hurried on to overtake the lead herds, then nearing Wichita. An ample range was found but twenty miles up the Arkansas River, and the third day all the Bell County men in the two outfits were sent home by train. The market was much the same as the year before: one herd of three thousand two-year-olds was our largest individual sale. Early in August the last herd was brought from the state line and the through help reduced to two outfits, one holding cattle at Wichita and the other bringing in shipments of beeves from the Medicine River range. The latter were splendid cattle, fatted to a finish for grass animals, and brought top prices in the different markets to which they were consigned. Omitting details, I will say it was an active year, as we bought and sold fully as many more as our drive amounted to, while I added to my stock of saddle horses an even three hundred head.

An amusing incident occurred with one of my men while

holding cattle that fall at Wichita. The boys were in and out of town frequently, and one of them returned to camp one evening and informed me that he wanted to quit work, as he intended to return to Wichita and kill a man. He was a good hand and I tried to persuade him out of the idea, but he insisted that it was absolutely necessary to preserve his honor. I threatened to refuse him a horse, but seeing that menace and persuasion were useless, I ordered him to pick my holdings of saddle stock, gave him his wages due, and told him to be sure and shoot first. He bade us all good-by, and a chum of his went with him. About an hour before daybreak they returned and awoke me, when the aggrieved boy said: "Mr. Anthony, I didn't kill him. No, I didn't kill him. He's a good man. You bet he's a game one. Oh, he's a good man all right." That morning when I awoke both lads were out on herd, and I had an early appointment to meet parties in town. Major Hunter gave me the story immediately on my arrival. The boys had located the offender in a store, and he anticipated the fact that they were on his trail. As our men entered the place, the enemy stepped from behind a pile of clothing with two six-shooters leveled in their faces, and ordered a clerk to relieve the pair of their pistols, which was promptly done. Once the particulars were known at camp, it was looked upon as a good joke on the lad, and whenever he was asked what he thought of Mr. Blank, his reply invariably was, "He's a good man."

The drive that year to the different markets in Kansas amounted to about five hundred thousand cattle. One half this number were handled at Wichita, the surrounding country absorbing them to such an extent that when it came time to restock our Medicine River range I was compelled to go to Great Bend to secure the needed cattle. All saddle horses, both purchased and my own remudas, with wagons, were sent to our winter camps by the shipping crew, so that the final start for Texas would be made from the Medicine River. It was the last of October that the last six trains of beeves were brought in to the railroad for shipment, the season's work drawing to an end. Meanwhile I had closed contracts on ten thousand three-year-old steers at "The Bend," so as fast as the three outfits were relieved of their consignment of beeves they pulled out up the Arkansas River to receive the last cattle of the year. It was nearly one hundred miles from Wichita, and on the arrival of the shipping crews the herds were received and started south for their winter range. Major Hunter and I accompanied the herds to the Medicine, and within a week after reaching the range the two through outfits started home with five wagons and eight hundred saddle horses.

It was the latter part of November when we left our winter camps and returned to The Grove for the annual settlement. Our silent partner was present, and we broke the necks of a number of champagne bottles in properly celebrating the success of the year's work. The wintered cattle had cleared the Dutchman's one per cent, while every hoof in the through and purchased herds was a fine source of profit. Congress would convene within a week, and our silent partner suggested that all three of us go down to Washington and attend the opening exercises. He had already looked into the contracting of beef to the government, and was particularly anxious to have my opinion on a number of contracts to be let the coming winter. It had been ten years since I left my old home in the Shenandoah Valley, my parents were still living, and all I asked was time enough to write a letter to my wife, and buy some decent clothing. The trio started in good time for the opening of Congress, but once we sighted the Potomac River the old home hunger came on me and I left the train at Harper's Ferry. My mother knew and greeted me just as if I had left home that morning on an errand, and had now returned. My father was breaking with years, yet had a mental alertness that was remarkable and a commercial instinct that understood the value of a Texas cow or a section of land scrip. The younger members of the family gathered from their homes to meet "Texas" Anthony, and for ten continuous days I did nothing but answer questions, running from the color of the baby's eyes to why we did not drive the fifteen thousand cattle in one herd, or how big a section of country would one thousand certificates of land scrip cover. My visit was broken by the necessity of conferring with my partners, so, promising to

Andy Adams

spend Christmas with my mother, I was excused until that date.

At the War and Interior departments I made many friends. I understood cattle so thoroughly that there was no feature of a delivery to the government that embarrassed me in the least. A list of contracts to be let from each department was courteously furnished us, but not wishing to scatter our business too wide, we submitted bids for six Indian contracts and four for delivery to army posts on the upper Missouri River. Two of the latter were to be northern wintered cattle, and we had them on the Medicine River; but we also had a sure market on them, and it was a matter of indifference whether we secured them or not. The Indian contracts called for cows, and I was anxious to secure as many as possible, as it meant a market for the aging she stuff on my ranch. Heretofore this class had fulfilled their mission in perpetuating their kind, had lived their day, and the weeds grew rankly where their remains enriched the soil. The bids would not be opened until the middle of January, and we should have notice at once if fortunate in securing any of the awards. The holiday season was approaching, Major Hunter was expected at home, and the firm separated for the time being.

CHAPTER XIII

THE CENTENNIAL YEAR

I returned to Texas early in January. Quite a change had come over the situation since my leaving home the spring before. Except on the frontier, business was booming in the new towns, while a regular revolution had taken place within the past month in land values. The cheapness of wild lands had attracted outside capital, resulting in a syndicate being formed by Northern capitalists to buy up the outstanding issue of land scrip. The movement had been handled cautiously, and had possibly been in active operation for a year or more, as its methods were conducted with the utmost secrecy. Options had been taken on all scrip voted to corporations in the State and still in their possession, agents of the syndicate were stationed at all centres where any amount was afloat, and on a given day throughout the State every certificate on the market was purchased. The next morning land scrip was worth fifty dollars a section, and on my return one hundred dollars a certificate was being freely bid, while every surveyor in the State was working night and day locating lands for individual holders of scrip.

This condition of affairs was largely augmented by a boom in sheep. San Antonio was the leading wool market in the State, many clips having sold as high as forty cents a pound for several years past on the streets of that city. Free range and the high price of wool was inviting every man and his cousin to come to Texas and make his fortune. Money was feverish for investment in sheep, flock-masters were buying land on which to run their bands, and a sheepman was an envied personage. Up to this time there had been little or no occasion to own the land on which the immense flocks grazed the year round, yet under existing cheap prices of land nearly all the watercourses in the immediate country had been taken up. Personally I was dumfounded at the sudden and unexpected change of affairs, and what nettled me most was that all the land adjoining my ranch had been filed on within the past month. The Clear Fork valley all the way up to Fort Griffin had been located, while every vacant acre on the mother Brazos, as far north as Belknap, was surveyed and recorded. I was mortified to think that I had been asleep, but then the change had come like a thief in the night. My wife's trunk was half full of scrip, I had had a surveyor on the ground only a year before, and now the opportunity had passed.

But my disappointment was my wife's delight, as there was no longer any necessity for keeping secret our holdings in land scrip. The little tin trunk held a snug fortune, and next to the babies, my wife took great pride in showing visitors the beautiful lithographed certificates. My ambition was land and cattle, but now that the scrip had a cash value, my wife took as much pride in those vouchers as if the land had been surveyed, recorded, and covered with our own herds. I had met so many reverses that I was grateful for any smile of fortune, and bore my disappointment with becoming grace. My ranch had branded over eight thousand calves that fall, and as long as it remained an open range I had room for my holdings of cattle. There was no question but that the public domain was bountiful, and if it were necessary I could go farther west and locate a new ranch. But it secretly grieved me to realize that what I had so fondly hoped for had come without warning and found me unprepared. I might as well have held title to half a million acres of the Clear Fork Valley as a paltry hundred and fifty sections.

Little time was given me to lament over spilt milk. On the return from my first trip to the Clear Fork, reports from the

War and Interior departments were awaiting me. Two contracts to the army and four to Indian agencies had been awarded us, all of which could be filled with through cattle. The military allotments would require six thousand heavy beeves for delivery on the upper Missouri River in Dakota, while the nation's wards would require thirteen thousand cows at four different agencies in the Indian Territory. My active partner was due in Fort Worth within a week, while bonds for the faithful fulfillment of our contracts would be executed by our silent partner at Washington, D.C. These awards meant an active year to our firm, and besides there was our established trade around The Grove, which we had no intention of abandoning. The government was a sure market, and as long as a healthy demand continued in Kansas for young cattle, the firm of Hunter, Anthony & Co. would be found actively engaged in supplying the same.

Major Hunter arrived under a high pressure of enthusiasm. By appointment we met in Fort Worth, and after carefully reviewing the situation we took train and continued on south to San Antonio. I had seen a herd of beeves, a few years before, from the upper Nueces River, and remembered them as good heavy cattle. There were two dollars a head difference, even in ages among younger stock, between the lower and upper counties in the State, and as it was pounds quantity that we wanted for the army, it was our intention to look over the cattle along the Nueces River before buying our supply of beeves. We met a number of acquaintances in San Antonio, all of whom recommended us to go west if in search of heavy cattle, and a few days later we reached Uvalde County. This was the section from which the beeves had come that impressed me so favorably; I even remembered the ranch brands, and without any difficulty we located the owners, finding them anxious to meet buyers for their mature surplus cattle. We spent a week along the Frio, Leona, and Nueces rivers, and closed contracts on sixty-one hundred five to seven year old beeves. The cattle were not as good a quality as prairie-raised north Texas stock, but the pounds avoirdupois were there, the defects being in their mongrel colors, length of legs, and breadth of horns, heritages from the original Spanish stock. Otherwise they were tall as a horse, clean-limbed as a deer, and active on their feet, and they looked like fine walkers. I estimated that two bits a head would drive them to Red River, and as we bought them at three dollars a head less than prevailing prices for the same-aged beeves north of or parallel to Fort Worth, we were well repaid for our time and trouble.

We returned to San Antonio and opened a bank account. The 15th of March was agreed on to receive. Two remudas of horses would have to be secured, wagons fitted up, and outfits engaged. Heretofore I had furnished all horses for trail work, but now, with our enlarging business, it would be necessary to buy others, which would be done at the expense of the firm. George Edwards was accordingly sent for, and met us at Waco. He was furnished a letter of credit on our San Antonio bank, and authorized to buy and equip two complete outfits for the Uvalde beeves. Edwards was a good judge of horses, there was an abundance of saddle stock in the country, and he was instructed to buy not less than one hundred and twenty-five head for each remuda, to outfit his wagons with four-mule teams, and announce us as willing to engage fourteen men to the herd. Once these details were arranged for, Major Hunter and myself bought two good horses and struck west for Coryell County, where we had put up two herds the spring before. Our return met with a flood of offerings, prices of the previous year still prevailed, and we let contracts for sixty-five hundred three-year-old steers and an equal number of dry and barren cows. We paid seven dollars a head for the latter, and in order to avoid any dispute at the final tender it was stipulated that the offerings must be in good flesh, not under five nor over eight years old, full average in weight, and showing no evidence of pregnancy. Under local customs, "a cow was a cow," and we had to be specific.

We did our banking at Waco for the Coryell herds. Hastening north, our next halt was in Hood County, where we bought thirty-three hundred two-year-old steers and three thousand and odd cows. This completed eight herds secured - three of young steers for the agricultural regions, and five intended for government delivery. We still lacked one for the Indian Bureau, and as I offered to make it up from my holdings, and on a credit, my active partner consented. I was putting in every dollar at my command, my partners were borrowing freely at home, and we were pulling together like a six-mule team to make a success of the coming summer's work. It was now the middle of February, and my active partner went to Fort Worth, where I did my banking, to complete his financial arrangements, while I returned to the ranch to organize the forces for the coming campaign. All the latter were intrusted to me, and while I had my old foremen at my beck and call, it was necessary to employ five or six new ones. With our deliveries scattered from the Indian Territory to the upper Missouri River, as well as our established trade at The Grove, two of us could not cover the field, and George Edwards had been decided on as the third and trusted man. In a practical way he was a better cowman than I was, and with my active Yankee partner for a running mate they made a team that would take care of themselves in any cow country.

A good foreman is a very important man in trail work. The drover or firm may or may not be practical cowmen, but the executive in the field must be the master of any possible situation that may arise, combining the qualities of generalship with the caution of an explorer. He must be a hail-fellow among his men, for he must command by deserving obedience; he must know the inmost thoughts of his herd, noting every sign of alarm or distress, and willingly sacrifice any personal comfort in the interest of his cattle or outfit. I had a few such men, boys who had grown up in my employ, several of whom I would rather trust in a dangerous situation with a herd than take active charge myself. No concern was given for their morals, but they must be capable, trustworthy, and honest, as they frequently handled large sums of money. All my old foremen swore by me, not one of them would accept a similar situation elsewhere, and in selecting the extra trail bosses their opinion was valued and given due consideration.

Andy Adams

Not having driven anything from my ranch the year before, a fine herd of twos, threes, and four-year-old steers could easily be made up. It was possible that a tenth and individual herd might be sent up the country, but no movement to that effect was decided on, and my regular ranch hands had orders only to throw in on the home range and gather outside steer cattle and dry cows. I had wintered all my saddle horses on the Clear Fork, and once the foremen were decided on, they repaired to the ranch and began outfitting for the start. The Coryell herds were to be received one week later than the beef cattle, and the outfits would necessarily have to start in ample time to meet us on our return from the upper Nueces River country. The two foremen allotted to Hood County would start a week later still, so that we would really move north with the advance of the season in receiving the cattle under contract. Only a few days were required in securing the necessary foremen, a remuda was apportioned to each, and credit for the commissary supplies arranged for, the employment of the men being left entirely to the trail bosses. Taking two of my older foremen with me, I started for Fort Worth, where an agreeable surprise awaited me. We had been underbidden at the War Department on both our proposals for northern wintered beeves. The fortunate bidder on one contract was refused the award, - for some duplicity in a former transaction, I learned later, - and the Secretary of War had approached our silent partner to fill the deficiency. Six weeks had elapsed, there was no obligation outstanding, and rather than advertise and relet the contract, the head of the War Department had concluded to allot the deficiency by private award. Major Hunter had been burning the wires between Fort Worth and Washington, in order to hold the matter open until I came in for a consultation. The department had offered half a cent a pound over and above our previous bid, and we bribed an operator to reopen his office that night and send a message of acceptance. We had ten thousand cattle wintering on the Medicine River, and it would just trim them up nicely to pick out all the heavy, rough beeves for filling an army contract.

When we had got a confirmation of our message, we

proceeded on south, accompanied by the two foremen, and reached Uvalde County within a week of the time set for receiving. Edwards had two good remudas in pastures, wagons and teams secured, and cooks and wranglers on hand, and it only remained to pick the men to complete the outfits. With three old trail foremen on the alert for good hands while the gathering and receiving was going on, the help would be ready in ample time to receive the herds. Gathering the beeves was in active operation on our arrival, a branding chute had been built to facilitate the work, and all five of us took to the saddle in assisting ranchmen in holding under herd, as we permitted nothing to be corralled night or day. The first herd was completed on the 14th, and the second a day later, both moving out without an hour's delay, the only instructions being to touch at Great Bend, Kansas, for final orders. The cattle more than came up to expectations, three fourths of them being six and seven years old, and as heavy as oxen. There was something about the days of the open range that left its impression on animals, as these two herds were as uniform in build as deer, and I question if the same country to-day has as heavy beeves.

Three days were lost in reaching Coryell County, where our outfits were in waiting and twenty others were at work gathering cattle. The herds were made up and started without a hitch, and we passed on to Hood County, meeting every date promptly and again finding the trail outfits awaiting us. Leaving my active partner and George Edwards to receive the two herds, I rode through to the Clear Fork in a single day. A double outfit had been at work for the past two weeks gathering outside cattle and had over a thousand under herd on my arrival. Everything had worked out so nicely in receiving the purchased herds that I finally concluded to send out my steers, and we began gathering on the home range. By making small round-ups, we disturbed the young calves as little as possible. I took charge of the extra outfit and my ranch foreman of his own, one beginning on the west end of my range, the other going north and coming down the Brazos. At the end of a week the two crews came together with nearly eight thousand cattle under herd. The next day we cut out thirty-five hundred cows and started them on the trail, turning free the remnant of she stuff, and began shaping up the steers, using only the oldest in making up thirty-two hundred head. There were fully two thousand threes, the remainder being nearly equally divided between twos and fours. No road branding was necessary; the only delay in moving out was in provisioning a wagon and securing a foreman. Failing in two or three quarters, I at last decided on a young fellow on my ranch, and he was placed in charge of the last herd. Great Bend was his destination, I instructed him where to turn off the Chisholm trail, - north of the Salt Fork in the Cherokee Outlet, - and he started like an army with banners.

I rejoined my active partner at Fort Worth. The Hood County cattle had started a week before, so taking George Edwards with us, we took train for Kansas. Major Hunter returned to his home, while Edwards and I lost no time in reaching the Medicine River. A fortnight was spent in riding our northern range, when we took horses and struck out for Pond Creek in the Outlet. The lead herds were due at this point early in May, and on our arrival a number had already passed. A road house and stage stand had previously been established, the proprietor of which kept a register of passing herds for the convenience of owners. None of ours were due, yet we looked over the "arrivals" with interest, and continued on down the trail to Red Fork. The latter was a branch of the Arkansas River, and at low water was inclined to be brackish, and hence was sometimes called the Salt Fork, with nothing to differentiate it from one of the same name sixty miles farther north. There was an old Indian trading post at Red Fork, and I lay over there while Edwards went on south to meet the cows. His work for the summer was to oversee the deliveries at the Indian agencies, Major Hunter was to look after the market at The Bend, and I was to attend to the contracts at army posts on the upper Missouri. Our first steer herd to arrive was from Hood County, and after seeing them safely on the Great Bend trail at Pond Creek, I waited for the other steer cattle from Coryell to arrive. Both herds came in within a day of each other, and I loitered along with them, finally overtaking the lead one when within fifty miles of The Bend. In fair weather it was a delightful existence to loaf along with the cattle; but once all three herds reached their destination, two outfits held them, and I took the Hood County lads and dropped back on the Medicine. Our ranch hands had everything shaped up nicely, and by working a double outfit and making round-ups at noon, when the cattle were on water, we quietly cut out three thousand head of our biggest beeves without materially disturbing our holdings on that range. These northern wintered cattle were intended for delivery at Fort Abraham Lincoln on the Missouri River in what is now North Dakota. The through heavy beeves from Uvalde County were intended for Fort Randall and intermediate posts, some of them for reissue to various Indian agencies. The reservations of half a dozen tribes were tributary to the forts along the upper Missouri, and the government was very liberal in supplying its wards with fresh beef.

The Medicine River beeves were to be grazed up the country to Fort Lincoln. We passed old Fort Larned within a week, and I left the outfit there and returned to The Bend. The outfit in charge of the wintered cattle had orders to touch at and cross the Missouri River at Fort Randall, where I would meet them again near the middle of July. The market had fairly opened at Great Bend, and I was kept busy assisting Major Hunter until the arrival of the Uvalde beef herds. Both came through in splendid condition, were admired by every buyer in the market, and passed on north under orders to graze ten miles a day until reaching their destination. By this time the whereabouts of all the Indian herds were known, yet not a word had reached me from the foreman of my individual cattle after crossing into the Nations. It was now the middle of June, and there were several points en route from which he might have mailed a letter, as did all the other foremen. Herds, which crossed at Red River Station a week after my steers, came into The Bend and reported having spoken no "44" cattle en route. I became uneasy and sent a courier as far south as the state line, who returned with a comfortless message. Finally a foreman in the employ of Jess Evens came to me and reported having taken dinner with a "44" outfit on the South Canadian; that the herd swam the river that afternoon, after which he never hailed them again. They were my own dear cattle, and I was worrying; I was overdue at Fort Randall, and in duty bound to look after the interests of the firm. Major Hunter came to the rescue, in his usual calm manner, and expressed his confidence that all would come out right in the end; that when the mystery was unraveled the foreman would be found blameless.

I took a night train for the north, connected with a boat on the Missouri River, and by finally taking stage reached Fort Randall. The mental worry of those four days would age an ordinary man, but on my arrival at the post a message from my active partner informed me that my cattle had reached Dodge City two weeks before my leaving. Then the scales fell from my eyes, as I could understand that when inquiries were made for the Salt Fork, some wayfarer had given that name to the Red Fork; and the new Dodge trail turned to the left, from the Chisholm, at Little Turkey, the first creek crossed after leaving the river. The message was supplemented a few days later by a letter, stating that Dodge City would possibly be a better market than the Bend, and that my interests would be looked after as well as if I were present. A load was lifted from my shoulders, and when the wintered cattle passed Randall, the whole post turned out to see the beef herd on its way up to Lincoln. The government line of forts along the Missouri River had the whitest lot of officers that it was ever my good fortune to meet. I was from Texas, my tongue and colloquialisms of speech proclaimed me Southern-born, and when I admitted having served in the Confederate army, interest and attention was only heightened, while every possible kindness was simply showered on me.

The first delivery occurred at Fort Lincoln. It was a very simple affair. We cut out half a dozen average beeves, killed, dressed, and weighed them, and an honest average on the herd was thus secured. The contract called for one and a half million pounds on foot; our tender overran twelve per cent; but this surplus was accepted and paid for. The second delivery was at Fort Pierre and the last at Randall, both of which passed pleasantly, the many acquaintances among army men that summer being one of my happiest memories. Leaving Randall, we put in to the nearest railroad point returning, where thirty men were sent home, after which we swept down the country and arrived at Great Bend during the last week in September. My active partner had handled his assignment of the summer's work in a masterly manner, having wholesaled my herd at Dodge City at as good figures as our other cattle brought in retail quantities at The Bend. The former point had received three hundred and fifty thousand Texas cattle that summer, while every one conceded that Great Bend's business as a trail terminal would close with that season. The latter had handled nearly a quarter-million cattle that year, but like Abilene, Wichita, and other trail towns in eastern Kansas, it was doomed to succumb to the advance guard of pioneer settlers.

The best sale of the year fell to my active partner. Before the shipping season opened, he sold, range count, our holdings on the Medicine River, including saddle stock, improvements, and good will. The cattle might possibly have netted us more by marketing them, but it was only a question of time until the flow of immigration would demand our range, and Major Hunter had sold our squatter's rights while they had a value. A new foreman had been installed on our giving up possession, and our old one had been skirmishing the surrounding country the past month for a new range, making a favorable report on the Eagle Chief in the Outlet. By paying a trifling rental to the Cherokee Nation, permission could be secured to hold cattle on these lands, set aside as a hunting ground. George Edwards had been rotting all summer in issuing cows at Indian agencies, but on the first of October the residue of his herds would be put in pastures or turned free for the winter. Major Hunter had wound up his affairs at The Bend, and nothing remained but a general settlement of the summer's work. This took place at Council Grove, our silent partner and Edwards both being present. The profits of the year staggered us all. I was anxious to go home, the different outfits having all gone by rail or overland with the remudas, with the exception of the two from Uvalde, which were property of the firm. I had bought three hundred extra horses at The Bend, sending them home with the others, and now nothing remained but to stock the new range in the Cherokee Outlet. Edwards and my active partner volunteered for this work, it being understood that the Uvalde remudas would be retained for ranch use, and that not over ten thousand cattle were to be put on the new range for the winter. Our silent partner was rapidly awakening to the importance of his usefulness in securing future contracts with the War and Indian departments, and vaguely outlining the future, we separated to three points of the compass.

CHAPTER XIV

ESTABLISHING A NEW RANCH

I hardly knew Fort Worth on my return. The town was in the midst of a boom. The foundations of many store buildings were laid on Monday morning, and by Saturday night they were occupied and doing a land-office business. Lots that could have been bought in the spring for one hundred dollars were now commanding a thousand, while land scrip was quoted as scarce at twenty-five cents an acre. I hurried home, spoke to my wife, and engaged two surveyors to report one week later at my ranch on the Clear Fork. Big as was the State and boundless as was her public domain, I could not afford to allow this advancing prosperity to catch me asleep again, and I firmly concluded to empty that little tin trunk of its musty land scrip. True enough, the present boom was not noticeable on the frontier, yet there was a buoyant feeling in the air that betokened a brilliant future. Something enthused me, and as my creed was land and cattle, I made up my mind to plunge into both to my full capacity.

The last outfit to return from the summer's drive was detained on the Clear Fork to assist in the fall branding. Another one of fifteen men all told was chosen from the relieved lads in making up a surveying party, and taking fifty saddle horses and a well-stocked commissary with us, we started due west. I knew the country for some distance beyond Fort Griffin, and from late maps in possession of the surveyors, we knew that by holding our course, we were due to strike a fork of the mother

Brazos before reaching the Staked Plain. Holding our course contrary to the needle, we crossed the Double Mountain Fork, and after a week out from the ranch the brakes which form the border between the lowlands and the Llano Estacado were sighted. Within view of the foothills which form the approach of the famous plain, the Salt and Double Mountain forks of the Brazos are not over twelve miles apart. We traveled up the divide between these two rivers, and when within thirty miles of the low-browed borderland a halt was called and we went into camp. From the view before us one could almost imagine the feelings of the discoverer of this continent when he first sighted land; for I remember the thrill which possessed our little party as we looked off into either valley or forward to the menacing Staked Plain in our front. There was something primal in the scene, - something that brought back the words, "In the beginning God created the heavens and the earth." Men who knew neither creed nor profession of faith felt themselves drawn very near to some great creative power. The surrounding view held us spellbound by its beauty and strength. It was like a rush of fern-scents, the breath of pine forests, the music of the stars, the first lovelight in a mother's eye; and now its pristine beauty was to be marred, as covetous eyes and a lust of possession moved an earth-born man to lay hands on all things created for his use.

Camp was established on the Double Mountain Fork. Many miles to the north, a spur of the Plain extended eastward, in the elbow of which it was my intention to locate the new ranch. A corner was established, a meridian line was run north beyond the Salt Fork and a random one west to the foothills. After a few days one surveyor ran the principal lines while the other did the cross-sectioning and correcting back, both working from the same camp, the wagon following up the work. Antelope were seen by the thousands, frequently buffaloes were sighted, and scarcely a day passed but our rifles added to the larder of our commissary supplies. Within a month we located four hundred sections, covering either side of the Double Mountain Fork, and embracing a country ten miles wide by forty long. Coming back to our original meridian line across to the Salt Fork, the work of surveying that valley was begun, when I was compelled to turn homeward. A list of contracts to be let by the War and Interior departments would be ready by December 1, and my partners relied on my making all the estimates. There was a noticeable advance of fully one dollar a head on steer cattle since the spring before, and I was supposed to have my finger on the pulse of supply and prices, as all government awards were let far in advance of delivery. George Edwards had returned a few days before and reported having stocked the new ranch in the Outlet with twelve thousand steers. The list of contracts to be let had arrived, and the two of us went over them carefully. The government was asking for bids on the delivery of over two hundred thousand cattle at various posts and agencies in the West, and confining ourselves to well-known territory, we submitted bids on fifteen awards, calling for forty-five thousand cattle in their fulfillment.

Our estimates were sent to Major Hunter for his approval, who in turn forwarded them to our silent partner at Washington, to be submitted to the proper departments. As the awards would not be made until the middle of January, nothing definite could be done until then, so, accompanied by George Edwards, I returned to the surveying party on the Salt Fork of the Brazos. We found them busy at their work, the only interruption having been an Indian scare, which only lasted a few days. The men still carried rifles against surprise, kept a scout on the lookout while at work, and maintained a guard over the camp and remuda at night. During my absence they had located a strip of country ten by thirty miles, covering the valley of the Salt Fork, and we still lacked three hundred sections of using up the scrip. The river, along which they were surveying, made an abrupt turn to the north, and offsetting by sections around the bend, we continued on up the valley for twenty miles or until the brakes of the Plain made the land no longer desirable. Returning to our commencement point with still one hundred certificates left, we extended the survey five miles down both rivers, using up the last acre of scrip. The new ranch was irregular in form, but it controlled the waters of fully one million acres of fine grazing land and was clothed with a carpet of nutritive grasses. This was the range of the buffalo, and the instinct of that animal could be relied on in choosing a range for its successor, the Texas cow.

The surveying over, nothing remained but the recording of the locations at the county seat to which for legal purposes this unorganized country was attached. All of us accompanied the outfit returning, and a gala week we spent, as no less than half a dozen buffalo robes were secured before reaching Fort Griffin. Deer and turkey were plentiful, and it was with difficulty that I restrained the boys from killing wantonly, as they were young fellows whose very blood yearned for the chase or any diverting excitement. We reached the ranch on the Clear Fork during the second week in January, and those of the outfit who had no regular homes were made welcome guests until work opened in the spring. My calf crop that fall had exceeded all expectations, nearly nine thousand having been branded, while the cattle were wintering in splendid condition. There was little or nothing to do, a few hunts with the hounds merely killing time until we got reports from Washington. In spite of all competition we secured eight contracts, five with the army and the remainder with the Indian Bureau.

Then the work opened in earnest. My active partner was due the first of February, and during the interim George Edwards and I rode a circle of five counties in search of brands of cattle for sale. In the course of our rounds a large number of whole stocks were offered us, but at firmer prices, yet we closed no trades, though many brands were bargains. It was my intention to stock the new ranch on the Double Mountain Fork the coming summer, and if arrangements could be agreed on with Major Hunter, I might be able to repeat my success of the summer of '74. Emigration to Texas was crowding the ranches to the frontier, many of them unwillingly, and it appealed to me strongly that the time was opportune for securing an ample holding of stock cattle. The appearance of my active partner was the beginning of active operations, and after we had outlined the programme for the summer and gone through all the details thoroughly, I asked for the privilege of supplying the cows on the Indian contracts. Never did partners stand more willingly by each other than did the firm of Hunter, Anthony & Co., and I only had to explain the opportunity of buying brands at wholesale, sending the young steers up the trail and the aging, dry, and barren cows to Indian agencies, to gain the hearty approval of the little Yankee major. He was entitled to a great deal of credit for my holdings in land, for from his first sight of Texas, day after day, line upon line, precept upon precept, he had urged upon me the importance of securing title to realty, while its equivalent in scrip was being hawked about, begging a buyer. Now we rejoiced together in the fulfillment of his prophecy, as I can lay little claim to any foresight, but am particularly anxious to give credit where credit is due.

With an asylum for any and all remnants of stock cattle, we authorized George Edwards to close trades on a number of brands. Taking with us the two foremen who had brought beef herds out of Uvalde County the spring before, the major and I started south on the lookout for beeves. The headwaters of the Nueces and its tributaries were again our destination, and the usual welcome to buyers was extended with that hospitality that only the days of the open range knew and practiced. We closed contracts with former customers without looking at their cattle. When a ranchman gave us his word to deliver us as good or better beeves than the spring before, there was no occasion to question his ability, and the cattle never deceived. There might arise petty wrangles over trifles, but the general hungering for a market among cowmen had not yet been satiated, and they offered us their best that we might come again. We placed our contracts along three rivers and over as many counties, limiting the number to ten thousand beeves of the same ages and paying one dollar a head above the previous spring. One of our foremen was provided with a letter of credit, and the two were left behind to make up three new and complete outfits for the trail.

This completed the purchase of beef cattle. Two of our contracts called for northern wintered beeves, which would be filled out of our holdings in the Cherokee Outlet. We again stopped in central Texas, but prices were too firm, and we passed on west to San Saba and Lampasas counties, where we effected trades on nine thousand five hundred three-year-old steers. My own outfits would drop down from the Clear Fork to receive these cattle, and after we had perfected our banking arrangements the major returned to San Antonio and I started homeward. George Edwards had in the mean time bargained for ten brands, running anywhere from one to five thousand head, paying straight through five to seven dollars, half cash and the balance in eight months, everything to be delivered on the Clear Fork. We intentionally made these deliveries late - during the last week in March and the first one in April - in order that Major Hunter might approve of the three herds of cows for Indian delivery. Once I had been put in possession of all necessary details, Edwards started south to join Major Hunter, as the receiving of the Nueces River beeves was set for from the 10th to the 15th of March.

I could see a busy time ahead. There was wood to haul for the branding, three complete outfits to start for the central part of the State, new wagons to equip for the trail, and others to care for the calf crop while en route to the Double Mountain Fork. There were oxen to buy in equipping teams to accompany the stock cattle to the new ranch, two yoke being allowed to each wagon, as it was strength and not speed that was desired. My old foremen rallied at a word and relieved me of the lesser details of provisioning the commissaries and engaging the help. Trusty men were sent to oversee and look out for my interests in gathering the different brands, the ranges of many of them being fifty to one hundred miles distant. The different brands were coming from six separate counties along the border, and on their arrival at my ranch we must be ready to receive, brand, and separate the herds into their respective classes, sending two grades to market and the remnant to their new home at the foot of the Staked Plain. The condition of the mules must be taken into consideration before the army can move, and in cattle life the same reliance is placed on the fitness for duty of the saddle horses. I had enough picked ones to make up a dozen remudas if necessary, and rested easy on that score. The date for receiving arrived and found us all ready and waiting.

The first herd was announced to arrive on the 25th of March. I met it ten miles from the ranch. My man assured me that the brand as gathered was intact and that it would run fifty per cent dry cows and steers over two years old. A number of mature beeves even were noticeable and younger steers were numerous, while the miscellany of the herd ran to every class and condition of the bovine race. Two other brands were expected the next day, and that evening the first one to arrive was counted and accepted. The next morning the entire herd was run through a branding chute and classified, all steers above a yearling and dry and aging cows going into one contingent and the mixed cattle into another. In order to save horseflesh, this work was easily done in the corrals. By hanging a gate at the exit of the branding chute, a man sat overhead and by swinging it a variation of two feet, as the cattle trailed through the trough in single file, the herd was cut into two classes. Those intended for the trail were put under herd, while the stock cattle were branded into the "44" and held separate. The second and third herds were treated in a similar manner, when we found ourselves with over eleven thousand cattle on hand, with two other brands due in a few days. But the evening of the fourth day saw a herd of thirty-three hundred steers on its way to Kansas, while a second one, numbering two hundred more than the first, was lopped off from the mixed stuff and started west for the Double Mountain Fork.

The situation was eased. A conveyance had been sent to the railroad to meet my partner, and before he and Edwards arrived two other brands had been received. A herd of thirty-five hundred dry cows was approved and started at once for the Indian Territory, while a second one moved out for the west, cleaning up the holdings of mixed stuff. The congestion was again relieved, and as the next few brands were expected to run light in steers, everything except cows was held under herd until all had been received. The final contingent came in from Wise County and were shaped up, and the last herd of cows, completing ten thousand five hundred, started for the Washita agency. I still had nearly sixty-five hundred steers on hand, and cutting back all of a small overplus of thin light cows, I had three brands of steers cut into one herd and four into another, both moving out for Dodge City. This left me with fully eight thousand miscellany on hand, with nothing but my ranch outfit to hold them, close-herding by day and bedding down and guarding them by night. Settlements were made with the different sellers, my outstanding obligations amounting to over one hundred thousand dollars, which the three steer herds were expected to liquidate. My active partner and George Edwards took train for the north. The only change in the programme was that Major Hunter was to look after our deliveries at army posts, while I was to meet our herds on their arrival in Dodge City. The cows were sold to the firm, and including my individual cattle, we had twelve herds on the trail, or a total of thirty-nine thousand five hundred head.

On the return of the first outfit from the west, some three weeks after leaving, the herd of stock cattle was cut in two and started. But a single man was left on the Clear Fork, my ranch foreman taking one herd, while I accompanied the other. It requires the patience of a saint to handle cows and calves, two wagons to the herd being frequently taxed to their capacity in picking up the youngsters. It was a constant sight to see some of the boys carrying a new-born calf across the saddle seat, followed by the mother, until camp or the wagon was reached. I was ashamed of my own lack of patience on that trip, while irritable men could while away the long hours, nursing along the drag end of a herd of cows and their toddling offspring. We averaged only about ten miles a day, the herds were large and unwieldy, and after twelve days out both were scattered along the Salt Fork and given their freedom. Leaving one outfit to locate the cattle on the new range, the other two hastened back to the Clear Fork and gathered two herds, numbering thirty-five hundred each, of young cows and heifers from the ranch stock. But a single day was lost in rounding-up, when they were started west, half a day apart, and I again took charge of an outfit, the trip being an easy one and made in ten days, as the calves were large enough to follow and there were no drag cattle among them. On our arrival at the new ranch, the cows and heifers were scattered among the former herds, and both outfits started back, one to look after the Clear Fork and the other to bring through the last herd in stocking my new possessions. This gave me fully twenty-five thousand mixed cattle on my new range, relieving the old ranch of a portion of its she stuff and shaping up both stocks to better advantage.

It was my intention to make my home on the Clear Fork thereafter, and the ranch outfit had orders to build a comfortable house during the summer. The frontier was rapidly moving westward, the Indian was no longer a dread, as it was only a question of time until the Comanche and his ally would imitate their red brethren and accept the dole of the superior race. I was due in Dodge City the first of June, the ranches would take care of themselves, and touching at the Edwards ranch for a day, I reached "Dodge" before any of the herds arrived. Here was a typical trail town, a winter resort for buffalo hunters, no settlement for fifty miles to the east, and an almost boundless range on which to hold through Texas cattle. The business was bound to concentrate at this place, as all other markets were abandoned within the State, while it was easily accessible to the mountain regions on the west. It was the logical meeting point for buyers and drovers; and while the town of that day has passed into history as "wicked Dodge," it had many redeeming features. The veneer of civilization may have fallen, to a certain extent, from the wayfaring man who tarried in this cow town, yet his word was a bond, and he reverenced the pure in womanhood, though to insult him invited death.

George Edwards and Major Hunter had become such great chums that I was actually jealous of being supplanted in the affections of the Yankee major. The two had been inseparable for months, visiting at The Grove, spending a fortnight together at the beef ranch in the Outlet, and finally putting in an appearance at Dodge. Headquarters for the summer were established at the latter point, our bookkeeper arrived, and we were ready for business. The market opened earlier than at more eastern points. The bulk of the sales were made to ranchmen, who used whole herds where the agricultural regions only bought cattle by the hundreds. It was more satisfactory than the retail trade; credit was out of the question, and there was no haggling over prices. Cattle companies were forming and stocking new ranges, and an influx of English and Scotch capital was seeking investment in ranches and live stock in the West, - a mere forerunner of what was to follow in later years.

Our herds began arriving, and as soon as an outfit could be freed it was started for the beef ranch under George Edwards, where a herd of wintered beeves was already made up to start for the upper Missouri River. Major Hunter followed a week later with the second relieved outfit, and our cattle were all moving for their destinations. The through beef herds from the upper Nueces River had orders to touch at old Fort Larned to the eastward, Edwards drifted on to the Indian agencies, and I bestirred myself to the task of selling six herds of young cattle at Dodge. Once more I was back in my old element, except that every feature of the latter market was on an enlarged scale. Two herds were sold to one man in Colorado, three others went under contract to the Republican River in Nebraska, and the last one was cut into blocks and found a market with feeders in Kansas. Long before deliveries were concluded to the War or Interior departments, headquarters were moved back to The Grove, my work being done. In the interim of waiting for the close of the year's business, our bookkeeper looked after two shipments of a thousand head each from the beef ranch, while I visited my brother in Missouri and surprised him by buying a carload of thoroughbred bulls. Arrangements were made for shipping them to Fort Worth during the last week in November, and promising to call for them, I returned to The Grove to meet my partners and adjust all accounts for the year.

CHAPTER XV

HARVEST HOME

The firm's profits for the summer of '77 footed up over two hundred thousand dollars. The government herds from the Cherokee Outlet paid the best, those sent to market next, while the through cattle remunerated us in the order of beeves, young steers, and lastly cows. There was a satisfactory profit even in the latter, yet the same investment in other classes paid a better per cent profit, and the banking instincts of my partners could be relied on to seek the best market for our capital. There was nothing haphazard about our business; separate accounts were kept on every herd, and at the end of the season the percentage profit on each told their own story. For instance, in the above year it cost us more to deliver a cow at an agency in the Indian Territory than a steer at Dodge City, Kansas. The herds sold in Colorado had been driven at an expense of eighty-five cents a head, those delivered on the Republican River ninety, and every cow driven that year cost us over one dollar a head in general expense. The necessity of holding the latter for a period of four months near agencies for issuing purposes added to the cost, and was charged to that particular department of our business.

George Edwards and my active partner agreed to restock our beef ranch in the Outlet, and I returned to Missouri. I make no claim of being the first cowman to improve the native cattle of Texas, yet forty years' keen observation has confirmed my original idea, - that improvement must come through the native and gradually. Climatic conditions in Texas are such that the best types of the bovine race would deteriorate if compelled to subsist the year round on the open range. The strongest point in the original Spanish cattle was their inborn ability as foragers, being inured for centuries to drouth, the heat of summer, and the northers of winter, subsisting for months on prickly pear, a species of the cactus family, or drifting like game animals to more favored localities in avoiding the natural afflictions that beset an arid country. In producing the ideal range animal it was more important to retain those rustling qualities than to gain a better color, a few pounds in weight, and a shortening of horns and legs, unless their possessor could withstand the rigors of a variable climate. Nature befriends the animal race. The buffalo of Montana could face the blizzard, while his brother on the plains of Texas sought shelter from the northers in cañons and behind sand-dunes, guided by an instinct that foretold the coming storm.

I accompanied my car of thoroughbred bulls and unloaded them at the first station north of Fort Worth. They numbered twenty-five, all two-year-olds past, and were representative of three leading beef brands of established reputation. Others had tried the experiment before me, the main trouble being in acclimation, which affects animals the same as the human family. But by wintering them at their destination, I had hopes of inuring the importation so that they would withstand the coming summer, the heat of which was a sore trial to a northern-bred animal. Accordingly I made arrangements with a farmer to feed my car of bulls during the winter, hay and grain both being plentiful. They had cost me over five thousand dollars, and rather than risk the loss of a single one by chancing them on the range, an additional outlay of a few hundred dollars was justified. Limiting the corn fed to three barrels to the animal a month, with plenty of rough feed, ought to bring them through the winter in good, healthy form. The farmer promised to report monthly on their condition, and agreeing to send for them by the first of April, I hastened on home.

My wife had taken a hand in the building of the new house on the Clear Fork. It was quite a pretentious affair, built of hewed logs, and consisted of two large rooms with a hallway between, a gallery on three sides, and a kitchen at the rear. Each of the main rooms had an ample fireplace, both hearths and chimneys built from rock, the only material foreign to the ranch being the lumber in the floors, doors, and windows. Nearly all the work was done by the ranch hands, even the clapboards were riven from oak that grew along the mother Brazos, and my wife showed me over the house as though it had been a castle that she had inherited from some feudal forbear. I was easily satisfied; the main concern was for the family, as I hardly lived at home enough to give any serious thought to the roof that sheltered me. The original buildings had been improved and enlarged for the men, and an air of prosperity pervaded the Anthony ranch consistent with the times and the success of its owner.

The two ranches reported a few over fifteen thousand calves branded that fall. A dim wagon road had been established between the ranches, by going and returning outfits during the stocking of the new ranch the spring before, and the distance could now be covered in two days by buckboard. The list of government contracts to be let was awaiting my attention, and after my estimates had been prepared, and forwarded to my active partner, it was nearly the middle of December before I found time to visit the new ranch. The hands at Double Mountain had not been idle, snug headquarters were established, and three line camps on the outskirts of the range were comfortably equipped to shelter men and horses. The cattle had located nicely, two large corrals had been built on each river, and the calves were as thrifty as weeds. Gray wolves were the worst enemy encountered, running in large bands and finding shelter in the cedar brakes in the cañons and foothills which border on the Staked Plain. My foreman on the Double Mountain ranch was using poison judiciously, all the line camps were supplied with the same, and an active winter of poisoning wolves was already inaugurated before my arrival. Long-range rifles would supplement the work, and a few years of relentless war on these pests would rid the ranch of this enemy of live stock.

Together my foreman and I planned for starting an improved herd of cattle. A cañon on the west was decided on as a range, as it was well watered from living springs, having a valley several miles wide, forming a park with ample range for two thousand cattle. The bluffs on either side were abrupt, almost an in closure, making it an easy matter for two men to loose-herd a small amount of stock, holding them adjoining my deeded range, yet separate. The survival of the fittest was adopted as the rule in beginning the herd, five hundred choice cows were to form the nucleus, to be the pick of the new ranch, thrift and formation to decide their selection. Solid colors only were to be chosen, every natural point in a cow was to be considered, with the view of reproducing the race in improved form. My foreman - an intelligent young fellow - was in complete sympathy, and promised me that he would comb the range in selecting the herd. The first appearance of grass in the spring was agreed on as the time for gathering the cows, when he would personally come to the Clear Fork and receive the importation of bulls, thus fully taking all responsibility in establishing the improved herd. By this method, unless our plans miscarried, in the course of a few years we expected to be raising quarter-bloods in the main ranch stock, and at the same time retaining all those essential qualities that distinguish the range-raised from the domestic-bred animal.

On my return to the Clear Fork, which was now my home, a letter from my active partner was waiting, informing me that he and Edwards would reach Texas about the time the list of awards would arrive. They had been unsuccessful in fully stocking our beef ranch, securing only three thousand head, as prices were against them, and the letter intimated that something must be done to provide against a repetition of this· unforeseen situation. The ranch in the Outlet had paid us a higher per cent on the investment than any of our ventures, and to neglect fully stocking it was contrary to the creed of

Hunter, Anthony & Co. True, we were double-wintering some four thousand head of cattle on our Cherokee range, but if a fair allowance of awards was allotted the firm, requiring northern wintered cattle in filling, it might embarrass us to supply the same when we did not have the beeves in hand; it was our business to have the beef.

At the appointed time the buckboard was sent to Fort Worth, and a few days later Major Hunter and our main segundo drove up to the Clear Fork. Omitting all preludes, atmosphere, and sunsets, we got down to business at once. If we could drive cattle to Dodge City and market them for eighty-five cents, we ought to be able to deliver them on our northern range for six bits, and the horses could be returned or sold at a profit. If any of our established trade must be sacrificed, why, drop what paid the least; but half stock our beef ranch? Never again! This was to be the slogan for the coming summer, and, on receiving the report from Washington, we were enabled to outline a programme for the year. The gradually advancing prices in cattle were alarming me, as it was now perceptible in cows, and in submitting our bids on Indian awards I had made the allowance of one dollar a head advance over the spring before. In spite of this we were allotted five contracts from the Interior Department and seven to the Army, three of the latter requiring ten thousand northern wintered beeves, - only oversold three thousand head. Major Hunter met my criticisms by taking the ground that we virtually had none of the cattle on hand, and if we could buy Southern stock to meet our requirements, why not the three thousand that we lacked in the North. Our bids had passed through his hands last; he knew our northern range was not fully stocked, and had forwarded the estimates to our silent partner at Washington, and now the firm had been assigned awards in excess of their holdings. But he was the kind of a partner I liked, and if he could see his way clear, he could depend on my backing him to the extent of my ability and credit.

The business of the firm had grown so rapidly that it was deemed advisable to divide it into three departments, - the

Army, the Indian, the beef ranch and general market. Major Hunter was specially qualified to handle the first division, the second fell to Edwards, and the last was assumed by myself. We were to consult each other when convenient, but each was to act separately for the firm, my commission requiring fifteen thousand cattle for our ranch in the Outlet, and three herds for the market at Dodge City. Our banking points were limited to Fort Worth and San Antonio, so agreeing to meet at the latter point on the 1st of February for a general consultation, we separated with a view to feeling the home market. Our man Edwards dropped out in the central part of the State, my active partner wished to look into the situation on the lower Nueces River, and I returned to the headwaters of that stream. During the past two summers we had driven five herds of heavy beeves from Uvalde and adjoining counties, and while we liked the cattle of that section, it was considered advisable to look elsewhere for our beef supply. Within a week I let contracts for five herds of two and three year old steers, then dropped back to the Colorado River and bought ten thousand more in San Saba and McCulloch counties. This completed the purchases in my department, and I hastened back to San Antonio for the expected consultation. Neither my active partner nor my trusted man had arrived, nor was there a line to indicate where they were or when they might be expected, though Major Hunter had called at our hotel a few days previously for his mail. The designated day was waning, and I was worried by the non-appearance of either, when I received a wire from Austin, saying they had just sublet the Indian contracts.

The next morning my active partner and Edwards arrived. The latter had met some parties at the capital who were anxious to fill our Indian deliveries, and had wired us in the firm's name, and Major Hunter had taken the first train for Austin. Both returned wreathed in smiles, having sublet our awards at figures that netted us more than we could have realized had we bought and delivered the cattle at our own risk. It was clear money, requiring not a stroke of work, while it freed a valuable man in outfitting, receiving, and starting our other herds, as well as relieving a snug sum for reinvestment. Our capital lay idle half the year, the spring months were our harvest, and, assigning Edwards full charge of the cattle bought on the Colorado River, we instructed him to buy for the Dodge market four herds more in adjoining counties, bringing down the necessary outfits to handle them from my ranch on the Clear Fork. Previous to his return to San Antonio my active partner had closed contracts on thirteen thousand heavy beeves on the Frio River and lower Nueces, thus completing our purchases. A healthy advance was noticeable all around in steer cattle, though hardly affecting cows; but having anticipated a growing appreciation in submitting our bids, we suffered no disappointment. A week was lost in awaiting the arrival of half a dozen old foremen. On their arrival we divided them between us and intrusted them with the buying of horses and all details in making up outfits.

The trails leading out of southern Texas were purely local ones, the only established trace running from San Antonio north, touching at Fort Griffin, and crossing into the Nations at Red River Station in Montague County. All our previous herds from the Uvalde regions had turned eastward to intercept this main thoroughfare, though we had been frequently advised to try a western outlet known as the Nueces Cañon route. The latter course would bring us out on high tablelands, but before risking our herds through it, I decided to ride out the country in advance. The cañon proper was about forty miles long, through which ran the source of the Nueces River, and if the way were barely possible it looked like a feasible route. Taking a pack horse and guide with me, I rode through and out on the mesa beyond. General McKinzie had used this route during his Indian campaigns, and had even built mounds of rock on the hills to guide the wayfarer, from the exit of the cañon across to the South Llano River. The trail was a rough one, but there was grass sufficient to sustain the herds and ample bed-grounds in the valleys, and I decided to try the western outlet from Uvalde. An early, seasonable spring favored us with fine grass on which to put up and start the herds, all five moving out within a week of each other. I promised my foremen to accompany them through the cañon, knowing that the passage would be a trial to man and beast, and asked the old bosses to loiter along, so that there would be but a few hours' difference between the rear and lead herds.

I received sixteen thousand cattle, and the four days required in passing through Nueces Cañon and reaching water beyond were the supreme physical test of my life. It was a wild section, wholly unsettled, between low mountains, the river-bed constantly shifting from one flank of the valley to the other, while cliffs from three to five hundred feet high alternated from side to side. In traveling the first twenty-five miles we crossed the bed of the river twenty-one times; and besides the river there were a great number of creeks and dry arroyos putting in from the surrounding hills, so that we were constantly crossing rough ground. The beds of the streams were covered with smooth, water-worn pebbles, white as marble, and then again we encountered limestone in lava formation, honeycombed with millions of sharp, up-turned cells. Some of the descents were nearly impossible for wagons, but we locked both hind wheels and just let them slide down and bounce over the boulders at the bottom. Half-way through the cañon the water failed us, with the south fork of the Llano forty miles distant in our front. We were compelled to allow the cattle to pick their way over the rocky trail, the herds not over a mile apart, and scarcely maintaining a snail's pace. I rode from rear to front and back again a dozen times in clearing the defile, and noted that splotches of blood from tender-footed cattle marked the white pebbles at every crossing of the river-bed. On the evening of the third day, the rear herd passed the exit of the cañon, the others having turned aside to camp for the night. Two whole days had now elapsed without water for the cattle.

I had not slept a wink the two previous nights. The south fork of the Llano lay over twenty miles distant, and although it had ample water two weeks before, one of the foremen and I rode through to it that night to satisfy ourselves. The supply was found sufficient, and before daybreak we were back in camp, arousing the outfits and starting the herds. In the spring of

1878 the old military trail, with its rocky sentinels, was still dimly defined from Nueces Cañon north to the McKinzie water-hole on the South Llano. The herds moved out with the dawn. Thousands of the cattle were travel-sore, while a few hundred were actually tender-footed. The evening before, as we came out into the open country, we had seen quite a local shower of rain in our front, which had apparently crossed our course nearly ten miles distant, though it had not been noticeable during our night's ride. The herds fell in behind one another that morning like columns of cavalry, and after a few miles their stiffness passed and they led out as if they had knowledge of the water ahead. Within two hours after starting we crossed a swell of the mesa, when the lead herd caught a breeze from off the damp hills to the left where the shower had fallen the evening before. As they struck this rise, the feverish cattle raised their heads and pulled out as if that vagrant breeze had brought them a message that succor and rest lay just beyond. The point men had orders to let them go, and as fast as the rear herds came up and struck this imaginary line or air current, a single moan would surge back through the herd until it died out at the rear. By noon there was a solid column of cattle ten miles long, and two hours later the drag and point men had trouble in keeping the different herds from mixing. Without a halt, by three o'clock the lead foremen were turning their charges right and left, and shortly afterward the lead cattle were plunging into the purling waters of the South Llano. The rear herds turned off above and below, filling the river for five miles, while the hollow-eyed animals gorged themselves until a half dozen died that evening and night.

Leaving orders with the foremen to rest their herds well and move out half a day apart, I rode night and day returning to Uvalde. Catching the first stage out, I reached San Antonio in time to overtake Major Hunter, who was awaiting the arrival of the last beef herd from the lower country, the three lead ones having already passed that point. All trail outfits from the south then touched at San Antonio to provision the wagons, and on the approach of our last herd I met it and spent half a day with it, - my first, last, and only glimpse of our heavy beeves. They were big rangy fellows many of them six and seven years old, and from the general uniformity of the herd, I felt proud of the cowman that my protégé and active partner had developed into. Major Hunter was anxious to reach home as soon as possible, in order to buy in our complement of northern wintered cattle; so, settling our business affairs in southern Texas, the day after the rear beeves passed we took train north. I stopped in the central part of the State, joining Edwards riding night and day in covering his appointments to receive cattle; and when the last trail herd moved out from the Colorado River there were no regrets.

Hastening on home, on my arrival I was assured by my ranch foreman that he could gather a trail herd in less than a week. My saddle stock now numbered over a thousand head, one hundred of which were on the Double Mountain ranch, seven remudas on the trail, leaving available over two hundred on the Clear Fork. I had the horses and cattle, and on the word being given my ranch foreman began gathering our oldest steers, while I outfitted and provisioned a commissary and secured half a dozen men. On the morning of the seventh day after my arrival, an individual herd, numbering thirty-five hundred, moved out from the Clear Fork, every animal in the straight ranch brand. An old trail foreman was given charge, Dodge City was the destination, and a finer herd of three-year-olds could not have been found in one brand within the boundaries of the State. This completed our cattle on the trail, and a breathing spell of a few weeks might now be indulged in, yet there was little rest for a cowman. Not counting the contracts to the Indian Bureau, sublet to others, and the northern wintered beeves, we had, for the firm and individually, seventeen herds, numbering fifty-four thousand five hundred cattle on the trail. In order to carry on our growing business unhampered for want of funds, the firm had borrowed on short time nearly a quarter-million dollars that spring, pledging the credit of the three partners for its repayment. We had been making money ever since the partnership was formed, and we had husbanded our profits, yet our business seemed to outgrow our means, compelling us to borrow every spring when buying trail herds.

In the mean time and while we were gathering the home cattle, my foreman and two men from the Double Mountain ranch arrived on the Clear Fork to receive the importation of bulls. The latter had not yet arrived, so pressing the boys into work, we got the trail herd away before the thoroughbreds put in an appearance. A wagon and three men from the home ranch had gone after them before my return, and they were simply loafing along, grazing five to ten miles a day, carrying corn in the wagon to feed on the grass. Their arrival found the ranch at leisure, and after resting a few days they proceeded on to their destination at a leisurely gait. The importation had wintered finely, - now all three-year-olds, - but hereafter they must subsist on the range, as corn was out of the question, and the boys had brought nothing but a pack horse from the western ranch. This was an experiment with me, but I was ably seconded by my foreman, who had personally selected every cow over a month before, and this was to make up the beginning of the improved herd. I accompanied them beyond my range and urged seven miles a day as the limit of travel. I then started for home, and within a week reached Dodge City, Kansas.

Headquarters were again established at Dodge. Fortunately a new market was being developed at Ogalalla on the Platte River in Nebraska, and fully one third the trail herds passed on to the upper point. Before my arrival Major Hunter had bought the deficiency of northern wintered beeves, and early in June three herds started from our range in the Outlet for the upper Missouri River army posts. We had wintered all horses belonging to the firm on the beef ranch, and within a fortnight after its desertion, the young steers from the upper Nueces River began arriving and were turned loose on the Eagle Chief, preempting our old range. One outfit was retained to locate the cattle, the remaining ones coming in to Dodge and returning home by train. George Edwards lent me valuable assistance in handling our affairs economically, but with the arrival of the herds at Dodge he was compelled to look after our sub-contracts at Indian agencies. The latter were delivered in our name, all money passed through our hands in settlement, so it was necessary to have a man on the ground to protect our interests. With nothing but the selling of eight herds of cattle in an active market like Dodge, I felt that the work of the summer was virtually over. One cattle company took ten thousand three-year-old steers, two herds were sold for delivery at Ogalalla, and the remaining three were placed within a month after their arrival. The occupation of the West was on with a feverish haste, and money was pouring into ranches and cattle, affording a ready market to the drover from Texas.

Nothing now remained for me but to draw the threads of our business together and await the season's settlement in the fall. I sold all the wagons and sent the remudas to our range in the Outlet, while from the first cattle sold the borrowed money was repaid. I visited Ogalalla to acquaint myself with its market, looked over our beef ranch in the Cherokee Strip during the lull, and even paid the different Indian agencies my respects to perfect my knowledge of the requirements of our business. Our firm was a strong one, enlarging its business year by year; and while we could not foresee the future, the present was a Harvest Home to Hunter, Anthony & Co.

CHAPTER XVI

AN ACTIVE SUMMER

The summer of 1878 closed with but a single cloud on the horizon. Like ourselves, a great many cattlemen had established beef ranches in the Cherokee Outlet, then a vacant country, paying a trifling rental to that tribe of civilized Indians. But a difference of opinion arose, some contending that the Cherokees held no title to the land; that the strip of country sixty miles wide by two hundred long set aside by treaty as a hunting ground, when no longer used for that purpose by the tribe, had reverted to the government. Some refused to pay the rent money, the council of the Cherokee Nation appealed to the general government, and troops were ordered in to preserve the peace. We felt no uneasiness over our holdings of cattle on the Strip, as we were paying a nominal rent, amounting to two bits a head a year, and were otherwise fortified in possession of our range. If necessary we could have secured a permit from the War Department, on the grounds of being government contractors and requiring a northern range on which to hold our cattle. But rather than do this, Major Hunter hit upon a happy solution of the difficulty by suggesting that we employ an Indian citizen as foreman, and hold the cattle in his name. The major had an old acquaintance, a half-breed Cherokee named LaFlors, who was promptly installed as owner of the range, but holding beeves for Hunter, Anthony & Co., government beef contractors.

I was unexpectedly called to Texas before the general

settlement that fall. Early in the summer, at Dodge, I met a gentleman who was representing a distillery in Illinois. He was in the market for a thousand range bulls to slop-feed, and as no such cattle ever came over the trail, I offered to sell them to him delivered at Fort Worth. I showed him the sights around Dodge and we became quite friendly, but I was unable to sell him his requirements unless I could show the stock. It was easily to be seen that he was not a range cattleman, and I humored him until he took my address, saying that if he were unable to fill his wants in other Western markets he would write me later. The acquaintance resulted in several letters passing between us that autumn, and finally an appointment was made to meet in Kansas City and go down to Texas together. I had written home to have the buckboard meet us at Fort Worth on October 1, and a few days later we were riding the range on the Brazos and Clear Fork. In the past there never had been any market for this class of drones, old age and death being the only relief, and from the great number of brands that I had purchased during my ranching and trail operations, my range was simply cluttered with these old cumberers. Their hides would not have paid freighting and transportation to a market, and they had become an actual drawback to a ranch, when the opportunity occurred and I sold twelve hundred head to the Illinois distillery. The buyer informed me that they fattened well; that there was a special demand for this quality in the export trade of dressed beef, and that owing to their cheapness and consequent profit they were in demand for distillery feeding.

Fifteen dollars a head was agreed on as the price, and we earned it a second time in delivering that herd at Fort Worth. Many of the animals were ten years old, surly when irritated, and ready for a fight when their day-dreams were disturbed. There was no treating them humanely, for every effort in that direction was resented by the old rascals, individually and collectively. The first day we gathered two hundred, and the attempt to hold them under herd was a constant fight, resulting in every hoof arising on the bed-ground at midnight and escaping to their old haunts. I worked as good a ranch outfit of men as the State ever bred, I was right there in the saddle with them, yet, in spite of every effort, to say nothing of the profanity wasted, we lost the herd. The next morning every lad armed himself with a prod-pole long as a lance and tipped with a sharp steel brad, and we commenced regathering. Thereafter we corralled them at night, which always called for a free use of ropes, as a number usually broke away on approaching the pens. Often we hog-tied as many as a dozen, letting them lie outside all night and freeing them back into the herd in the morning. Even the day-herding was a constant fight, as scarcely an hour passed but some old resident would scorn the restraint imposed upon his liberties and deliberately make a break for freedom. A pair of horsemen would double on the deserter, and with a prod-pole to his ear and the pressure of a man and horse bearing their weight on the same, a circle would be covered and Toro always reëntered the day-herd. One such lesson was usually sufficient, and by reaching corrals every night and penning them, we managed, after two weeks' hard work, to land them in the stockyards at Fort Worth. The buyer remained with and accompanied us during the gathering and en route to the railroad, evidently enjoying the continuous performance. He proved a good mixer, too, and returned annually thereafter. For years following I contracted with him, and finally shipped on consignment, our business relations always pleasant and increasing in volume until his death.

Returning with the outfit, I continued on west to the new ranch, while the men began the fall branding at home. On arriving on the Double Mountain range, I found the outfit in the saddle, ironing up a big calf crop, while the improved herd was the joy and pride of my foreman. An altitude of about four thousand feet above sea-level had proved congenial to the thoroughbreds, who had acclimated nicely, the only loss being one from lightning. Two men were easily holding the isolated herd in their cañon home, the sheltering bluffs affording them ample protection from wintry weather, and there was nothing henceforth to fear in regard to the experiment. I spent a week with the outfit; my ranch foreman assured me that the brand could turn out a trail herd of three-year-old steers the following spring and a second one of twos, if it was my wish to send them to market. But it was too soon to anticipate the coming summer; and then it seemed a shame to move young steers to a northern climate to be matured, yet it was an economic necessity. Ranch headquarters looked like a trapper's cave with wolf-skins and buffalo-robes taken the winter before, and it was with reluctance that I took my leave of the cosy dugouts on the Double Mountain Fork.

On returning home I found a statement for the year and a pressing invitation awaiting me to come on to the national capital at once. The profits of the summer had exceeded the previous one, but some bills for demurrage remained to be adjusted with the War and Interior departments, and my active partner and George Edwards had already started for Washington. It was urged on me that the firm should make themselves known at the different departments, and the invitation was supplemented by a special request from our silent partner, the Senator, to spend at least a month at the capital. For years I had been promising my wife to take her on a visit to Virginia, and now when the opportunity offered, womanlike, she pleaded her nakedness in the midst of plenty. I never had but one suit at a time in my life, and often I had seen my wife dressed in the best the frontier of Texas afforded, which was all that ought to be expected. A day's notice was given her, the eldest children were sent to their grandparents, and taking the two youngest with us, we started for Fort Worth. I was anxious that my wife should make a favorable impression on my people, and in turn she was fretting about my general appearance. Out of a saddle a cowman never looks well, and every effort to improve his personal appearance only makes him the more ridiculous. Thus with each trying to make the other presentable, we started. We stopped a week at my brother's in Missouri, and finally reached the Shenandoah Valley during the last week in November. Leaving my wife to speak for herself and the remainder of the family, I hurried on to Washington and found the others quartered at a prominent hotel. A less pretentious one would have suited me, but then a

United States senator must befittingly entertain his friends. New men had succeeded to the War and Interior departments, and I was properly introduced to each as the Texas partner of the firm of Hunter, Anthony & Co. Within a week, several little dinners were given at the hotel, at which from a dozen to twenty men sat down, all feverish to hear about the West and the cattle business in particular. Already several companies had been organized to engage in ranching, and the capital had been over-subscribed in every instance; and actually one would have supposed from the chat that we were holding a cattle convention in the West instead of dining with a few representatives and government officials at Washington.

I soon became the object of marked attention. Possibly it was my vocabulary, which was consistent with my vocation, together with my ungainly appearance, that differentiated me from my partners. George Edwards was neat in appearance, had a great fund of Western stories and experiences, and the two of us were constantly being importuned for incidents of a frontier nature. Both my partners, especially the Senator, were constantly introducing me and referring to me as a man who, in the course of ten years, had accumulated fifty thousand cattle and acquired title to three quarters of a million acres of land. I was willing to be a sociable fellow among my friends, but notoriety of this character was offensive, and in a private lecture I took my partners to task for unnecessary laudation. The matter was smoothed over, our estimates for the coming year were submitted, and after spending the holidays with my parents in Virginia, I returned to the capital to await the allotments for future delivery of cattle to the Army and Indian service. Pending the date of the opening of the bids a dinner was given by a senator from one of the Southern States, to which all members of our firm were invited, when the project was launched of organizing a cattle company with one million dollars capital. The many advantages that would accrue where government influence could be counted on were dwelt upon at length, the rapid occupation of the West was cited, the concentration of all Indian tribes on reservations, and the necessary requirements of beef in feeding the same was openly commented on as the opportunity of the hour. I took no hand in the general discussion, except to answer questions, but when the management of such a company was tendered me, I emphatically declined. My partners professed surprise at my refusal, but when the privacy of our rooms was reached I unburdened myself on the proposition. We had begun at the foot of the hill, and now having established ourselves in a profitable business, I was loath to give it up or share it with others. I argued that our trade was as valuable as realty or cattle in hand; that no blandishments of salary as manager could induce me to forsake legitimate channels for possibilities in other fields. "Go slow and learn to peddle," was the motto of successful merchants; I had got out on a limb before and met with failure, and had no desire to rush in where angels fear for their footing. Let others organize companies and we would sell them the necessary cattle; the more money seeking investment the better the market.

Major Hunter was Western in his sympathies and coincided with my views, the Senator was won over from the enterprise, and the project failed to materialize. The friendly relations of our firm were slightly strained over the outcome, but on the announcement of the awards we pulled together again like brothers. In the allotment for delivery during the summer and fall of 1879, some eighteen contracts fell to us, - six in the Indian Bureau and the remainder to the Army, four of the latter requiring northern wintered beeves. A single award for Fort Buford in Dakota called for five million pounds on foot and could be filled with Southern cattle. Others in the same department ran from one and a half to three million pounds, varying, as wanted for future or present use, to through or wintered beeves. The latter fattened even on the trail and were ready for the shambles on their arrival, while Southern stock required a winter and time to acclimate to reach the pink of condition. The government maintained several distributing points in the new Northwest, one of which was Fort Buford, where for many succeeding years ten thousand cattle were annually received and assigned to lesser posts. This was the market that I knew. I had felt every throb of its pulse ever since

I had worked as a common hand in driving beef to Fort Sumner in 1866. The intervening years had been active ones, and I had learned the lessons of the trail, knew to a fraction the cost of delivering a herd, and could figure on a contract with any other cowman.

Leaving the arrangement of the bonds to our silent partner, the next day after the awards were announced we turned our faces to the Southwest. February 1 was agreed on for the meeting at Fort Worth, so picking up the wife and babies in Virginia, we embarked for our Texas home. My better half was disappointed in my not joining in the proposed cattle company, with its officers, its directorate, annual meeting, and other high-sounding functions. I could have turned into the company my two ranches at fifty cents an acre, could have sold my brand outright at a fancy figure, taking stock in lieu for the same, but I preferred to keep them private property. I have since known other cowmen who put their lands and cattle into companies, and after a few years' manipulation all they owned was some handsome certificates, possibly having drawn a dividend or two and held an honorary office. I did not then have even the experience of others to guide my feet, but some silent monitor warned me to stick to my trade, cows.

Leaving the family at the Edwards ranch, I returned to Fort Worth in ample time for the appointed meeting. My active partner and our segundo had become as thick as thieves, the two being inseparable at idle times, and on their arrival we got down to business at once. The remudas were the first consideration. Besides my personal holdings of saddle stock, we had sent the fall before one thousand horses belonging to the firm back to the Clear Fork to winter. Thus equipped with eighteen remudas for the trail, we were fairly independent in that line. Among the five herds driven the year before to our beef ranch in the Outlet, the books showed not over ten thousand coming four years old that spring, leaving a deficiency of northern wintered beeves to be purchased. It was decided to restock the range with straight threes, and we again divided the buying into departments, each taking the same division as the year before. The purchase of eight herds of heavy beeves would thus fall to Major Hunter. Austin and San Antonio were decided on as headquarters and banking points, and we started out on a preliminary skirmish. George Edwards had an idea that the Indian awards could again be relet to advantage, and started for the capital, while the major and I journeyed on south. Some former sellers whom we accidentally met in San Antonio complained that we had forsaken them and assured us that their county, Medina, had not less than fifty thousand mature beeves. They offered to meet any one's prices, and Major Hunter urged that I see a sample of the cattle while en route to the Uvalde country. If they came up to requirements, I was further authorized to buy in sufficient to fill our contract at Fort Buford, which would require three herds, or ten thousand head. It was an advantage to have this delivery start from the same section, hold together en route, and arrive at their destination as a unit. I was surprised at both the quality and the quantity of the beeves along the tributaries of the Frio River, and readily let a contract to a few leading cowmen for the full allotment. My active partner was notified, and I went on to the headwaters of the Nueces River. I knew the cattle of this section so well that there was no occasion even to look at them, and in a few days contracted for five herds of straight threes. While in the latter section, word reached me that Edwards had sublet four of our Indian contacts, or those intended for delivery at agencies in the Indian Territory. The remaining two were for tribes in Colorado, and notifying our segundo to hold the others open until we met, I took stage back to San Antonio. My return was awaited by both Major Hunter and Edwards, and casting up our purchases on through cattle, we found we lacked only two herds of cows and the same of beeves. I offered to make up the Indian awards from my ranches, the major had unlimited offerings from which to pick, and we turned our attention to securing young steers for the open market. Our segundo was fully relieved and ordered back to his old stamping-ground on the Colorado River to contract for six herds of young cattle. It was my intention to bring remudas down from the Clear Fork to handle the cattle from Uvalde and Medina counties, but my active partner would have to look out for his own saddle stock for the other beef herds. Hurrying home, I started eight hundred saddle horses belonging to the firm to the lower country, assigned two remudas to leave for the Double Mountain ranch, detailed the same number for the Clear Fork, and authorized the remaining six to report to Edwards on the Colorado River.

This completed the main details for moving the herds. There was an increase in prices over the preceding spring throughout the State, amounting on a general average to fully one dollar a head. We had anticipated the advance in making our contracts, there was an abundance of water everywhere, and everything promised well for an auspicious start. Only a single incident occurred to mar the otherwise pleasant relations with our ranchmen friends. In contracting for the straight threes from Uvalde County, I had stipulated that every animal tendered must be full-aged at the date of receiving; we were paying an extra price and the cattle must come up to specifications. Major Hunter had moved his herds out in time to join me in receiving the last one of the younger cattle, and I had pressed him into use as a tally clerk while receiving. Every one had been invited to turn in stock in making up the herd, but at the last moment we fell short of threes, when I offered to fill out with twos at the customary difference in price. The sellers were satisfied. We called them by ages as they were cut out, when a row threatened over a white steer. The foreman who was assisting me cut the animal in question for a two-year-old, Major Hunter repeated the age in tallying the steer, when the owner of the brand, a small ranchman, galloped up and contended that the steer was a three-year-old, though he lacked fully two months of that age. The owner swore the steer had been raised a milk calf; that he knew his age to a day; but Major Hunter firmly yet kindly told the man that he must observe the letter of the contract and that the steer must go as a two-year-old or not at all. In reply a six-shooter was thrown in the major's face, when a number of us rushed in on our horses and the pistol was struck from the man's hand. An explanation was demanded, but the only intelligent reply that could be elicited from the owner of the white steer was, "No G - - d - - Yankee can classify my cattle." One of the ranchmen with whom we were contracting took the insult off my hands and gave the man his choice, - to fight or apologize. The seller cooled down, apologies followed, and the unfortunate incident passed and was forgotten with the day's work.

A week later the herds on the Colorado River moved out. Major Hunter and I looked them over before they got away, after which he continued on north to buy in the deficiency of three thousand wintered beeves, while I returned home to start my individual cattle. The ranch outfit had been at work for ten days previous to my arrival gathering the three-year-old steers and all dry and barren cows. On my return they had about eight thousand head of mixed stock under herd and two trail outfits were in readiness, so cutting them separate and culling them down, we started them, the cows for Dodge and the steers for Ogalalla, each thirty-five hundred strong. Two outfits had left for the Double Mountain range ten days before, and driving night and day, I reached the ranch to find both herds shaped up and ready for orders. Both foremen were anxious to strike due north, several herds having crossed Red River as far west as Doan's Store the year before; but I was afraid of Indian troubles and routed them northeast for the old ford on the Chisholm trail. They would follow down the Brazos, cross over to the Wichita River, and pass about sixty miles to the north of the home ranch on the Clear Fork. I joined them for the first few days out, destinations were the same as the other private herds, and promising to meet them in Dodge, I turned homeward. The starting of these last two gave the firm and me personally twenty-three herds, numbering seventy-six thousand one hundred cattle on the trail.

An active summer followed. Each one was busy in his department. I met Major Hunter once for an hour during the spring months, and we never saw each other again until late fall. Our segundo again rendered valuable assistance in meeting outfits on their arrival at the beef ranch, as it was deemed advisable to hold the through and wintered cattle separate for fear of Texas fever. All beef herds were routed to touch at headquarters in the Outlet, and thence going north, they skirted the borders of settlement in crossing Kansas and Nebraska. Where possible, all correspondence was conducted by wire, and with the arrival of the herds at Dodge I was kept in the saddle thenceforth. The demand for cattle was growing with each succeeding year, prices were firmer, and a general advance was maintained in all grades of trail stock. On the arrival of the cattle from the Colorado River, I had them reclassed, sending three herds of threes on to Ogalalla. The upper country wanted older stock, believing that it withstood the rigors of winter better, and I trimmed my sail to catch the wind. The cows came in early and were started west for their destination, the rear herds arrived and were located, while Dodge and Ogalalla howled their advantages as rival trail towns. The three herds of two-year-olds were sold and started for the Cherokee Strip, and I took train for the west and reached the Platte River, to find our cattle safely arrived at Ogalalla. Near the middle of July a Wyoming cattle company bought all the central Texas steers for delivery a month later at Cheyenne, and we grazed them up the South Platte and counted them out to the buyers, ten thousand strong. My individual herds classed as Pan-Handle cattle, exempt from quarantine, netted one dollar a head above the others, and were sold to speculators from the corn regions on the western borders of Nebraska. One herd of cows was intended for the Southern and the other for the Uncompahgre Utes, and they had been picking their way through and across the mountains to those agencies during the summer mouths. Late in August both deliveries were made wholesale to the agents of the different tribes, and my work was at an end. All unsold remudas returned to Dodge, the outfits were sent home, and the saddle stock to our beef ranch, there to await the close of the summer's drive.

CHAPTER XVII

FORESHADOWS

I returned to Texas early in September. My foreman on the Double Mountain ranch had written me several times during the summer, promising me a surprise on the half-blood calves. There was nothing of importance in the North except the shipping of a few trainloads of beeves from our ranch in the Outlet, and as the bookkeeper could attend to that, I decided to go back. I offered other excuses for going, but home-hunger and the improved herd were the main reasons. It was a fortunate thing that I went home, for it enabled me to get into touch with the popular feeling in my adopted State over the outlook for live stock in the future. Up to this time there had been no general movement in cattle, in sympathy with other branches of industry, notably in sheep and wool, supply always far exceeding demand. There had been a gradual appreciation in marketable steers, first noticeable in 1876, and gaining thereafter about one dollar a year per head on all grades, yet so slowly as not to disturb or excite the trade. During the fall of 1879, however, there was a feeling of unrest in cattle circles in Texas, and predictions of a notable advance could be heard on every side. The trail had been established as far north as Montana, capital by the millions was seeking investment in ranching, and everything augured for a brighter future. That very summer the trail had absorbed six hundred and fifty thousand cattle, or possibly ten per cent of the home supply, which readily found a market at army posts, Indian agencies, and two little cow towns in the North. Investment in Texas steers was paying fifty to one hundred per cent annually, the whole Northwest was turning into one immense pasture, and the feeling was general that the time had come for the Lone Star State to expect a fair share in the profits of this immense industry.

Cattle associations, organized for mutual protection and the promotion of community interests, were active agencies in enlarging the Texas market. National conventions were held annually, at which every live-stock organization in the West was represented, and buyer and seller met on common ground. Two years before the Cattle Raisers' Association of Texas was formed, other States and Territories founded similar organizations, and when these met in national assembly the cattle on a thousand hills were represented. No one was more anxious than myself that a proper appreciation should follow the enlargement of our home market, yet I had hopes that it would come gradually and not excite or disturb settled conditions. In our contracts with the government, we were under the necessity of anticipating the market ten months in advance, and any sudden or unseen change in prices in the interim between submitting our estimates and buying in the cattle to fill the same would be ruinous. Therefore it was important to keep a finger on the pulse of the home market, to note the drift of straws, and to listen for every rumor afloat. Lands in Texas were advancing in value, a general wave of prosperity had followed self-government and the building of railroads, and cattle alone was the only commodity that had not proportionally risen in value.

In spite of my hopes to the contrary, I had a well-grounded belief that a revolution in cattle prices was coming. Daily meeting with men from the Northwest, at Dodge and Ogalalla, during the summer just passed, I had felt every throb of the demand that pulsated those markets. There was a general inquiry for young steers, she stuff with which to start ranches was eagerly snapped up, and it stood to reason that if this reckless Northern demand continued, its influence would soon be felt on the plains of Texas. Susceptible to all these influences, I had returned home to find both my ranches littered with a big calf crop, the brand actually increasing in numbers in spite of the drain of trail herds annually cut out. But the idol of my eye was those half-blood calves. Out of a possible five hundred, there were four hundred and fifty odd by actual count, all big as yearlings and reflecting the selection of their parents. I loafed away a week at the cañon camp, rode through them daily, and laughed at their innocent antics as they horned the bluffs or fought their mimic fights. The Double Mountain ranch was my pride, and before leaving, the foreman and I outlined some landed additions to fill and square up my holdings, in case it should ever be necessary to fence the range.

On my return to the Clear Fork, the ranch outfit had just finished gathering from my own and adjoining ranges fifteen hundred bulls for distillery feeding. The sale had been effected by correspondence with my former customer, and when the herd started the two of us drove on ahead into Fort Worth. The Illinois man was an extensive dealer in cattle and had followed the business for years in his own State, and in the week we spent together awaiting the arrival of his purchase, I learned much of value. There was a distinct difference between a range cowman and a stockman from the older Western States; but while the occupations were different, there was much in common between the two. Through my customer I learned that Western range cattle, when well fatted, were competing with grass beeves from his own State; that they dressed more to their gross weight than natives, and that the quality of their flesh was unsurpassed. As to the future, the Illinois buyer could see little to hope for in his own country, but was enthusiastic over the outlook for us ranchmen in the Southwest. All these things were but straws which foretold the course of the wind, yet neither of us looked for the cyclone which was hovering near.

I accompanied the last train of the shipment as far as Parsons, Kansas, where our ways parted, my customer going to Peoria, Illinois, while I continued on to The Grove. Both my partners and our segundo were awaiting me, the bookkeeper had all accounts in hand, and the profits of the year were enough to turn ordinary men's heads. But I sounded a note of warning, - that there were breakers ahead, - though none of them took me seriously until I called for the individual herd accounts. With all the friendly advantages shown us by the War and Interior departments, the six herds from the Colorado River, taking their chances in the open market, had cleared more money per head than had the heavy beeves requiring thirty-three per cent a larger investment. In summing up my warning, I suggested that now, while we were winners, would be a good time to drop contracting with the government and confine ourselves strictly to the open market. Instead of ten months between assuming obligations and their fulfillment, why not reduce the chances to three or four, with the hungry, clamoring West for our market?

The powwow lasted several days. Finally all agreed to sever our dealings with the Interior Department, which required cows for Indian agencies, and confine our business to the open market and supplying the Army with beef. Our partner the Senator reluctantly yielded to the opinions of Major Hunter and myself, urging our loss of prestige and its reflection on his standing at the national capital. But we countered on him, arguing that as a representative of the West the opportunity of the hour was his to insist on larger estimates for the coming year, and to secure proportionate appropriations for both the War and Interior departments, if they wished to attract responsible bidders. If only the ordinary estimates and allowances were made, it would result in a deficiency in these departments, and no one cared for vouchers, even against the government, when the funds were not available to meet the same on presentation. Major Hunter suggested to our partner that as beef contractors we be called in consultation with the head of each department, and allowed to offer our views for the general benefit of the service. The Senator saw his opportunity, promising to hasten on to Washington at once, while the rest of us agreed to hold ourselves in readiness to respond to any call.

Edwards and I returned to Texas. The former was stationed for the winter at San Antonio, under instructions to keep in touch with the market, while I loitered between Fort Worth and the home ranch. The arrival of the list of awards came promptly as usual, but beyond a random glance was neglected pending state developments. An advance of two dollars and a half a head was predicted on all grades, and buyers and superintendents of cattle companies in the North and West were quietly dropping down into Texas for the winter, inquiring for and offering to contract cattle for spring delivery at Dodge and Ogalalla. I was quietly resting on my oars at the ranch, when a special messenger arrived summoning me to Washington. The motive was easily understood, and on my reaching Fort Worth the message was supplemented by another one from Major Hunter, asking me to touch at Council Grove en route. Writing Edwards fully what would be expected of him during my absence, I reached The Grove and was joined by my partner, and we proceeded on to the national capital. Arriving fully two weeks in advance of the closing day for bids, all three of us called and paid our respects to the heads of the War and Interior departments. On special request of the Secretaries, an appointment was made for the following day, when the Senator took Major Hunter and me under his wing and coached us in support of his suggestions to either department. There was no occasion to warn me, as I had just come from the seat of beef supply, and knew the feverish condition of affairs at home.

The appointments were kept promptly. At the Interior Department we tarried but a few minutes after informing the Secretary that we were submitting no bids that year in his division, but allowed ourselves to be drawn out as to the why and wherefore. Major Hunter was a man of moderate schooling, apt in conversation, and did nearly all the talking, though I put in a few general observations. We were cordially greeted at the War Office, good cigars were lighted, and we went over the situation fully. The reports of the year before were gone over, and we were complimented on our different deliveries to the Army. We accepted all flatteries as a matter of course, though the past is poor security for the future. When the matter of contracting for the present year was broached, we confessed our ability to handle any awards in our territory to the number of fifty to seventy-five thousand beeves, but would like some assurance that the present or forthcoming appropriations would be ample to meet all contracts. Our doubts were readily removed by the firmness of the Secretary when as we arose to leave, Major Hunter suggested, by way of friendly advice, that the government ought to look well to the bonds of contractors, saying that the beef-producing regions of the West and South had experienced an advance in prices recently, which made contracting cattle for future delivery extremely hazardous. At parting regret was expressed that the sudden change in affairs would prevent our submitting estimates only so far as we had the cattle in hand.

Three days before the limit expired, we submitted twenty bids to the War Department. Our figures were such that we felt fully protected, as we had twenty thousand cattle on our Northern range, while advice was reaching us daily from the beef regions of Texas. The opening of proposals was no surprise, only seven falling to us, and all admitting of Southern beeves. Within an hour after the result was known, a wire was sent to Edwards, authorizing him to contract immediately for twenty-two thousand heavy steer cattle and advance money liberally on every agreement. Duplicates of our estimates had been sent him the same day they were submitted at the War Office. Our segundo had triple the number of cattle in sight, and was then in a position to act intelligently. The next morning Major Hunter and I left the capital for San Antonio, taking a southern route through Virginia, sighting old battle-fields where both had seen service on opposing sides, but now standing shoulder to shoulder as trail drovers and army contractors. We arrived at our destination promptly. Edwards was missing, but inquiry among our bankers developed the fact that he had been drawing heavily the past few days, and we knew that all was well. A few nights later he came in, having secured our requirements at an advance of two to three dollars a head over the prices of the preceding spring.

The live-stock interests of the State were centring in the coming cattle convention, which would be held at Fort Worth in February. At this meeting heavy trading was anticipated for present and future delivery, and any sales effected would establish prices for the coming spring. From the number of Northern buyers that were in Texas, and others expected at the convention, Edwards suggested buying, before the meeting, at least half the requirements for our beef ranch and trail cattle. Major Hunter and I both fell in with the idea of our segundo, and we scattered to our old haunts under agreement to report at Fort Worth for the meeting of the clans. I spent two weeks among my ranchmen friends on the headwaters of the Frio and Nueces rivers, and while they were fully awake to the advance in prices, I closed trades on twenty-one thousand two and three year old steers for March delivery. It was always a weakness in me to overbuy, and in receiving I could never hold a herd down to the agreed numbers, but my shortcomings in this instance proved a boon. On arriving at Fort Worth, the other two reported having combed their old stamping-grounds of half a dozen counties along the Colorado River, and having secured only fifteen thousand head. Every one was waiting until after the cattle convention, and only those who had the stock in hand could be induced to talk business or enter into agreements.

The convention was a notable affair. Men from Montana and intervening States and Territories rubbed elbows and clinked their glasses with the Texans to "Here's to a better acquaintance." The trail drovers were there to a man, the very atmosphere was tainted with cigar smoke, the only sounds were cattle talk, and the nights were wild and sleepless. "I'll sell ten thousand Pan-Handle three-year-old steers for delivery at Ogalalla," spoken in the lobby of a hotel or barroom, would instantly attract the attention of half a dozen men in fur overcoats and heavy flannel. "What are your cattle worth laid down on the Platte?" was the usual rejoinder, followed by a drink, a cigar, and a conference, sometimes ending in a deal or terminating in a friendly acquaintance. I had met many of these men at Abilene, Wichita, and Great Bend, and later at

Dodge City and Ogalalla, and now they had invaded Texas, and the son of a prophet could not foretell the future. Our firm never offered a hoof, but the three days of the convention were forewarnings of the next few years to follow. I was personally interested in the general tendency of the men from the upper country to contract for heifers and young cows, and while the prices offered for Northern delivery were a distinct advance over those of the summer before, I resisted all temptations to enter into agreements. The Northern buyers and trail drovers selfishly joined issues in bearing prices in Texas; yet, in spite of their united efforts, over two hundred thousand cattle were sold during the meeting, and at figures averaging fully three dollars a head over those of the previous spring.

The convention adjourned, and those in attendance scattered to their homes and business. Between midnight and morning of the last day of the meeting, Major Hunter and I closed contracts for two trail herds of sixty-five hundred head in Erath and Comanche counties. Within a week two others of straight three-year-olds were secured, - one in my home county and the other fifty miles northwest in Throckmorton. This completed our purchases for the present, giving us a chain of cattle to receive from within one county of the Rio Grande on the south to the same distance from Red River on the north. The work was divided into divisions. One thousand extra saddle horses were needed for the beef herds and others, and men were sent south, to secure them. All private and company remudas had returned to the Clear Fork to winter, and from there would be issued wherever we had cattle to receive. A carload of wagons was bought at the Fort, teams were sent in after them, and a busy fortnight followed in organizing the forces. Edwards was assigned to assist Major Hunter in receiving the beef cattle along the lower Frio and Nueces, starting in ample time to receive the saddle stock in advance of the beeves. There was three weeks' difference in the starting of grass between northern and southern Texas, and we made our dates for receiving accordingly, mine for Medina and Uvalde counties following on the heels of the beef herds from the lower country.

From the 12th of March I was kept in the saddle ten days, receiving cattle from the headwaters of the Frio and Nueces rivers. All my old foremen rendered valuable assistance, two and three herds being in the course of formation at a time, and, as usual, we received eleven hundred over and above the contracts. The herds moved out on good grass and plenty of water, the last of the heavy beeves had passed north on my return to San Antonio, and I caught the first train out to join the others in central Texas. My buckboard had been brought down with the remudas and was awaiting me at the station, the Colorado River on the west was reached that night, and by noon the next day I was in the thick of the receiving. When three herds had started, I reported in Comanche and Erath counties, where gathering for our herds was in progress; and fixing definite dates that would allow Edwards and my partner to arrive, I drove on through to the Clear Fork. Under previous instructions, a herd of thirty-five hundred two-year-old heifers was ready to start, while nearly four thousand steers were in hand, with one outfit yet to come in from up the Brazos. We were gathering close that year, everything three years old or over must go, and the outfits were ranging far and wide. The steer herd was held down to thirty-two hundred, both it and the heifers moving out the same day, with a remnant of over a thousand three-year-old steers left over.

The herd under contract to the firm in the home county came up full in number, and was the next to get away. A courier arrived from the Double Mountain range and reported a second contingent of heifers ready, but that the steers would overrun for a wieldy herd. The next morning the overplus from the Clear Fork was started for the new ranch, with orders to make up a third steer herd and cross Red River at Doan's. This cleaned the boards on my ranches, and the next day I was in Throckmorton County, where everything was in readiness to pass upon. This last herd was of Clear Fork cattle, put up within twenty-five miles of Fort Griffin, every brand as familiar as my own, and there was little to do but count and receive. Road-branding was necessary, however; and while this work was in progress, a relay messenger arrived from the ranch, summoning me to Fort Worth posthaste. The message was from Major Hunter, and from the hurried scribbling I made out that several herds were tied up when ready to start, and that they would be thrown on the market. I hurried home, changed teams, and by night and day driving reached Fort Worth and awakened my active partner and Edwards out of their beds to get the particulars. The responsible man of a firm of drovers, with five herds on hand, had suddenly died, and the banks refused to advance the necessary funds to complete their payments. The cattle were under herd in Wise and Cook counties, both Major Hunter and our segundo had looked them over, and both pronounced the herds gilt-edged north Texas steers. It would require three hundred thousand dollars to buy and clear the herds, and all our accounts were already overdrawn, but it was decided to strain our credit. The situation was fully explained in a lengthy message to a bank in Kansas City, the wires were kept busy all day answering questions; but before the close of business we had authority to draw for the amount needed, and the herds, with remudas and outfits complete, passed into our hands and were started the next day. This gave the firm and me personally thirty-three herds, requiring four hundred and ninety-odd men and over thirty-five hundred horses, while the cattle numbered one hundred and four thousand head.

Two thirds of the herds were routed by way of Doan's Crossing in leaving Texas, while all would touch at Dodge in passing up the country. George Edwards accompanied the north Texas herds, and Major Hunter hastened on to Kansas City to protect our credit, while I hung around Doan's Store until our last cattle crossed Red River. The annual exodus from Texas to the North was on with a fury, and on my arrival at Dodge all precedents in former prices were swept aside in the eager rush to secure cattle. Herds were sold weeks before their arrival, others were met as far south as Camp Supply, and it was easily to be seen that it was a seller's market. Two thirds of the trail herds merely took on new supplies at Dodge and passed on to the Platte. Once our heavy beeves had crossed the Arkansas, my partner and I swung round to Ogalalla and met our advance herd, the foreman of which reported meeting buyers as far south as the Republican River. It was actually dangerous to price cattle for fear of being under the market; new classifications were being introduced, Pan-Handle and north Texas steers commanding as much as three dollars a head over their brethren from the coast and far south.

The boom in cattle of the early '80's was on with a vengeance. There was no trouble to sell herds that year. One morning, while I was looking for a range on the north fork of the Platte, Major Hunter sold my seven thousand heifers at twenty-five dollars around, commanding two dollars and a half a head over steers of the same age. Edwards had been left in charge at Dodge, and my active partner reluctantly tore himself away from the market at Ogalalla to attend our deliveries of beef at army posts. Within six weeks after arriving at Dodge and Ogalalla the last of our herds had changed owners, requiring another month to complete the transfers at different destinations. Many of the steers went as far north as the Yellowstone River, and Wyoming and Nebraska were liberal buyers at the upper market, while Colorado, Kansas, and the Indian Territory absorbed all offerings at the lower point. Horses were even in demand, and while we made no effort to sell our remudas, over half of them changed owners with the herds they had accompanied into the North.

The season closed with a flourish. After we had wound up our affairs, Edwards and I drifted down to the beef ranch with the unsold saddle stock, and the shipping season opened. The Santa Fé Railway had built south to Caldwell that spring, affording us a nearer shipping point, and we moved out five to ten trainloads a week of single and double wintered beeves. The through cattle for restocking the range had arrived early and were held separate until the first frost, when everything would be turned loose on the Eagle Chief. Trouble was still brewing between the Cherokee Nation and the government on the one side and those holding cattle in the Strip, and a clash occurred that fall between a lieutenant of cavalry and our half-breed foreman LaFlors. The troops had been burning hay and destroying improvements belonging to cattle outfits, and had paid our range a visit and mixed things with our foreman. The latter stood firm on his rights as a Cherokee citizen and cited his employers as government beef contractors, but the young lieutenant haughtily ignored all statements and ordered the hay, stabling, and dug-outs burned. Like a flash of light, LaFlors aimed a six-shooter at the officer's breast, and was instantly covered by a dozen carbines in the hands of troopers.

"Order them to shoot if you dare," smilingly said the Cherokee to the young lieutenant, a cocked pistol leveled at the latter's heart, "and she goes double. There isn't a man under you can pull a trigger quicker than I can." The hay was not burned, and the stabling and dug-outs housed our men and horses for several winters to come.

CHAPTER XVIII

THE BEGINNING OF THE BOOM

The great boom in cattle which began in 1880 and lasted nearly five years was the beginning of a ruinous end. The frenzy swept all over the northern and western half of the United States, extended into the British possessions in western Canada, and in the receding wave the Texan forgot the pit from which he was lifted and bowed down and worshiped the living calf. During this brief period the great breeding grounds of Texas were tested to their utmost capacity to supply the demand, the canebrakes of Arkansas and Louisiana were called upon for their knotty specimens of the bovine race, even Mexico responded, and still the insatiable maw of the early West called for more cattle. The whirlpool of speculation and investment in ranches and range stock defied the deserts on the west, sweeping across into New Mexico and Arizona, where it met a counter wave pushing inland from California to possess the new and inviting pastures. Naturally the Texan was the last to catch the enthusiasm, but when he found his herds depleted to a remnant of their former numbers, he lost his head and plunged into the vortex with the impetuosity of a gambler. Pasture lands that he had scorned at ten cents an acre but a decade before were eagerly sought at two and three dollars, and the cattle that he had bartered away he bought back at double and triple their former prices.

How I ever weathered those years without becoming bankrupt is unexplainable. No credit or foresight must be claimed, for the opinions of men and babes were on a parity; yet I am inclined to think it was my dread of debt, coupled with an innate love of land and cattle, that saved me from the almost universal fate of my fellow cowmen. Due acknowledgment must be given my partners, for while I held them in check in certain directions, the soundness of their advice saved my feet from many a stumble. Major Hunter was an unusually shrewd man, a financier of the rough and ready Western school; and while we made our mistakes, they were such as human foresight could not have avoided. Nor do I withhold a word of credit from our silent partner, the Senator, who was the keystone to the arch of Hunter, Anthony & Co., standing in the shadow in our beginning as trail drovers, backing us with his means and credit, and fighting valiantly for our mutual interests when the firm met its Waterloo.

The success of our drive for the summer of 1880 changed all plans for the future. I had learned that percentage was my ablest argument in suggesting a change of policy, and in casting up accounts for the year we found that our heavy beeves had paid the least in the general investment. The banking instincts of my partners were unerring, and in view of the open market that we had enjoyed that summer it was decided to withdraw from further contracting with the government. Our profits for the year were dazzling, and the actual growth of our beeves in the Outlet was in itself a snug fortune, while the five herds bought at the eleventh hour cleared over one hundred thousand dollars, mere pin-money. I hurried home to find that fortune favored me personally, as the Texas and Pacific Railway had built west from Fort Worth during the summer as far as Weatherford, while the survey on westward was within easy striking distance of both my ranches. My wife was dazed and delighted over the success of the summer's drive, and when I offered her the money with which to build a fine house at Fort Worth, she balked, but consented to employ a tutor at the ranch for the children.

I had a little leisure time on my hands that fall. Activity in wild lands was just beginning to be felt throughout the State, and

Andy Adams

the heavy holders of scrip were offering to locate large tracts to suit the convenience of purchasers. Several railroads held immense quantities of scrip voted to them as bonuses, all the charitable institutions of the State were endowed with liberal grants, and the great bulk of certificates issued during the Reconstruction régime for minor purposes had fallen into the hands of shrewd speculators. Among the latter was a Chicago firm, who had opened an office at Fort Worth and employed a corps of their own surveyors to locate lands for customers. They held millions of acres of scrip, and I opened negotiations with them to survey a number of additions to my Double Mountain range. Valuable water-fronts were becoming rather scarce, and the legislature had recently enacted a law setting apart every alternate section of land for the public schools, out of which grew the State's splendid system of education. After the exchange of a few letters, I went to Fort Worth and closed a contract with the Chicago firm to survey for my account three hundred thousand acres adjoining my ranch on the Salt and Double Mountain forks of the Brazos. In my own previous locations, the water-front and valley lands were all that I had coveted, the tracts not even adjoining, the one on the Salt Fork lying like a boot, while the lower one zigzagged like a stairway in following the watercourse. The prices agreed on were twenty cents an acre for arid land, forty for medium, and sixty for choice tracts, every other section to be set aside for school purposes in compliance with the law. My foreman would designate the land wanted, and the firm agreed to put an outfit of surveyors into the field at once.

My two ranches were proving a valuable source of profit. After starting five herds of seventeen thousand cattle on the trail that spring, and shipping on consignment fifteen hundred bulls to distilleries that fall, we branded nineteen thousand five hundred calves on the two ranges. In spite of the heavy drain, the brand was actually growing in numbers, and as long as it remained an open country I had ample room for my cattle even on the Clear Fork. Each stock was in splendid shape, as the culling of the aging and barren of both sexes to Indian agencies and distilleries had preserved the brand vigorous and productive. The first few years of its establishment I am satisfied that the Double Mountain ranch increased at the rate of ninety calves to the hundred cows, and once the Clear Fork range was rid of its drones, a similar ratio was easily maintained on that range. There was no such thing as counting one's holdings; the increase only was known, and these conclusions, with due allowance for their selection, were arrived at from the calf crop of the improved herd. Its numbers were known to an animal, all chosen for their vigor and thrift, the increase for the first two years averaging ninety-four per cent.

There is little rest for the wicked and none for a cowman. I was planning an enjoyable winter, hunting with my hounds, when the former proposition of organizing an immense cattle company was revived at Washington. Our silent partner was sought on every hand by capitalists eager for investment in Western enterprises, and as cattle were absorbing general attention at the time, the tendency of speculation was all one way. The same old crowd that we had turned down two winters before was behind the movement, and as certain predictions that were made at that time by Major Hunter and myself had since come true, they were all the more anxious to secure our firm as associates. Our experience and resultant profits from wintering cattle in southern Kansas and the Cherokee Strip were well known to the Senator, and, to judge from his letters and frequent conversations, he was envied by his intimate acquaintances in Congress. In the revival of the original proposition it was agreed that our firm might direct the management of the enterprise, all three of us to serve on the directorate and to have positions on the executive committee. This sounded reasonable, and as there was a movement on foot to lease the entire Cherokee Outlet from that Nation, if an adequate range could be secured, such a cattle company as suggested ought to be profitable.

Major Hunter and I were a unit in business matters, and after an exchange of views by letter, it was agreed to run down to the capital and hold a conference with the promoters of the proposed company. My parents were aging fast, and now that I was moderately wealthy it was a pleasure to drop in on them for a week and hearten their declining years. Accordingly with the expectation of combining filial duty and business, I took Edwards with me and picked up the major at his home, and the trio of us journeyed eastward. I was ten days late in reaching Washington. It was the Christmas season in the valley; every darky that our family ever owned renewed his acquaintance with Mars' Reed, and was remembered in a way befitting the season. The recess for the holidays was over on my reaching the capital, yet in the mean time a crude outline of the proposed company was under consideration. On the advice of our silent partner, who well knew that his business associates were slightly out of their element at social functions and might take alarm, all banquets were cut out, and we met in little parties at cafés and swell barrooms. In the course of a few days all the preliminaries were agreed on, and a general conference was called.

Neither my active partner nor myself was an orator, but we had coached the silent member of the firm to act in our behalf. The Senator was a flowery talker, and in prefacing his remarks he delved into antiquity, mentioning the Aryan myth wherein the drifting clouds were supposed to be the cows of the gods, driven to and from their feeding grounds. Coming down to a later period, he referred to cattle being figured on Egyptian monuments raised two thousand years before the Christian era, and to the important part they were made to play in Greek and Roman mythology. Referring to ancient biblical times, he dwelt upon the pastoral existence of the old patriarchs, as they peacefully led their herds from sheltered nook to pastures green. Passing down and through the cycles of change from ancient to modern times, he touched upon the relation of cattle to the food supply of the world, and finally the object of the meeting was reached. In few and concise words, an outline of the proposed company was set forth, its objects and limitations. A pound of beef, it was asserted, was as staple as a loaf of bread, the production of the one was as simple as the making of the other, and both were looked upon equally as the staff of life. Other remarks of a general nature followed. The capital was limited to one million dollars, though double the capitalization could have been readily placed at the first meeting. Satisfactory committees were appointed on organization and other preliminary steps, and books were opened for subscriptions. Deference was shown our firm, and I subscribed the same amount as my partners, except that half my subscription was made in the name of George Edwards, as I wanted him on the executive committee if the company ever got beyond its present embryo state. The trio of us taking only one hundred and fifty thousand dollars, there was a general scramble for the remainder.

The preliminary steps having been taken, nothing further could be done until a range was secured. My active partner, George Edwards, and myself were appointed on this committee, and promising to report at the earliest convenience, we made preparations for returning West. A change of administration was approaching, and before leaving the capital, Edwards, my partners, and myself called on Secretaries Schurz of the Interior Department and Ramsey of the War Department. We had done an extensive business with both departments in the past, and were anxious to learn the attitude of the government in regard to leasing lands from the civilized Indian nations. A lease for the Cherokee Outlet was pending, but for lack of precedent the retiring Secretary of the Interior, for fear of reversal by the succeeding administration, lent only a qualified approval of the same. There were six million acres of land in the Outlet, a splendid range for maturing beef, and if an adequate-sized ranch could be secured the new company could begin operations at once. The Cherokee Nation was anxious to secure a just rental, an association had offered $200,000 a year for the Strip, and all that was lacking was a single word of indorsement from the paternal government.

Hoping that the incoming administration would take favorable action permitting civilized Indian tribes to lease their surplus lands, we returned to our homes. The Cherokee Strip Cattle Association had been temporarily organized some time previous, - not being chartered, however, until March, 1883, -

and was the proposed lessee of the Outlet in which our beef ranch lay. The organization was a local one, created for the purpose of removing all friction between the Cherokees and the individual holders of cattle in the Strip. The officers and directors of the association were all practical cattlemen, owners of herds and ranges in the Outlet, paying the same rental as others into the general treasury of the organization. Major Hunter was well acquainted with the officers, and volunteered to take the matter up at once, by making application in person for a large range in the Cherokee Strip. There was no intention on the part of our firm to forsake the trail, this cattle company being merely a side issue, and active preparations were begun for the coming summer.

The annual cattle convention would meet again in Fort Worth in February. With the West for our market and Texas the main source of supply, there was no occasion for any delay in placing our contracts for trail stock. The closing figures obtainable at Dodge and Ogalalla the previous summer had established a new scale of prices for Texas, and a buyer must either pay the advance or let the cattle alone. Edwards and I were in the field fully three weeks before the convention met, covering our old buying grounds and venturing into new ones, advancing money liberally on all contracts, and returning to the meeting with thirty herds secured. Major Hunter met us at the convention, and while nothing definite was accomplished in securing a range, a hopeful word had reached us in regard to the new administration. Starting the new company that spring was out of the question, and all energies were thrown into the forthcoming drive. Representatives from the Northwest again swept down on the convention, all Texas was there, and for three days and nights the cattle interests carried the keys of the city. Our firm offered nothing, but, on the other hand, bought three herds of Pan-Handle steers for acceptance early in April. Three weeks of active work were required to receive the cattle, the herds starting again with the grass. My individual contingent included ten thousand three-year-old steers, two full herds of two-year-old heifers, and seven thousand cows. The latter were driven in two herds; extra wagons with oxen attached accompanied each in order to save the calves, as a youngster was an assistance in selling an old cow. Everything was routed by Doan's Crossing, both Edwards and myself accompanying the herds, while Major Hunter returned as usual by rail. The new route, known as the Western trail, was more direct than the Chisholm though beset by Comanche and Kiowa Indians once powerful tribes, but now little more than beggars. The trip was nearly featureless, except that during a terrible storm on Big Elk, a number of Indians took shelter under and around one of our wagons and a squaw was killed by lightning. For some unaccountable reason the old dame defied the elements and had climbed up on a water barrel which was ironed to the side of the commissary wagon, when the bolt struck her and she tumbled off dead among her people. The incident created quite a commotion among the Indians, who set up a keening, and the husband of the squaw refused to be comforted until I gave him a stray cow, when he smiled and asked for a bill of sale so that he could sell the hide at the agency. I shook my head, and the cook told him in Spanish that no one but the owner could give a hill of sale, when he looked reproachfully at me and said, "Mebby so you steal him."

I caught a stage at Camp Supply and reached Dodge a week in advance of the herds. Major Hunter was awaiting me with the report that our application for an extra lease in the Cherokee Strip had been refused. Those already holding cattle in the Outlet were to retain their old grazing grounds, and as we had no more range than we needed for the firm's holding of stock, we must look elsewhere to secure one for the new company. A movement was being furthered in Washington, however, to secure a lease from the Cheyenne and Arapahoe tribes, blanket Indians, whose reservation lay just south of the Strip, near the centre of the Territory and between the Chisholm and Western trails. George Edwards knew the country, having issued cows at those agencies for several summers, and reported the country well adapted for ranging cattle. We had a number of congressmen and several distinguished senators in our company, and if there was such a thing as pulling the wires with the new administration, there was little doubt but it would be done. Kirkwood of Iowa had succeeded Schurz in the Interior Department, and our information was that he would at least approve of any lease secured. We were urged at the earliest opportunity to visit the Cheyenne and Arapahoe agency, and open negotiations with the ruling chiefs of those tribes. This was impossible just at present, for with forty herds, numbering one hundred and twenty-six thousand cattle, on the trail and for our beef ranch, a busy summer lay before us. Edwards was dispatched to meet and turn off the herds intended for our range in the Outlet, Major Hunter proceeded on to Ogalalla, while I remained at Dodge until the last cattle arrived or passed that point.

The summer of 1881 proved a splendid market for the drover. Demand far exceeded supply and prices soared upward, while she stuff commanded a premium of three to five dollars a head over steers of the same age. Pan-Handle and north Texas cattle topped the market, their quality easily classifying them above Mexican, coast, and southern breeding. Herds were sold and cleared out for their destination almost as fast as they arrived; the Old West wanted the cattle and had the range and to spare, all of which was a tempered wind to the Texas drover. I spent several months in Dodge, shaping up our herds as they arrived, and sending the majority of them on to Ogalalla. The cows were the last to arrive on the Arkansas, and they sold like pies to hungry boys, while all the remainder of my individual stock went on to the Platte and were handled by our segundo and my active partner. Near the middle of the summer I closed up our affairs at Dodge, and, taking the assistant bookkeeper with me, moved up to Ogalalla. Shortly after my arrival there, it was necessary to send a member of the firm to Miles City, on the Yellowstone River in Montana, and the mission fell to me. Major Hunter had sold twenty thousand threes for delivery at that point, and the cattle were already en route to their destination on my arrival. I took train and stage and met the herds on the Yellowstone.

On my return to Ogalalla the season was drawing to a feverish close. All our cattle were sold, the only delay being in deliveries and settlements. Several of our herds were received on the Platte, but, as it happened, nearly all our sales were effected with new cattle companies, and they had too much confidence in the ability of the Texas outfits to deliver to assume the risk themselves. Everything was fish to our net, and if a buyer had insisted on our delivering in Canada, I think Major Hunter would have met the request had the price been satisfactory. We had the outfits and horses, and our men were plainsmen and were at home as long as they could see the north star. Edwards attended a delivery on the Crazy Woman in Wyoming, Major Hunter made a trip for a similar purpose to the Niobrara in Nebraska, and various trail foremen represented the firm at minor deliveries. All trail business was closed before the middle of September, the bookkeepers made up their final statements, and we shook hands all round and broke the necks of a few bottles.

But the climax of the year's profits came from the beef ranch in the Outlet. The Eastern markets were clamoring for well-fatted Western stock, and we sent out train after train of double wintered beeves that paid one hundred per cent profit on every year we had held them. The single wintered cattle paid nearly as well, and in making ample room for the through steers we shipped out eighteen thousand head from our holdings on the Eagle Chief. The splendid profits from maturing beeves on Northern ranges naturally made us anxious to start the new company. We were doing fairly well as a firm and personally, and with our mastery of the business it was but natural that we should enlarge rather than restrict our operations. There had been no decrease of the foreign capital, principally Scotch and English, for investment in ranges and cattle in the West during the summer just past, and it was contrary to the policy of Hunter, Anthony & Co. to take a backward step. The frenzy for organizing cattle companies was on with a fury, and half-breed Indians and squaw-men, with rights on reservations, were in demand as partners in business or as managers of cattle syndicates.

An amusing situation developed during the summer of 1881 at Dodge. The Texas drovers formed a social club and rented and furnished quarters, which immediately became the rendezvous of the wayfaring mavericks. Cigars and refreshments were added, social games introduced, and in burlesque of the general craze of organizing stock companies to engage in cattle ranching, our club adopted the name of The Juan-Jinglero Cattle Company, Limited. The capital stock was placed at five million, full-paid and non-assessable, with John T. Lytle as treasurer, E.G. Head as secretary, Jess Pressnall as attorney, Captain E.G. Millet as fiscal agent for placing the stock, and a dozen leading drovers as vice-presidents, while the presidency fell to me. We used the best of printed stationery, and all the papers of Kansas City and Omaha innocently took it up and gave the new cattle company the widest publicity. The promoters of the club intended it as a joke, but the prominence of its officers fooled the outside public, and applications began to pour in to secure stock in the new company. No explanation was offered, but all applications were courteously refused, on the ground that the capital was already over-subscribed. All members were freely using the club stationery, thus daily advertising us far and wide, while no end of jokes were indulged in at the expense of the burlesque company. For instance, Major Seth Mabry left word at the club to forward his mail to Kansas City, care of Armour's Bank, as he expected to be away from Dodge for a week. No sooner had he gone than every member of the club wrote him a letter, in care of that popular bank, addressing him as first vice-president and director of The Juan-Jinglero Cattle Company. While attending to business Major Mabry was hourly honored by bankers and intimate friends desiring to secure stock in the company, to all of whom he turned a deaf ear, but kept the secret. "I told the boys," said Major Seth on his return, "that our company was a close corporation, and unless we increased the capital stock, there was no hope of them getting in on the ground floor."

In Dodge practical joking was carried to the extreme, both by citizens and cowmen. One night a tipsy foreman, who had just arrived over the trail, insisted on going the rounds with a party of us, and in order to shake him we entered a variety theatre, where my maudlin friend soon fell asleep in his seat. The rest of us left the theatre, and after seeing the sights I wandered back to the vaudeville, finding the performance over and my friend still sound asleep. I awoke him, never letting him know that I had been absent for hours, and after rubbing his eyes open, he said: "Reed, is it all over? No dance or concert? They give a good show here, don't they?"

CHAPTER XIX

THE CHEYENNE AND
ARAPAHOE CATTLE COMPANY

The assassination of President Garfield temporarily checked our plans in forming the new cattle company. Kirkwood of the Interior Department was disposed to be friendly to all Western enterprises, but our advices from Washington anticipated a reorganization of the cabinet under Arthur. Senator Teller was slated to succeed Kirkwood, and as there was no question about the former being fully in sympathy with everything pertaining to the West, every one interested in the pending project lent his influence in supporting the Colorado man for the Interior portfolio. Several senators and any number of representatives were subscribers to our company, and by early fall the outlook was so encouraging that we concluded at least to open negotiations for a lease on the Cheyenne and Arapahoe reservation. A friendly acquaintance was accordingly to be cultivated with the Indian agent of these tribes. George Edwards knew him personally, and, well in advance of Major Hunter and myself, dropped down to the agency and made known his errand. There were already a number of cattle being held on the reservation by squaw-men, sutlers, contractors, and other army followers stationed at Fort Reno. The latter ignored all rights of the tribes, and even collected a rental from outside cattle for grazing on the reservation, and were naturally antagonistic to any interference with their personal plans. There had been more or less friction between the Indian agent and these usurpers of the grazing privileges, and a proposition to lease a million acres at an annual rental of fifty thousand dollars at once met with the sanction of the agent. Major Hunter and I were notified of the outlook, and at the close of the beef-shipping season we took stage for the Cheyenne and Arapahoe Agency. Our segundo had thoroughly ridden over the country, the range was a desirable one, and we soon came to terms with the agent. He was looked upon as a necessary adjunct to the success of our company, a small block of stock was set aside for his account, while his usefulness in various ways would entitle his name to grace the salary list. For the present the opposition of the army followers was to be ignored, as no one gave them credit for being able to thwart our plans.

The Indian agent called the head men of the two tribes together. The powwow was held at the summer encampment of the Cheyennes, and the principal chiefs of the Arapahoes were present. A beef was barbecued at our expense, and a great deal of good tobacco was smoked. Aside from the agent, we employed a number of interpreters; the council lasted two days, and on its conclusion we held a five years' lease, with the privilege of renewal, on a million acres of as fine grazing land as the West could boast. The agreement was signed by every chief present, and it gave us the privilege to fence our range, build shelter and stabling for our men and horses, and otherwise equip ourselves for ranching. The rental was payable semiannually in advance, to begin with the occupation of the country the following spring, and both parties to the lease were satisfied with the terms and conditions. In the territory allotted to us grazed two small stocks of cattle, one of which had comfortable winter shelters on Quartermaster Creek. Our next move was to buy both these brands and thus gain the good will of the only occupants of the range. Possession was given at once, and leaving Edwards and a few men to hold the range, the major and I returned to Kansas and reported our success to Washington.

The organization was perfected, and The Cheyenne and Arapahoe Cattle Company began operations with all the rights and privileges of an individual. One fourth of the capital stock was at once paid into the hands of the treasurer, the lease and cattle on hand were transferred to the new company, and the executive committee began operations for the future. Barbed wire by the carload was purchased sufficient to build one hundred miles of four-strand fence, and arrangements were made to have the same freighted one hundred and fifty miles inland by wagon from the railway terminal to the new ranch on Quartermaster Creek. Contracts were let to different men for cutting the posts and building the fence, and one of the old trail bosses came on from Texas and was installed as foreman of the new range. The first meeting of stockholders - for permanent organization - was awaiting the convenience of the Western contingent; and once Edwards was relieved, he and Major Hunter took my proxy and went on to the national capital. Every interest had been advanced to the farthest possible degree: surveyors would run the lines, the posts would be cut and hauled during the winter, and by the first of June the fences would be up and the range ready to receive the cattle.

I returned to Texas to find everything in a prosperous condition. The Texas and Pacific railway had built their line westward during the past summer, crossing the Colorado River sixty miles south of headquarters on the Double Mountain ranch and paralleling my Clear Fork range about half that distance below. Previous to my return, the foreman on my Western ranch shipped out four trains of sixteen hundred bulls on consignment to our regular customer in Illinois, it being the largest single shipment made from Colorado City since the railway reached that point. Thrifty little towns were springing up along the railroad, land was in demand as a result of the boom in cattle, and an air of prosperity pervaded both city and hamlet and was reflected in a general activity throughout the State. The improved herd was the pride of the Double Mountain ranch, now increased by over seven hundred half-blood heifers, while the young males were annually claimed for the improvement of the main ranch stock. For fear of in-and-in breeding, three years was the limit of use of any bulls among the improved cattle, the first importation going to the main stock, and a second consignment supplanting them at the head of the herd.

In the permanent organization of The Cheyenne and Arapahoe Cattle Company, the position of general manager fell to me. It was my wish that this place should have gone to Edwards, as he was well qualified to fill it, while I was busy looking after the firm and individual interests. Major Hunter likewise favored our segundo, but the Eastern stockholders were insistent that the management of the new company should rest in the hands of a successful cowman. The salary contingent with the position was no inducement to me, but, with the pressure brought to bear and in the interests of harmony, I was finally prevailed on to accept the management. The proposition was a simple one, - the maturing and marketing of beeves; we had made a success of the firm's beef ranch in the Cherokee Outlet, and as far as human foresight went, all things augured for a profitable future.

There was no intention on the part of the old firm to retire from the enviable position that we occupied as trail drovers. Thus enlarging the scope of our operations as cowmen simply meant that greater responsibility would rest on the shoulders of the active partners and our trusted men. Accepting the management of the new company meant, to a certain extent, a severance of my personal connection with the firm, yet my every interest was maintained in the trail and beef ranch. One of my first acts as manager of the new company was to serve a notice through our secretary-treasurer calling for the capital stock to be paid in on or before February 1, 1882. It was my intention to lay the foundation of the new company on a solid basis, and with ample capital at my command I gave the practical experiences of my life to the venture. During the winter I bought five hundred head of choice saddle horses, all bred in north Texas and the Pan-Handle, every one of which I passed on personally before accepting.

Thus outfitted, I awaited the annual cattle convention. Major Hunter and our segundo were present, and while we worked in harmony, I was as wide awake for a bargain in the interests of the new company as they were in that of the old firm. I let contracts for five herds of fifteen thousand Pan-Handle three-year-old steers for delivery on the new range in the Indian Territory, and bought nine thousand twos to be driven on company account. There was the usual whoop and hurrah at the convention, and when it closed I lacked only six thousand head of my complement for the new ranch. I was confining myself strictly to north Texas and Pan-Handle cattle, for through Montana cowmen I learned that there was an advantage, at maturity, in the northern-bred animal. Major Hunter and our segundo bought and contracted in a dozen counties from the Rio Grande to Red River during the convention, and at the close we scattered to the four winds in the interests of our respective work. In order to give my time and attention to the new organization, I assigned my individual cattle to the care of the firm, of which I was sending out ten thousand three-year-old steers and two herds of aging and dry cows. They would take their chances in the open market, though I would have dearly loved to take over the young steers for the new company rather than have bought their equivalent in numbers. I had a dislike to parting with an animal of my own breeding, and to have brought these to a ripe maturity under my own eye would have been a pleasure and a satisfaction. But such an action might have caused distrust of my management, and an honest name is a valuable asset in a cowman's capital.

My ranch foremen made up the herds and started my individual cattle on the trail. I had previously bought the two remaining herds in Archer and Clay counties, and in the five that were contracted for and would be driven at company risk and account, every animal passed and was received under my personal inspection. Three of the latter were routed by way of the Chisholm trail, and two by the Western, while the cattle under contract for delivery at the company ranch went by any route that their will and pleasure saw fit. I saw very little of my old associates during the spring months, for no sooner had I started the herds than I hastened to overtake the lead one so as to arrive with the cattle at their new range. I had kept in touch with the building of fences, and on our arrival, near the middle of May, the western and southern strings were completed. It was not my intention to inclose the entire range, only so far as to catch any possible drift of cattle to the south or west. A twenty-mile spur of fence on the east, with half that line and all the north one open, would be sufficient until further encroachments were made on our range. We would have to ride the fences daily, anyhow, and where there was no danger of drifting, an open line was as good as a fence.

As fast as the cattle arrived they were placed under loose herd for the first two weeks. Early in June the last of the contracted herds arrived and were scattered over the range, the outfits returning to Texas. I reduced my help gradually, as the cattle quieted down and became located, until by the middle of summer we were running the ranch with thirty men, which were later reduced to twenty for the winter. Line camps were established on the north and east, comfortable quarters were built for fence-riders and their horses, and aside from head-quarters camp, half a dozen outposts were maintained. Hay contracts were let for sufficient forage to winter forty horses, the cattle located nicely within a month, and time rolled by without a cloud on the horizon of the new cattle company. I paid a flying visit to Dodge and Ogalalla, but, finding the season drawing to a close and the firm's cattle all sold, I contentedly returned to my accepted task. I had been buried for several months in the heart of the Indian Territory, and to get out where one could read the daily papers was a treat. During my banishment, Senator Teller had been confirmed as Secretary of the Interior, an appointment that augured well for the future of the Cheyenne and Arapahoe Cattle Company. Advices from Washington were encouraging, and while the new secretary lacked authority to sanction our lease, his tacit approval was assured.

The firm of Hunter, Anthony & Co. made a barrel of money in trailing cattle and from their beef ranch during the summer of 1882. I actually felt grieved over my portion of the season's work for while I had established a promising ranch, I had little to show, the improvement account being heavy, owing to our isolation. It was doubtful if we could have sold the ranch and cattle at a profit, yet I was complimented on my management, and given to understand that the stockholders were anxious to double the capitalization should I consent. Range was becoming valuable, and at a meeting of the directors that fall a resolution was passed, authorizing me to secure a lease adjoining our present one. Accordingly, when paying the second installment of rent money, I took the Indian agent of the two tribes with me. The leading chiefs were pleased with my punctuality in meeting the rental, and a proposition to double their income of "grass" money met with hearty grunts of approval. I made the council a little speech, - my maiden endeavor, - and when it was interpreted to the squatting circle I had won the confidence of these simple aborigines. A duplicate of our former lease in acreage and terms was drawn up and signed; and during the existence of our company the best teepee in the winter or summer encampments, of either the Cheyennes or Arapahoes, was none too good for Reed Anthony when he came with the rent money or on other business.

Our capital stock was increased to two million dollars, in the latter half of which, one hundred thousand was asked for and allotted to me. I stayed on the range until the first of December, freighting in a thousand bushels of corn for the horses and otherwise seeing that the camps were fully provisioned before returning to my home in Texas. The winter proved dry and cold, the cattle coming through in fine condition, not one per cent of loss being sustained, which is a good record for through stock. Spring came and found me on the trail, with five herds on company account and eight herds under contract, - a total of forty thousand cattle intended for the enlarged range. All these had been bought north of the quarantine line in Texas, and were turned loose with the wintered ones, fever having been unknown among our holdings of the year before. In the mean time the eastern spur of fence had been taken down and the southern line extended forty miles eastward and north the same distance. The northern line of our range was left open, the fences being merely intended to catch any possible drift from summer storms or wintry blizzards. Yet in spite of this precaution, two round-up outfits were kept in the field through the early summer, one crossing into the Chickasaw Nation and the other going as far south as Red River, gathering any possible strays from the new range.

I was giving my best services to the new company. Save for the fact that I had capable foremen on my individual ranches in Texas, my absence was felt in directing the interests of the firm and personally. Major Hunter had promoted an old foreman to a trusted man, and the firm kept up the volume of business on the trail and ranch, though I was summoned once to Dodge and twice to Ogalalla during the summer of 1883. Issues had arisen making my presence necessary, but after the last trail herd was sold I returned to my post. The boom was still on in cattle at the trail markets, and Texas was straining every energy to supply the demand, yet the cry swept down from the North for more cattle. I was branding twenty thousand calves a year on my two ranches, holding the increase down to that number by sending she stuff up the country on sale, and from half a dozen sources of income I was coining money beyond human need or necessity. I was then in the physical prime of my life and was master of a profitable business, while vistas of a brilliant future opened before me on every hand.

When the round-up outfits came in for the summer, the beef shipping began. In the first two contingents of cattle purchased in securing the good will of the original range, we now had five thousand double wintered beeves. It was my intention to ship out the best of the single wintered ones, and five separate outfits were ordered into the saddle for that purpose. With the exception of line and fence riders, - for two hundred and forty miles were ridden daily, rain or shine, summer or winter, - every man on the ranch took up his abode with the wagons. Caldwell and Hunnewell, on the Kansas state line were the nearest shipping points, requiring fifteen days' travel with beeves, and if there was no delay in cars, an outfit could easily gather the cattle and make a round trip in less than a month. Three or four trainloads, numbering from one thousand and fifty to fourteen hundred head, were cut out at a time and handled by a single outfit. I covered the country between the ranch and shipping points, riding night and day ahead in ordering cars, and dropping back to the ranch to superintend the cutting out of the next consignment of cattle. Each outfit made three trips, shipping out fifteen thousand beeves that fall, leaving sixty thousand cattle to winter on the range.

Several times that fall, when shipping beeves from Caldwell, we met up with the firm's outfits from the Eagle Chief in the Cherokee Outlet. Naturally the different shipping crews looked over each other's cattle, and an intense rivalry sprang up between the different foremen and men. The cattle of the new company outshone those of the old firm, and were outselling them in the markets, while the former's remudas were in a class by themselves, all of which was salt to open wounds and magnified the jealousy between our own outfits. The rivalry amused me, and until petty personalities were freely indulged in, I encouraged and widened the breach between the rival crews. The outfits under my direction had accumulated a large supply of saddle and sleeping blankets procured from the Indians, gaudy in color, manufactured in sizes for papoose, squaw, and buck. These goods were of the finest quality, but during the annual festivals of the tribe Lo's hunger for gambling induced him to part, for a mere song, with the blanket that the paternal government intended should shelter him during the storms of winter. Every man in my outfits owned from six to ten blankets, and the Eagle Chief lads rechristened the others, including myself, with the most odious of Indian names. In return, we refused to visit or eat at their wagons, claiming that they lived slovenly and were lousy. The latter had an educated Scotchman with them, McDougle by name, the ranch bookkeeper, who always went into town in advance to order cars. McDougle had a weakness for the cup, and on one occasion he fell into the hands of my men, who humored his failing, marching him through the streets, saloons, and hotels shouting at the top of his voice, "Hunter, Anthony & Company are going to ship!" The expression became a byword among the citizens of the town, and every reappearance of McDougle was accepted as a herald that our outfits from the Eagle Chief were coming in with cattle.

A special meeting of the stockholders was called at Washington that fall, which all the Western members attended. Reports were submitted by the secretary-treasurer and myself, the executive committee made several suggestions, the proposition, to pay a dividend was overwhelmingly voted down, and a further increase of the capital stock was urged by the Eastern contingent. I sounded a note of warning, called attention to the single cloud on the horizon, which was the enmity that we had engendered in a clique of army followers in and around Fort Reno. These men had in the past, were even then, collecting toll from every other holder of cattle on the Cheyenne and Arapahoe reservation. That this coterie of usurpers hated the new company and me personally was a well-known fact, while its influence was proving much stronger than at first anticipated, and I cheerfully admitted the same to the stockholders assembled. The Eastern mind, living under established conditions, could hardly realize the chaotic state of affairs in the West, with its vicious morals, and any attempt to levy tribute in the form of blackmail was repudiated by the stockholders in assembly. Major Hunter understood my position and delicately suggested coming to terms with the company's avowed enemies as the only feasible solution of the impending trouble. To further enlarge our holdings of cattle and leased range, he urged, would be throwing down the gauntlet in defiance of the clique of army attaches. Evidently no one took us seriously, and instead, ringing resolutions passed, enlarging the capital stock by another million, with instructions to increase our leases accordingly.

The Western contingent returned home with some misgivings as to the future. Nothing was to be feared from the tribes from whom we were leasing, nor the Comanche and his allies on the southwest, though there were renegades in both; but the danger lay in the flotsam of the superior race which infested the frontier. I felt no concern for my personal welfare, riding in and out from Fort Reno at my will and pleasure, though I well knew that my presence on the reservation was a thorn in the flesh of my enemies. There was little to fear, however, as the latter class of men never met an adversary in the open, but by secret methods sought to accomplish their objects. The breach between the Indian agent and these parasites of the army was constantly widening, and an effort had been made to have the former removed, but our friends at the national capital took a hand, and the movement was thwarted. Fuel was being constantly added to the fire, and on our taking a third lease on a million acres, the smoke gave way to flames. Our usual pacific measures were pursued, buying out any cattle in conflict, but fencing our entire range. The last addition to our pasture embraced a strip of country twenty miles wide, lying north of and parallel to the two former leases, and gave us a range on which no animal need ever feel the restriction of a fence. Ten to fifteen acres were sufficient to graze a steer the year round, but owing to the fact that we depended entirely on running water, much of the range would be valueless during the dry summer months. I readily understood the advantages of a half-stocked range, and expected in the future to allow twenty-five acres in the summer and thirty in the winter to the pasture's holdings. Everything being snug for the winter, orders were left to ride certain fences twice a day, - lines where we feared fence-cutting, - and I took my departure for home.

CHAPTER XX

HOLDING THE FORT

As in many other lines of business, there were ebb and flood tides in cattle. The opening of the trail through to the extreme Northwest gave the range live stock industry its greatest impetus. There have always been seasons of depression and advances, the cycles covering periods of ten to a dozen years, the duration of the ebb and stationary tides being double that of the flood. Outside influences have had their bearing, and the wresting of an empire from its savage possessors in the West, and its immediate occupancy by the dominant race in ranching, stimulated cattle prices far beyond what was justified by the laws of supply and demand. The boom in live stock in the Southwest which began in the early '80's stands alone in the market variations of the last half-century. And as if to rebuke the folly of man and remind him that he is but grass, Nature frowned with two successive severe winters, humbling the kings and princes of the range.

Up to and including the winter of 1883-84 the loss among range cattle was trifling. The country was new and open, and when the stock could drift freely in advance of storms, their instincts carried them to the sheltering coulees, cut banks, and broken country until the blizzard had passed. Since our firm began maturing beeves ten years before, the losses attributable to winter were never noticed, nor did they in the least affect our profits. On my ranches in Texas the primitive law of survival of the fittest prevailed, the winter-kill falling sorest

Andy Adams

among the weak and aging cows. My personal loss was always heavier than that of the firm, owing to my holdings being mixed stock, and due to the fact that an animal in the South never took on tallow enough to assist materially in resisting a winter. The cattle of the North always had the flesh to withstand the rigors of the wintry season, dry, cold, zero weather being preferable to rain, sleet, and the northers that swept across the plains of Texas. The range of the new company was intermediate between the extremes of north and south, and as we handled all steer cattle, no one entertained any fear from the climate.

I passed a comparatively idle winter at my home on the Clear Fork. Weekly reports reached me from the new ranch, several of which caused uneasiness, as our fences were several times cut on the southwest, and a prairie fire, the work of an incendiary, broke out at midnight on our range. Happily the wind fell, and by daybreak the smoke arose in columns, summoning every man on the ranch, and the fire was soon brought under control. As a precaution to such a possibility we had burned fire-guards entirely around the range by plowing furrows one hundred feet apart and burning out the middle. Taking advantage of creeks and watercourses, natural boundaries that a prairie fire could hardly jump, we had cut and quartered the pasture with fire-guards in such a manner that, unless there was a concerted action on the part of any hirelings of our enemies, it would have been impossible to have burned more than a small portion of the range at any one time. But these malicious attempts at our injury made the outfit doubly vigilant, and cutting fences and burning range would have proven unhealthful occupations had the perpetrators, red or white, fallen into the hands of the foreman and his men. I naturally looked on the bright side of the future, and in the hope that, once the entire range was fenced, we could keep trespassers out, I made preparations for the spring drive.

With the first appearance of grass, all the surplus horses were ordered down to Texas from the company ranch. There was a noticeable lull at the cattle convention that spring, and an absence of buyers from the Northwest was apparent, resulting in little or no trouble in contracting for delivery on the ranch, and in buying on company account at the prevailing prices of the spring before. Cattle were high enough as it was; in fact the market was top-heavy and wobbling on its feet, though the brightest of us cowmen naturally supposed that current values would always remain up in the pictures. As manager of the new company, I bought and contracted for fifty thousand steers, ten herds of which were to be driven on company account. All the cattle came from the Pan-Handle and north Texas, above the quarantine line, the latter precaution being necessary in order to avoid any possibility of fever, in mixing through and northern wintered stock. With the opening of spring two of my old foremen were promoted to assist in the receiving, as my contracts called for everything to be passed upon on the home range before starting the herds. Some little friction had occurred the summer before with the deliveries at the company ranch in an effort to turn in short-aged cattle. All contracts this year and the year before called for threes, and frequently several hundred long twos were found in a single herd, and I refused to accept them unless at the customary difference in price. More or less contention arose, and, for the present spring, I proposed to curb all friction at home, allotting to my assistants the receiving of the herds for company risk, and personally passing on seven under contract.

The original firm was still in the field, operating exclusively in central Texas and Pan-Handle cattle. Both my ranches sent out their usual contribution of steers and cows, consigned to the care of the firm, which was now giving more attention to quality than quantity. The absence of the men from the Northwest at the cattle convention that spring was taken as an omen that the upper country would soon be satiated, a hint that retrenchment was in order, and a better class of stock was to receive the firm's attention in its future operations. My personal contingent of steers would have passed muster in any country, and as to my consignment of cows, they were pure velvet, and could defy competition in the upper range markets. Everything moved out with the grass as usual, and when the last of the company herds had crossed Red River, I rode through to the new ranch. The north and east line of fence was nearing completion, the western string was joined to the original boundary, and, with the range fully inclosed, my ranch foreman, the men, and myself looked forward to a prosperous future.

The herds arrived and were located, the usual round-up outfits were sent out wherever there was the possibility of a stray, and we settled down in pastoral security. The ranch outfit had held their own during the winter just passed, had trailed down stolen cattle, and knew to a certainty who the thieves were and where they came from. Except what had been slaughtered, all the stock was recovered, and due notice given to offenders that Judge Lynch would preside should any one suspected of fence-cutting, starting incendiary fires, or stealing cattle be caught within the boundaries of our leases. Fortunately the other cowmen were tiring of paying tribute to the usurpers, and our determined stand heartened holders of cattle on the reservation, many of whom were now seeking leases direct from the tribes. I made it my business personally to see every other owner of live stock occupying the country, and urge upon them the securing of leases and making an organized fight for our safety. Lessees in the Cherokee Strip had fenced as a matter of convenience and protection, and I urged the same course on the Cheyenne and Arapahoe reservation, offering the free use of our line fences to any one who wished to adjoin our pastures. In the course of a month, nearly every acre of the surrounding country was taken, only one or two squaw-men holding out, and these claiming their ranges under Indian rights. The movement was made so aggressive that the usurpers were driven into obscurity, never showing their hand again until after the presidential election that fall.

During the summer a deputation of Cheyennes and Arapahoes visited me at ranch headquarters. On the last lease taken, and now inclosed in our pasture, there were a number of wild plum groves, covering thousands of acres, and the Indians wanted permission to gather the ripening fruit. Taking advantage of the opportunity, in granting the request I made it a point to fortify the friendly relations, not only with ourselves, but with all other cattlemen on the reservation. Ten days' permission was given to gather the wild plums, camps were allotted to the Indians, and when the fruit was all gathered, I barbecued five stray beeves in parting with my guests. The Indian agent and every cowman on the reservation were invited, and at the conclusion of the festival the Quaker agent made the assembled chiefs a fatherly talk. Torpid from feasting, the bucks grunted approval of the new order of things, and an Arapahoe chief, responding in behalf of his tribe, said that the rent from the grass now fed his people better than under the old buffalo days. Pledging anew the fraternal bond, and appointing the gathering of the plums as an annual festival thereafter, the tribes took up their march in returning to their encampment.

I was called to Dodge but once during the summer of 1884. My steers had gone to Ogalalla and were sold, the cows remaining at the lower market, all of which had changed owners with the exception of one thousand head. The demand had fallen off, and a dull close of the season was predicted, but I shaded prices and closed up my personal holdings before returning. Several of the firm's steer herds were unsold at Dodge, but on the approach of the shipping season I returned to my task, and we began to move out our beeves with seven outfits in the saddle. Four round trips were made to the crew, shipping out twenty thousand double and half that number of single wintered cattle. The grass had been fine that summer, and the beeves came up in prime condition, always topping the market as range cattle at the markets to which they were consigned. That branch of the work over, every energy was centred in making the ranch snug for the winter. Extra fire-guards were plowed, and the middles burned out, cutting the range into a dozen parcels, and thus, as far as possible, the winter forage was secured for our holdings of eighty thousand cattle. Hay and grain contracts had been previously let, the latter to be freighted in from southern Kansas, when the news reached us that the recent election had resulted in a political change of administration. What effect this would have on our holding cattle on Indian lands was pure conjecture, though our enemies came out of hiding, gloating over the change, and swearing vengeance on the cowmen on the Cheyenne and Arapahoe reservation.

The turn of the tide in cattle prices was noticeable at all the range markets that fall. A number of herds were unsold at Dodge, among them being one of ours, but we turned it southeast early in September and wintered it on our range in the Outlet. The largest drive in the history of the trail had taken place that summer, and the failure of the West and Northwest to absorb the entire offerings of the drovers made the old firm apprehensive of the future. There was a noticeable shrinkage in our profits from trail operations, but with the supposition that it was merely an off year, the matter was passed for the present. It was the opinion of the directors of the new company that no dividends should he declared until our range was stocked to its full capacity, or until there was a comfortable surplus. This suited me, and, returning home, I expected to spend the winter with my family, now increased to four girls and six boys.

But a cowman can promise himself little rest or pleasure. After a delightful week spent on my western ranch, I returned to the Clear Fork, and during the latter part of November a terrible norther swept down and caught me in a hunting-camp twenty-five miles from home. My two oldest boys were along, a negro cook, and a few hands, and in spite of our cosy camp, we all nearly froze to death. Nothing but a roaring fire saved us during the first night of its duration, and the next morning we saddled our horses and struck out for home, riding in the face of a sleet that froze our clothing like armor. Norther followed norther, and I was getting uneasy about the company ranch, when I received a letter from Major Hunter, stating that he was starting for our range in the Outlet and predicting a heavy loss of cattle. Headquarters in the Indian Territory were fully two hundred and fifty miles due north, and within an hour after receiving the letter, I started overland on horseback, using two of my best saddlers for the trip. To have gone by rail and stage would have taken four days, and if fair weather favored me I could nearly divide that time by half. Changing horses frequently, one day out I had left Red River in my rear, but before me lay an uninhabited country, unless I veered from my course and went through the Chickasaw Nation. For the sake of securing grain for the horses, this tack was made, following the old Chisholm trail for nearly one hundred miles. The country was in the grip of winter, sleet and snow covering the ground, with succor for man and horse far apart. Mumford Johnson's ranch on the Washita River was reached late the second night, and by daybreak the next morning I was on the trail, making Quartermaster Creek by one o'clock that day. Fortunately no storms were encountered en route, but King Winter ruled the range with an iron hand, fully six inches of snow covering the pasture, over which was a crusted sleet capable of carrying the weight of a beef. The foreman and his men were working night and day to succor the cattle. Between storms, two crews of the boys drifted everything back from the south line of fence, while others cut ice and opened the water to the perishing animals. Scarcity of food was the most serious matter; being unable to reach the grass under its coat of sleet and snow, the cattle had eaten the willows down to the ground. When a boy in Virginia I had often helped cut down basswood and maple trees in the spring for the cattle to browse upon, and, sending to the agency for new axes, I armed every man on the ranch with one, and we began felling the cottonwood and other edible timber along the creeks and rivers in the pasture. The cattle followed the axemen like sheep, eating the tender branches of the softer woods to the size of a man's wrist, the crash of a falling tree bringing them by the dozens to browse and stay their hunger. I swung an axe with the men, and never did slaves under the eye of a task-master work as faithfully or as long as we did in cutting ice and falling timber in succoring our holding of cattle. Several times the sun shone warm for a few days, melting the snow off the southern slopes, when we took to our saddles, breaking the crust with long poles, the cattle following to where the range was bared that they might get a bit of grass. Had it not been for a few such sunny days, our loss would have been double what it was; but as it was, with the general range in the clutches of sleet and snow for over fifty days, about twenty per cent, of our holdings were winter-killed, principally of through cattle.

Our saddle stock, outside of what was stabled and grain-fed, braved the winter, pawing away the snow and sleet in foraging for their subsistence. A few weeks of fine balmy weather in January and February followed the distressing season of wintry storms, the cattle taking to the short buffalo-grass and rapidly recuperating. But just when we felt that the worst was over, simultaneously half a dozen prairie fires broke out in different portions of the pasture, calling every man to a fight that lasted three days. Our enemies, not content with havoc wrought by the elements, were again in the saddle, striking in the dark and escaping before dawn, inflicting injuries on dumb animals in harassing their owners. That it was the work of hireling renegades, more likely white than red, there was little question; but the necessity of preserving the range withheld us from trailing them down and meting out a justice they so richly deserved. Dividing the ranch help into half a dozen crews, we rode to the burning grass and began counter-firing and otherwise resorting to every known method in checking the consuming flames. One of the best-known devices, in short grass and flank-fires, was the killing of a light beef, beheading and splitting it open, leaving the hide to hold the parts together. By turning the animal flesh side down and taking ropes from a front and hind foot to the pommels of two saddles, the men, by riding apart, could straddle the flames, virtually rubbing the fire out with the dragging carcass. Other men followed with wet blankets and beat out any remaining flames, the work being carried on at a gallop, with a change of horses every mile or so, and the fire was thus constantly hemmed in to a point. The variations of the wind sometimes entirely checked all effort, between midnight and morning being the hours in which most progress was accomplished. No sooner was one section of the fire brought under control than we divided the forces and hastened to lend assistance to the next nearest section, the cooks with commissaries following up the firefighters. While a single blade of grass was burning, no one thought of sleeping, and after one third of the range was consumed, the last of the incendiary fires was stamped out, when we lay down around the wagons and slept the sleep of exhaustion.

There was still enough range saved to bring the cattle safely through until spring. Leaving the entire ranch outfit to ride the fences - several lines of which were found cut by the renegades in entering and leaving the pasture - and guard the gates, I took train and stage for the Grove. Major Hunter had returned from the firm's ranch in the Strip, where heavy losses were encountered, though it then rested in perfect security from any influence except the elements. With me, the burning of the company range might be renewed at any moment, in which event we should have to cut our own fences and let the cattle drift south through an Indian country, with nothing to check them except Red River. A climax was approaching in the company's existence, and the delay of a day or week might mean inestimable loss. In cunning and craftiness our enemies were expert; they knew their control of the situation fully, and nothing but cowardice would prevent their striking the final, victorious blow. My old partner and I were a unit as to the only course to pursue, - one which meant a dishonorable compromise with our enemies, as the only hope of saving the cattle. A wire was accordingly sent East, calling a special meeting of the stockholders. We followed ourselves within an hour. On arriving at the national capital, we found that all outside shareholders had arrived in advance of ourselves, and we went into session with closed doors and the committee on entertainment and banquets inactive. In as plain words as the English language would permit, as general manager of the company, I stated the cause for calling the meeting, and bluntly suggested the only avenue of escape. Call it tribute, blackmail, or what you will, we were at the mercy of as heartless a set of scoundrels as ever missed a rope, whose mercenaries, like the willing hirelings that they were, would cheerfully do the bidding of their superiors. Major Hunter, in his remarks before the meeting, modified my rather radical statement, with the more plausible argument that this tribute money was merely insurance, and what was five or ten thousand dollars a year, where an original investment of three millions and our surplus were in jeopardy? Would any line - life, fire, or marine - carry our risk as cheaply? These men had been receiving toll from our predecessors, and were then in a position to levy tribute or wreck the company.

Notwithstanding our request for immediate action, an adjournment was taken. A wire could have been sent to a friend in Fort Reno that night, and all would have gone well for the future security of the Cheyenne and Arapahoe Cattle Company. But I lacked authority to send it, and the next morning at the meeting, the New England blood that had descended from the Puritan Fathers was again in the saddle, shouting the old slogans of no compromise while they had God and right on their side. Major Hunter and I both keenly felt the rebuke, but personal friends prevented an open rupture, while the more conservative ones saw brighter prospects in the political change of administration which was soon to assume the reins of government. A number of congressmen and senators among our stockholders were prominent in the ascendant party, and once the new régime took charge, a general shake-up of affairs in and around Fort Reno was promised. I remembered the old maxim of a new broom; yet in spite of the blandishments that were showered down in silencing my active partner and me, I could almost smell the burning range, see the horizon lighted up at night by the licking flames, hear the gloating of our enemies, in the hour of their victory, and the click of the nippers of my own men, in cutting the wire that the cattle might escape and live.

I left Washington somewhat heartened. Major Hunter, ever inclined to look on the bright side of things, believed that the crisis had passed, even bolstering up my hopes in the next administration. It was the immediate necessity that was worrying me, for it meant a summer's work to gather our cattle on Red River and in the intermediate country, and bring them back to the home range. The mysterious absence of any report from my foreman on my arrival at the Grove did not mislead me to believe that no news was good news, and I accordingly hurried on to the front. There was a marked respect shown me by the civilians located at Fort Reno, something unusual; but I hurried on to the agency, where all was quiet, and thence to ranch headquarters. There I learned that a second attempt to burn the range had been frustrated; that one of our boys had shot dead a white man in the act of cutting the east string of fence; that the same night three fires had broken out in the pasture, and that a squad of our men, in riding to the light, had run afoul of two renegade Cheyennes armed with wire-nippers, whose remains then lay in the pasture unburied. Both horses were captured and identified as not belonging to the Indians, while their owners were well known. Fortunately the wind veered shortly after the fires started, driving the flames back against the plowed guards, and the attempt to burn the range came to naught. A salutary lesson had been administered to the hirelings of the usurpers, and with a new moon approaching its full, it was believed that night marauding had ended for that winter. None of our boys recognized the white man, there being no doubt but he was imported for the purpose, and he was buried where he fell; but I notified the Indian agent, who sent for the remains of the two renegades and took possession of the horses. The season for the beginning of active operations on trail and for ranch account was fast approaching, and, leaving the boys to hold the fort during my absence, I took my private horses and turned homeward.

Andy Adams

CHAPTER XXI

THE FRUITS OF CONSPIRACY

With a loss of fully fifteen thousand cattle staring me in the face, I began planning to recuperate the fortunes of the company. The cattle convention, which was then over, was conspicuous by the absence of all Northern buyers. George Edwards had attended the meeting, was cautious enough to make no contracts for the firm, and fully warned me of the situation. I was in a quandary; with an idle treasury of over a million, my stewardship would be subject to criticism unless I became active in the interests of my company. On the other hand, a dangerous cloud hung over the range, and until that was removed I felt like a man who was sent for and did not want to go. The falling market in Texas was an encouragement, but my experience of the previous winter had had a dampening effect, and I was simply drifting between adverse winds. But once it was known that I had returned home, my old customers approached me by letter and personally, anxious to sell and contract for immediate delivery. Trail drovers were standing aloof, afraid of the upper markets, and I could have easily bought double my requirements without leaving the ranch. The grass was peeping here and there, favorable reports came down from the reservation, and still I sat idle.

The appearance of Major Hunter acted like a stimulus. Reports about the new administration were encouraging - not from our silent partner, who was not in sympathy with the dominant party, but from other prominent stockholders who were. The original trio - the little major, our segundo, and myself - lay around under the shade of the trees several days and argued the possibilities that confronted us on trail and ranch. Edwards reproached me for my fears, referring to the time, nineteen years before, when as common hands we fought our way across the Staked Plain and delivered the cattle safely at Fort Sumner. He even taunted me with the fact that our employers then never hesitated, even if half the Comanche tribe were abroad, roving over their old hunting grounds, and that now I was afraid of a handful of army followers, contractors, and owners of bar concessions. Edwards knew that I would stand his censure and abuse as long as the truth was told, and with the major acting as peacemaker between us I was finally whipped into line. With a fortune already in hand, rounding out my forty-fifth year, I looted the treasury by contracting and buying sixty thousand cattle for my company.

The surplus horses were ordered down from above, and the spring campaign began in earnest. The old firm was to confine its operations to fine steers, handling my personal contribution as before, while I rallied my assistants, and we began receiving the contracted cattle at once. Observation had taught me that in wintering beeves in the North it was important to give the animals every possible moment of time to locate before the approach of winter. The instinct of a dumb beast is unexplainable yet unerring. The owner of a horse may choose a range that seems perfect in every appointment, but the animal will spurn the human selection and take up his abode on some flinty hills, and there thrive like a garden plant. Cattle, especially steers, locate slowly, and a good summer's rest usually fortifies them with an inward coat of tallow and an outward one of furry robe, against the wintry storms. I was anxious to get the through cattle to the new range as soon as practicable, and allowed the sellers to set their dates as early as possible, many of them agreeing to deliver on the reservation as soon as the middle of May. Ten wagons and a thousand horses came down during the last days of March, and early in April started back with thirty thousand cattle at company risk.

All animals were passed upon on the Texas range, and on their arrival at the pasture there was little to do but scatter them over the ranch to locate. I reached the reservation with the lead herd, and was glad to learn from neighboring cowmen that a suggestion of mine, made the fall before, had taken root. My proposition was to organize all the cattlemen on the Cheyenne and Arapahoe reservation into an association for mutual protection. By coöperation we could present a united front to our enemies, the usurpers, and defy them in their nefarious schemes of exacting tribute. Other ranges besides ours had suffered by fire and fence-cutters during the winter just passed, and I returned to find my fellow cowmen a unit for organization. A meeting was called at the agency, every owner of cattle on the reservation responded, and an association was perfected for our mutual interest and protection. The reservation was easily capable of carrying half a million cattle, the tribes were pleased with the new order of things, and we settled down with a feeling of security not enjoyed in many a day.

But our tranquil existence received a shock within a month, when a cowboy from a neighboring ranch, and without provocation, was shot down by Indian police in a trader's store at the agency. The young fellow was a popular Texan, and as nearly all the men employed on the reservation came from the South, it was with difficulty that our boys were restrained from retaliating. Those from Texas had little or no love for an Indian anyhow, and nothing but the plea of policy in preserving peaceful relations with the tribes held them in check. The occasional killing of cattle by Indians was overlooked, until they became so bold as to leave the hides and heads in the pasture, when an appeal was made to the agent. But the aborigine, like his white brother, has sinful ways, and the influence of one evil man can readily combat the good advice of half a dozen right-minded ones, and the Quaker agent found his task not an easy one. Cattle were being killed in remote and unfrequented places, and still we bore with it, the better class of Indians, however, lending their assistance to check the abuse. On one occasion two boys and myself detected a band of five young bucks skinning a beef in our pasture, and nothing but my presence prevented a clash between my men and the thieves. But it was near the wild-plum season, and as we were making preparations to celebrate that event, the killing of a few Indians might cause distrust, and we dropped out of sight and left them to the enjoyment of their booty. It was pure policy on my part, as we could shame or humble the Indian, and if the abuse was not abated, we could remunerate ourselves by with-holding from the rent money the value of cattle killed.

Our organization for mutual protection was accepted by our enemies as a final defiance. A pirate fights as valiantly as if his cause were just, and, through intermediaries, the gauntlet was thrown back in our faces and notice served that the conflict had reached a critical stage. I never discussed the issue direct with members of the clique, as they looked upon me as the leader in resisting their levy of tribute, but indirectly their grievances were made known. We were accused of having taken the bread out of their very mouths, which was true in a sense, but we had restored it tenfold where it was entitled to go, - among the Indians. With the exception of an occasional bottle of whiskey, none of the tribute money went to the tribes, but was divided among the usurpers. They waxed fat in their calling and were insolent and determined, while our replies to all overtures looking to peace were firm and to the point. Even at that late hour I personally knew that the clique had strength in reserve, and had I enjoyed the support of my company, would willingly have stood for a compromise. But it was out of the question to suggest it, and, trusting to the new administration, we politely told them to crack their whips.

The *fiesta* which followed the plum gathering was made a notable occasion. All the cowmen on the reservation had each contributed a beef to the barbecue, the agent saw to it that all the principal chiefs of both tribes were present, and after two days of feasting, the agent made a Quaker talk, insisting that the bond between the tribes and the cowmen must be observed to the letter. He reviewed at length the complaints that had reached him of the killing of cattle, traceable to the young and thoughtless, and pointed out the patience of the cattlemen in not retaliating, but in spreading a banquet instead to those who had wronged them. In concluding, he warned them that the patience of the white man had a limit, and, while they hoped to live in peace, unless the stealing of beef was stopped immediately, double the value of the cattle killed would be withheld from the next payment of grass money. It was in the power of the chiefs present to demand this observance of faith among their young men, if the bond to which their signatures were attached was to be respected in the future. The leading chiefs of both tribes spoke in defense, pleading their inability to hold their young men in check as long as certain evil influences were at work among their people. The love of gambling and strong drink was yearly growing among their men, making them forget their spoken word, until they were known as thieves and liars. The remedy lay in removing these evil spirits and trusting the tribes to punish their own offenders, as the red man knew no laws except his own.

The festival was well worth while and augured hopefully for the future. Clouds were hovering on the horizon, however, and, while at Ogalalla, I received a wire that a complaint had been filed against us at the national capital, and that the President had instructed the Lieutenant-General of the Army to make an investigation. Just what the inquiry was to be was a matter of conjecture; possibly to determine who was supplying the Indians with whiskey, or probably our friends at Washington were behind the movement, and the promised shake-up of army followers in and around Fort Reno was materializing. I attended to some unsettled business before returning, and, on my arrival at the reservation, a general alarm was spreading among the cattle interests, caused by the cock-sure attitude of the usurpers and a few casual remarks that had been dropped. I was appealed to by my fellow cowmen, and, in turn, wired our friends at Washington, asking that our interests be looked after and guarded. Pending a report, General P.H. Sheridan arrived with a great blare of trumpets at Fort Reno for the purpose of holding the authorized investigation. The general's brother, Michael, was the recognized leader of the clique of army followers, and was interested in the bar concessions under the sutler. Matters, therefore, took on a serious aspect. All the cowmen on the reservation came in, expecting to be called before the inquiry, as it was then clear that a fight must be made to protect our interests. No opportunity, however, was given the Indians or cattlemen to present their side of the question, and when a committee of us cowmen called on General Sheridan we were cordially received and politely informed that the investigation was private. I believe that forty years have so tempered the animosities of the Civil War that an honest opinion is entitled to expression. And with due consideration to the record of a gallant soldier, I submit the question, Were not the owners of half a million cattle on the Cheyenne and Arapahoe reservation entitled to a hearing before a report was made that resulted in an order for their removal?

I have seen more trouble at a country dance, more bloodshed in a family feud, than ever existed or was spilled on the Cheyenne and Arapahoe reservation. The Indians were pleased, the lessees were satisfied, yet by artfully concealing the true cause of any and all strife, a report, every word of which was as sweet as the notes of a flute, was made to the President, recommending the removal of the cattle. It was found that there had been a gradual encroachment on the liberties of the tribes; that the rental received from the surplus pasture lands had a bad tendency on the morals of the Indians, encouraging them in idleness; and that the present system retarded all progress in agriculture and the industrial arts. The report was superficial, religiously concealing the truth, but dealing with broad generalities. Had the report emanated from some philanthropical society, it would have passed unnoticed or been commented on as an advance in the interest of a worthy philanthropy but taken as a whole, it was a splendid specimen of the use to which words can be put in concealing the truth and cloaking dishonesty.

An order of removal by the President followed the report. Had we been subjects of a despotic government and bowed our necks like serfs, the matter would have ended in immediate compliance with the order. But we prided ourselves on our liberties as Americans, and an appeal was to be made to the first citizen of the land, the President of the United States. A committee of Western men were appointed, which would be augmented by others at the national capital, and it was proposed to lay the bare facts in the chief executive's hands and at least ask for a modification of the order. The latter was ignorant in its conception, brutal and inhuman in its intent, ending in the threat to use the military arm of the government, unless the terms and conditions were complied with within a given space of time. The Cheyenne and Arapahoe Cattle Company, alone, not to mention the other members of our association equally affected, had one hundred and twenty-five thousand head of beeves and through steers on its range, and unless some relief was granted, a wayfaring man though a fool could see ruin and death and desolation staring us in the face. Fortunately Major Hunter had the firm's trail affairs so well in hand that Edwards could close up the business, thus relieving my active partner to serve on the committee, he and four others offering to act in behalf of our association in calling on the President. I was among the latter, the only one in the delegation from Texas, and we accordingly made ready and started for Washington.

Meanwhile I had left orders to start the shipping with a vengeance. The busy season was at hand on the beef ranges, and men were scarce; but I authorized the foreman to comb the country, send to Dodge if necessary, and equip ten shipping outfits and keep a constant string of cattle moving to the markets. We had about sixty-five thousand single and double wintered beeves, the greater portion of which were in prime condition; but it was the through cattle that were worrying me, as they were unfit to ship and it was too late in the season to relocate them on a new range. But that blessed hope that springs eternal in the human breast kept us hopeful that the President had been deceived into issuing his order, and that he would right all wrongs. The more sanguine ones of the Western delegation had matters figured down to a fraction; they believed that once the chief executive understood the true cause of the friction existing on the reservation, apologies would follow, we should all be asked to remain for lunch, and in the most democratic manner imaginable everything would be righted. I had no opinions, but kept anticipating the worst; for if the order stood unmodified, go we must and in the face of winter and possibly accompanied by negro troops. To return to Texas meant to scatter the cattle to the four winds; to move north was to court death unless an open winter favored us.

On our arrival at Washington, all senators and congressmen shareholders in our company met us by appointment. It was an inactive season at the capital, and hopes were entertained that the President would grant us an audience at once; but a delay of nearly a week occurred. In the mean time several conferences were held, at which a general review of the situation was gone over, and it was decided to modify our demands, asking for nothing personally, only a modification of the order in the interest of humanity to dumb animals. Before our arrival, a congressman and two senators, political supporters of the chief executive, had casually called to pay their respects, and incidentally inquired into the pending trouble between the cattlemen and the Cheyenne and Arapahoe Indians. Reports were anything but encouraging; the well-known obstinacy of the President was admitted; it was also known that he possessed a rugged courage in pursuance of an object or purpose. Those who were not in political sympathy with the party in power characterized the President as an opinionated executive, and could see little or no hope in a personal appeal.

However, the matter was not to be dropped. The arrival of a deputation of cattlemen from the West was reported by the press, their purposes fully, set forth, and in the interim of waiting for an appointment, all of us made hay with due diligence. Major Hunter and I had a passing acquaintance at both the War and Interior departments, and taking along senators and representatives in political sympathy with the heads of those offices, we called and paid our respects. A number of old acquaintances were met, hold-overs from the former régime, and a cordial reception was accorded us. Now that the boom in cattle was over, we expressed a desire to resume our former business relations as contractors with the government. At both departments, the existent trouble on the Indian reservations was well known, and a friendly inquiry resulted, which gave us an opportunity to explain our position fully. There was a hopeful awakening to the fact that there had been a conspiracy to remove us, and the most friendly advances of assistance were proffered in setting the matter right. Public opinion is a strong factor, and with the press of the capital airing our grievances daily, sympathy and encouragement were simply showered down upon us.

Finally an audience with the President was granted. The Western delegation was increased by senators and representatives until the committee numbered an even dozen. Many of the latter were personal friends and ardent supporters of the chief executive. The rangemen were introduced, and we proceeded at once to the matter at issue. A congressman from New York stated the situation clearly, not mincing his words in condemning the means and procedure by which this order was secured, and finally asking for its revocation, or a modification that would permit the evacuation of the country without injury to the owners and their herds. Major Hunter, in replying to a question of the President, stated our position: that we were in no sense intruders, that we paid our rental in advance, with the knowledge and sanction of the two preceding Secretaries of the Interior, and only for lack of precedent was their indorsement of our leases withheld. It soon became evident that countermanding the order was out of the question, as to vacillate or waver in a purpose, right or wrong, was not a characteristic of the chief executive. Our next move was for a modification of the order, as its terms required us to evacuate that fall, and every cowman present accented the fact that to move cattle in the mouth of winter was an act that no man of experience would countenance. Every step, the why and wherefore, must be explained to the President, and at the request of the committee, I went into detail in making plain what the observations of my life had taught me of the instincts and habits of cattle, - why in the summer they took to the hills, mesas, and uplands, where the breezes were cooling and protected them from insect life; their ability to foretell a storm in winter and seek shelter in coulees and broken country. I explained that none of the cattle on the Cheyenne and Arapahoe reservation were native to that range, but were born anywhere from three to five hundred miles to the south, fully one half of them having arrived that spring; that to acquaint an animal with its new range, in cattle parlance to "locate" them, was very important; that every practical cowman moved his herds to a new range with the grass in the spring, in order that ample time should be allowed to acclimate and familiarize them with such shelters as nature provided to withstand the storms of winter. In concluding, I stated that if the existent order could be so modified as to permit all through cattle and those unfit for market to remain on their present range for the winter, we would cheerfully evacuate the country with the grass in the spring. If such relief could be consistently granted, it would no doubt save the lives of hundreds and thousands of cattle.

The President evidently was embarrassed by the justice of our prayer. He consulted with members of the committee, protesting that he should be spared from taking what would be considered a backward step, and after a stormy conference with intimate friends, lasting fully an hour, he returned and in these words refused to revoke or modify his order: "If I had known," said he, "what I know now, I never would have made the order; but having made it, I will stand by it."

Laying aside all commercial considerations, we had made our entreaty in behalf of dumb animals, and the President's answer angered a majority of the committee. I had been rebuked too often in the past by my associates easily to lose my temper, and I naturally looked at those whose conscience balked at paying tribute, while my sympathies were absorbed for the future welfare of a quarter-million cattle affected by the order. We broke into groups in taking our leave, and the only protest that escaped any one was when the York State representative refused the hand of the executive, saying, "Mr. President, I have my opinion of a man who admits he is wrong and refuses to right it." Two decades have passed since those words, rebuking wrong in high places, were uttered, and the speaker has since passed over to the silent majority. I should feel that these memoirs were incomplete did I not mention the sacrifice and loss of prestige that the utterance of these words cost, for they were the severance of a political friendship that was never renewed.

The autocratic order removing the cattle from the Cheyenne and Arapahoe reservation was born in iniquity and bore a harvest unequaled in the annals of inhumanity. With the last harbor of refuge closed against us, I hastened back and did all that was human to avert the impending doom, every man and horse available being pressed into service. Our one hope lay in a mild winter, and if that failed us the affairs of the company would be closed by the merciless elements. Once it was known that the original order had not been modified, and in anticipation of a flood of Western cattle, the markets broke, entailing a serious commercial loss. Every hoof of single and double wintered beeves that had a value in the markets was shipped regardless of price, while I besought friends in the Cherokee Strip for a refuge for those unfit and our holding of through cattle. Fortunately the depreciation in live stock and the heavy loss sustained the previous winter had interfered with stocking the Outlet to its fall capacity, and by money, prayers, and entreaty I prevailed on range owners and secured pasturage for seventy-five thousand head. Long before the shipping season ended I pressed every outfit belonging to the firm on the Eagle Chief into service, and began moving out the through cattle to their new range. Squaw winter and snow-squalls struck us on the trail, but with a time-limit hanging over our heads, and rather than see our cattle handled by nigger soldiers, we bore our burdens, if not meekly, at least in a manner consistent with our occupation. I have always deplored useless profanity, yet it was music to my ears to hear the men arraign our enemies, high and low, for our present predicament. When the last beeves were shipped, a final round-up was made, and we started out with over fifty thousand cattle in charge of twelve outfits. Storms struck us en route, but we weathered them, and finally turned the herds loose in the face of a blizzard.

The removed cattle, strangers in a strange land, drifted to the fences and were cut to the quick by the biting blasts. Early in January the worst blizzard in the history of the plains swept down from the north, and the poor wandering cattle were driven to the divides and frozen to death against the line fences. Of all the appalling sights that an ordinary lifetime on the range affords, there is nothing to compare with the suffering and death that were daily witnessed during the month of January in the winter of 1885-86. I remained on the range, and left men at winter camps on every pasture in which we had stock, yet we were powerless to relieve the drifting cattle. The morning after the great storm, with others, I rode to a south string of fence on a divide, and found thousands of our cattle huddled against it, many frozen to death, partially through and hanging on the wire. We cut the fences in order to allow them to drift on to shelter, but the legs of many of them were so badly frozen that, when they moved, the skin cracked open and their hoofs dropped off. Hundreds of young steers were wandering aimlessly around on hoofless stumps, while their tails cracked and broke like icicles. In angles and nooks of the fence, hundreds had perished against the wire, their bodies forming a scaling ladder, permitting late arrivals to walk over the dead and dying as they passed on with the fury of the storm. I had been a soldier and seen sad sights, but nothing to compare to this; the moaning of the cattle freezing to death would have melted a heart of adamant. All we could do was to cut the fences and let them drift, for to halt was to die; and when the storm abated one could have walked for miles on the bodies of dead animals. No pen could describe the harrowing details of that winter; and for years afterward, or until their remains had a commercial value, a wayfarer could have traced the south-line fences by the bleaching bones that lay in windrows, glistening in the sun like snowdrifts, to remind us of the closing chapter in the history of the Cheyenne and Arapahoe Cattle Company.

CHAPTER XXII

IN CONCLUSION

The subsequent history of the ill-fated Cheyenne and Arapahoe Cattle Company is easily told. Over ninety per cent of the cattle moved under the President's order were missing at the round-up the following spring. What few survived were pitiful objects, minus ears and tails, while their horns, both root and base, were frozen until they drooped down in unnatural positions. Compared to the previous one, the winter of 1885-86, with the exception of the great January blizzard, was the less severe of the two. On the firm's range in the Cherokee Strip our losses were much lighter than during the previous winter, owing to the fact that food was plentiful, there being little if any sleet or snow during the latter year. Had we been permitted to winter in the Cheyenne and Arapahoe country, considering our sheltered range and the cattle fully located, ten per cent would have been a conservative estimate of loss by the elements. As manager of the company I lost five valuable years and over a quarter-million dollars. Time has mollified my grievances until now only the thorn of inhumanity to dumb beasts remains. Contrasted with results, how much more humane it would have been to have ordered out negro troops from Fort Reno and shot the cattle down, or to have cut the fences ourselves, and, while our holdings were drifting back to Texas, trusted to the mercy of the Comanches.

I now understand perfectly why the business world dreads a

Andy Adams

political change in administration. Whatever may have been the policy of one political party, the reverse becomes the slogan of the other on its promotion to power. For instance, a few years ago, the general government offered a bounty on the home product of sugar, stimulating the industry in Louisiana and also in my adopted State. A change of administration followed, the bounty was removed, and had not the insurance companies promptly canceled their risks on sugar mills, the losses by fire would have been appalling. Politics had never affected my occupation seriously; in fact I profited richly through the extravagance and mismanagement of the Reconstruction régime in Texas, and again met the defeat of my life at the hands of the general government.

With the demand for trail cattle on the decline, coupled with two severe winters, the old firm of Hunter, Anthony & Co. was ripe for dissolution. We had enjoyed the cream of the trade while it lasted, but conditions were changing, making it necessary to limit and restrict our business. This was contrary to our policy, though the spring of 1886 found us on the trail with sixteen herds for the firm and four from my own ranches, one half of which were under contract. A dry summer followed, and thousands of weak cattle were lost on the trail, while ruin and bankruptcy were the portion of a majority of the drovers. We weathered the drouth on the trail, selling our unplaced cattle early, and before the beef-shipping season began, our range in the Outlet, including good will, holding of beeves, saddle horses, and general improvements, was sold to a Kansas City company, and the old firm passed out of existence. Meanwhile I had closed up the affairs of the Cheyenne and Arapahoe Company, returning a small pro rata of the original investment to shareholders, charging my loss to tuition in rounding out my education as a cowman.

The productive capacity of my ranches for years past safely tided me over all financial difficulties. With all outside connections severed, I was then enabled to give my personal attention to ranching in Texas. I was fortunate in having capable ranch foremen, for during my almost continued absence there was a steady growth, together with thorough management of my mixed cattle. The improved herd, now numbering over two thousand, was the pride of my operations in live stock, while my quarter and three-eighths blood steers were in a class by themselves. We were breeding over a thousand half and three-quarters blood bulls annually, and constantly importing the best strains to the head of the improved herd. Results were in evidence, and as long as the trail lasted, my cattle were ready sellers in the upper range markets. For the following few years I drove my own growing of steers, usually contracting them in advance. The days of the trail were numbered; 1889 saw the last herd leave Texas, many of the Northern States having quarantined against us, and we were afterward compelled to ship by rail in filling contracts on the upper ranges.

When Kansas quarantined against Texas cattle, Dodge was abandoned as a range market. The trail moved West, first to Lakin and finally to Trail City, on the Colorado line. In attempting to pass the former point with four Pan-Handle herds in the spring of 1888, I ran afoul of a quarantine convention. The cattle were under contract in Wyoming, and it was my intention not even to halt the herds, but merely to take on supplies in passing. But a deputation met us south of the river, notifying me that the quarantine convention was in session, and requesting me not to attempt to cross the Arkansas. I explained that my cattle were from above the dead line in Texas, had heretofore gone unmolested wherever they wished, and that it was out of my way to turn west and go up through Colorado. The committee was reasonable, looked over the lead herd, and saw that I was driving graded cattle, and finally invited me in to state my case before the convention. I accompanied the men sent to warn me away, and after considerable parley I was permitted to address the assembly. In a few brief words I stated my destination, where I was from, and the quality of cattle making up my herds, and invited any doubters to accompany me across the river and look the stock over. Fortunately a number of the cattlemen in the convention knew me, and I was excused while the assembly went into executive session to consider my case. Prohibition was in effect at Lakin, and I was compelled to resort to diplomacy in order to cross the Arkansas River with my cattle. It was warm, sultry weather in the valley, and my first idea was to secure a barrel of bottled beer and send it over to the convention, but the town was dry. I ransacked all the drug stores, and the nearest approach to anything that would cheer and stimulate was Hostetter's Bitters. The prohibition laws were being rigidly enforced, but I signed a "death warrant" and ordered a case, which the druggist refused me until I explained that I had four outfits of men with me and that we had contracted malaria while sleeping on the ground. My excuse won, and taking the case of bitters on my shoulder, I bore it away to the nearest livery stable, where I wrote a note, with my compliments, and sent both by a darkey around to the rear door of the convention hall.

On adjournment for dinner, my case looked hopeless. There was a strong sentiment against admitting any cattle from Texas, all former privileges were to be set aside, and the right to quarantine against any section or state was claimed as a prerogative of a free people. The convention was patiently listening to all the oratorical talent present, and my friends held out a slender hope that once the different speakers had relieved their minds they might feel easier towards me, and possibly an exception would be made in my case. During the afternoon session I received frequent reports from the convention, and on the suggestion of a friend I began to skirmish around for a second case of bitters. There were only three drug stores in the town, and as I was ignorant of the law, I naturally went back to the druggist from whom I secured the first case. To my surprise he refused to supply my wants, and haughtily informed me that one application a day was all the law permitted him to sell to any one person. Rebuffed, I turned to another drug store, and was greeted by the proprietor, who formerly ran a saloon in Dodge. He recognized me, calling me by name; and after we had pledged our acquaintance anew behind the prescription case, I was confidentially informed that I could have his whole house and welcome, even if the State of Kansas did object and he had to go to jail. We both regretted that the good old days in the State were gone, but I sent around another case of bitters and a box of cigars, and sat down patiently to await results. With no action taken by the middle of the afternoon, I sent around a third installment of refreshments, and an hour later called in person at the door of the convention. The doorkeeper refused to admit me, but I caught his eye, which was glassy, and received a leery wink, while a bottle of bitters nestled cosily in the open bosom of his shirt. Hopeful that the signs were favorable, I apologized and withdrew, but was shortly afterwards sent for and informed that an exception had been made in my favor, and that I might cross the river at my will and pleasure. In the interim of waiting, in case I was successful, I had studied up a little speech of thanks, and as I arose to express my appreciation, a chorus of interruptions greeted me: "G' on, Reed! G' on, you d -- d old cow-thief! Git out of town or we'll hang you!"

With the trail a thing of the past, I settled down to the peaceful pursuits of a ranchman. The fencing of ranges soon became necessary, the Clear Fork tract being first inclosed, and a few years later owners of pastures adjoining the Double Mountain ranch wished to fence, and I fell in with the prevailing custom. On the latter range I hold title to a little over one million acres, while there are two hundred sections of school land included in my western pasture, on which I pay a nominal rental for its use. All my cattle are now graded, and while no effort is made to mature them, the advent of cotton-seed oil mills and other sources of demand have always afforded me an outlet for my increase. I have branded as many as twenty-five thousand calves in a year, and to this source of income alone I attribute the foundation of my present fortune. As a source of wealth the progeny of the cow in my State has proven a perennial harvest, with little or no effort on the part of the husbandman. Reversing the military rule of moving against the lines of least resistance, experience has taught me to follow those where Nature lends its greatest aid. Mine being strictly a grazing country, by preserving the native grasses and breeding only the best quality of cattle, I have always achieved success. I have brought up my boys to observe these economics of nature, and no plow shall ever mar the surface where my cows have grazed, generation after generation, to the profit and satisfaction of their owner. Where once I was a buyer in carload lots of the best strains of blood in the country, now I am a seller by hundreds and thousands of head, acclimated and native to the soil. One man to his trade and another to his merchandise, and the mistakes of my life justly rebuke me for dallying in paths remote from my legitimate calling.

There is a close relationship between a cowman and his herds. My insight into cattle character exceeds my observation of the human family. Therefore I wish to confess my great love for the cattle of the fields. When hungry or cold, sick or distressed, they express themselves intelligently to my understanding, and when dangers of night and storm and stampede threaten their peace and serenity, they instinctively turn to the refuge of a human voice. When a herd was bedded at night, and wolves howled in the distance, the boys on guard easily calmed the sleeping cattle by simply raising their voices in song. The desire of self-preservation is innate in the animal race, but as long as the human kept watch and ward, the sleeping cattle had no fear of the common enemy. An incident which I cannot explain, but was witness to, occurred during the war. While holding cattle for the Confederate army we received a consignment of beeves from Texas. One of the men who accompanied the herd through called my attention to a steer and vouchsafed the statement that the animal loved music, - that he could be lured out of the herd with singing. To prove his assertion, the man sang what he termed the steer's favorite, and to the surprise of every soldier present, a fine, big mottled beef walked out from among a thousand others and stood entranced over the simple song. In my younger days my voice was considered musical; I could sing the folk-songs of my country better than the average, and when the herdsmen left us, I was pleased to see that my vocal efforts fascinated the late arrival from Texas. Within a week I could call him out with a song, when I fell so deeply in love with the broad-horn Texan that his life was spared through my disloyalty. In the daily issue to the army we kept him back as long as possible; but when our supply was exhausted, and he would have gone to the shambles the following day, I secretly cut him out at night and drove him miles to our rear, that his life might be spared. Within a year he returned with another consignment of beef; comrades who were in the secret would not believe me; but when a quartette of us army herders sang "Rock of Ages," the steer walked out and greeted us with mute appreciation. We enjoyed his company for over a month, I could call him with a song as far as my voice reached, and when death again threatened him, we cut him to the rear and he was never spoken again. Loyal as I was to the South, I would have deserted rather than have seen that steer go to the shambles.

In bringing these reminiscences to a close, I wish to bear testimony in behalf of the men who lent their best existence that success should crown my efforts. Aside from my family, the two pleasantest recollections of my life are my old army comrades and the boys who worked with me on the range and trail. When men have roughed it together, shared their hardships in field and by camp-fire like true comrades, there is an indescribable bond between them that puts to shame any pretense of fraternal brotherhood. Among the hundreds, yes, the thousands, of men who worked for our old firm on the trail, all feel a pride in referring to former associations. I never leave home without meeting men, scattered everywhere, many of them prosperous, who come to me and say, "Of course you don't remember me, but I made a trip over the trail with your cattle, - from San Saba County in '77. Jake de Poyster was foreman. By the way, is your old partner, the little Yankee major, still living?" The acquaintance, thus renewed by chance, was always a good excuse for neglecting any business, and many a happy hour have I spent, living over again with one of my old boys the experiences of the past.

I want to say a parting word in behalf of the men of my occupation. Sterling honesty was their chief virtue. A drover with an established reputation could enter any trail town a month in advance of the arrival of his cattle, and any merchant or banker would extend him credit on his spoken word. When the trail passed and the romance of the West was over, these same men were in demand as directors of banks or custodians of trust funds. They were simple as truth itself, possessing a rugged sense of justice that seemed to guide and direct their lives. On one occasion a few years ago, I unexpectedly dropped down from my Double Mountain ranch to an old cow town on the railroad. It was our regular business point, and I kept a small bank account there for current ranch expenses. As it happened, I needed some money, but on reaching the village found the banks closed, as it was Labor Day. Casually meeting an old cowman who was a director in the bank with which I did business, I pretended to take him to task over my disappointment, and wound up my arraignment by asking, "What kind of a jim-crow bank are you running, anyhow?"

"Well, now, Reed," said he in apology, "I really don't know why the bank should close to-day, but there must be some reason for it. I don't pay much attention to those things, but there's our cashier and bookkeeper, - you know Hank and Bill, - the boys in charge of the bank. Well, they get together every once in a while and close her up for a day. I don't know why they do it, but those old boys have read history, and you can just gamble your last cow that there's good reasons for closing."

The fraternal bond between rangemen recalls the sad end of one of my old trail bosses. The foreman in question was a faithful man, working for the firm during its existence and afterwards in my employ. I would have trusted my fortune to his keeping, my family thought the world of him, and many was the time that he risked his life to protect my interests. When my wife overlooks the shortcomings of a man, it is safe to say there is something redeemable in him, even though the offense is drinking. At idle times and with convivial company, this man would drink to excess, and when he was in his cups a spirit of harmless mischief was rampant in him, alternating with uncontrollable flashes of anger. Though he was usually as innocent as a kitten, it was a deadly insult to refuse drinking with him, and one day he shot a circle of holes around a stranger's feet for declining an invitation. A complaint was lodged against him, and the sheriff, not knowing the man, thoughtlessly sent a Mexican deputy to make the arrest. Even then, had ordinary courtesy been extended, the unfortunate occurrence might have been avoided. But an undue officiousness on the part of the officer angered the old trail boss, who flashed into a rage, defying the deputy, and an exchange of shots ensued. The Mexican was killed at the first fire, and my man mounted his horse unmolested, and returned to the ranch. I was absent at the time, but my wife advised him to go in and surrender to the proper authorities, and he obeyed her like a child.

We all looked upon him as one of the family, and I employed the best of counsel. The circumstances were against him, however, and in spite of an able defense he received a sentence of ten years. No one questioned the justice of the verdict, the law must be upheld, and the poor fellow was taken to the penitentiary to serve out the sentence. My wife and I concealed the facts from the younger children, who were constantly inquiring after his return, especially my younger girls, with whom he was a great favorite. The incident was worse than a funeral; it would not die out, as never a day passed but inquiry was made after the missing man; the children dreamed about him, and awoke from their sleep to ask if he had come and if he had brought them anything. The matter finally affected my wife's nerves, the older boys knew the truth, and the younger children were becoming suspicious of the veracity of their parents. The truth was gradually leaking out, and after he had served a year in prison, I began a movement with the view of securing his pardon. My influence in state politics was always more or less courted, and appealing to my friends, I drew up a petition, which was signed by every prominent politician in that section, asking that executive clemency be extended in behalf of my old foreman. The governor was a good friend of mine, anxious to render me a service, and through his influence we managed to have the sentence so reduced that after serving two years the prisoner was freed and returned to the ranch. He was the same lovable character, tolerated by my wife and fondled by the children, and he refused to leave home for over a year. Ever cautious to remove temptation from him, both my wife and I hoped that the lesson would last him through life, but in an unguarded hour he took to drink, and shot to death his dearest friend.

For the second offense he received a life sentence. My regret over securing his pardon, and the subsequent loss of human life, affected me as no other event has ever done in my career. This man would have died for me or one of mine, and what I thought to be a generous act to a man in prison proved a curse that haunted me for many years. But all is well now between us. I make it a point to visit him at least once a year; we have talked the matter over and have come to the conclusion that the law is just and that he must remain in confinement the remainder of his days. That is now the compact, and, strange to say, both of us derive a sense of security and peace from our covenant such as we had never enjoyed during the year of his liberty. The wardens inform me that he is a model prisoner, perfectly content in his restraint; and I have promised him that on his death, whether it occurs before or after mine, his remains will be brought back to the home ranch and be given a quiet grave in some secluded spot.

For any success that I may have achieved, due acknowledgment must be given my helpmate. I was blessed with a wife such as falls to the lot of few men. Once children were born to our union and a hearthstone established, the family became the magnet of my life. It mattered not where my occupation carried me, or how long my absence from home, the lodestar of a wife and family was a sustaining help. Our first cabin, long since reduced to ashes, lives in my memory as a palace. I was absent at the time of its burning, but my wife's father always enjoyed telling the story on his daughter. The elder Edwards was branding calves some five miles distant from the home ranch, but on sighting the signal smoke of the burning house, he and his outfit turned the cattle loose, mounted their horses, and rode to the rescue at a break-neck pace. When they reached the scene our home was enveloped in flames, and there was no prospect of saving any of its contents. The house stood some distance from the other ranch buildings, and as there was no danger of the fire spreading, there was nothing that could be done and the flames held undisputed sway. The cause of the fire was unknown, my wife being at her father's house at the time; but on discovering the flames, she picked up the baby and ran to the burning cabin, entered it and rescued the little tin trunk that held her girlhood trinkets and a thousand certificates of questionable land scrip. When the men dashed up, my wife was sitting on the tin trunk, surrounded by the children, all crying piteously, fully unconscious of the fact that she had saved the foundation of my present landed holdings. The cabin had cost two weeks' labor to build, its contents were worthless, but I had no record of the numbers of the certificates, and to my wife's presence of mind or intuition in an emergency all credit is given for saving the land scrip. Many daughters have done virtuously, but thou excellest them all. The compiling of these memoirs has been a pleasant task. In this summing-up of my active life, much has been omitted; and then again, there seems to have been a hopeless repetition with the recurring years, for seedtime and harvest come to us all as the seasons roll round. Four of my boys have wandered far afield, forging out for themselves, not content to remain under the restraint of older brothers who have assumed the active management of my ranches. One bad general is still better than two good ones, and there must be a head to a ranch if it is to be made a success. I still keep an eye over things, but the rough, hard work now falls on younger shoulders, and I find myself delegated to amuse and be amused by the third generation of the Anthonys. In spite of my years, I still enjoy a good saddle horse, scarcely a day passing but I ride from ten to twenty miles. There is a range maxim that "the eyes of the boss make a fat horse," and at deliveries of cattle, rounds-ups, and branding, my mere presence makes things move with alacrity. I can still give the boys pointers in handling large bodies of cattle, and the ranch outfits seem to know that we old-time cowmen have little use for the modern picturesque cowboy,

Andy Adams

unless he is an all-round man and can deliver the goods in any emergency.

With but a few years of my allotted span yet to run, I find myself in the full enjoyment of all my faculties, ready for a romp with my grandchildren or to crack a joke with a friend. My younger girls are proving splendid comrades, always ready for a horseback ride or a trip to the city. It has always been a characteristic of the Anthony family that they could ride a horse before they could walk, and I find the third generation following in the footsteps of their elders. My grandsons were all expert with a rope before they could read, and it is one of the evidences of a merciful providence that their lives have been spared, as it is nearly impossible to keep them out of mischief and danger. To forbid one to ride a certain dangerous horse only serves to heighten his anxiety to master the outlaw, and to banish him from the branding pens means a prompt return with or without an excuse. On one occasion, on the Double Mountain ranch, with the corrals full of heavy cattle, I started down to the pens, but met two of my grandsons coming up the hill, and noticed at a glance that there had been trouble. I stopped the boys and inquired the cause of their tears, when the youngest, a barefooted, chubby little fellow, said to me between his sobs, "Grandpa, you'd - you'd - you'd better keep away from those corrals. Pa's as mad as a hornet, and - and - and he quirted us - yes, he did. If you fool around down there, he'll - he'll - he'll just about wear you out."

Should this transcript of my life ever reach the dignity of publication, the casual reader, in giving me any credit for success, should bear in mind the opportunities of my time. My lot was cast with the palmy days of the golden West, with its indefinable charm, now past and gone and never to return. In voicing this regret, I desire to add that my mistakes are now looked back to as the chastening rod, leading me to an appreciation of higher ideals, and the final testimony that life is well worth the living.

Choose from Thousands of 1stWorldLibrary Classics By

A. M. Barnard
Ada Leverson
Adolphus William Ward
Aesop
Agatha Christie
Alexander Aaronsohn
Alexander Kielland
Alexandre Dumas
Alfred Gatty
Alfred Ollivant
Alice Duer Miller
Alice Turner Curtis
Alice Dunbar
Ambrose Bierce
Amelia E. Barr
Amory H. Bradford
Andrew Lang
Andrew McFarland Davis
Andy Adams
Anna Sewell
Annie Besant
Annie Hamilton Donnell
Annie Payson Call
Annonaymous
Anton Chekhov
Arnold Bennett
Arthur Conan Doyle
Arthur M. Winfield
Arthur Ransome
Atticus
B.H. Baden-Powell
B. M. Bower
Baroness Emmuska Orczy
Baroness Orczy
Basil King
Bayard Taylor
Ben Macomber
Bertha Muzzy Bower
Bjornstjerne Bjornson
Booth Tarkington
Boyd Cable
Bram Stoker
C. Collodi
C. E. Orr
C. M. Ingleby
Carolyn Wells
Catherine Parr Traill
Charles A. Eastman
Charles Dickens

Charles Dudley Warner
Charles Farrar Browne
Charles Ives
Charles Kingsley
Charles Klein
Charles Amory Beach
Charles Hanson Towne
Charles Lathrop Pack
Charles Whibley
Charles Willing Beale
Charlotte M. Braeme
Charlotte M. Yonge
Charlotte Perkins Stetson
Clair W. Hayes
Clarence Day Jr.
Clarence E. Mulford
Clemence Housman
Confucius
Cornelis DeWitt Wilcox
Cyril Burleigh
D. H. Lawrence
Daniel Defoe
David Garnett
Dinah Craik
Don Carlos Janes
Donald Keyhoe
Dorothy Kilner
Dougan Clark
Douglas Fairbanks
E. Nesbit
E.P.Roe
E. Phillips Oppenheim
Earl Barnes
Edgar Rice Burroughs
Edith Van Dyne
Edith Wharton
Edward J. O'Biren
Edward S. Ellis
Edwin L. Arnold
Eleanor Atkins
Eliot Gregory
Elizabeth Gaskell
Elizabeth McCracken
Elizabeth Von Arnim
Ellem Key
Emerson Hough
Emilie F. Carlen
Emily Dickinson
Enid Bagnold

Enilor Macartney Lane
Erasmus W. Jones
Ernie Howard Pie
Ethel Turner
Ethel Watts Mumford
Eugenie Foa
Eugene Wood
Eustace Hale Ball
Evelyn Everett-green
Everard Cotes
F. H. Cheley
F. J. Cross
Federick Austin Ogg
Ferdinand Ossendowski
Francis Bacon
Francis Darwin
Frances Hodgson Burnett
Frances Parkinson Keyes
Frank Gee Patchin
Frank Harris
Frank Jewett Mather
Frank L. Packard
Frank V. Webster
Frederic Stewart Isham
Frederick Trevor Hill
Frederick Winslow Taylor
Friedrich Kerst
Friedrich Nietzsche
Fyodor Dostoyevsky
G.A. Henty
G.K. Chesterton
Gabrielle E. Jackson
Garrett P. Serviss
Gaston Leroux
George A. Warren
George Ade
Geroge Bernard Shaw
George Durston
George Ebers
George Eliot
George Gissing
George MacDonald
George Meredith
George Orwell
George Sylvester Viereck
George Tucker
George W. Cable
George Wharton James
Gertrude Atherton

Grace E. King	J. Henri Fabre	Katherine Stokes
Grace Gallatin	J. M. Barrie	L. A. Abbot
Grant Allen	J. Macdonald Oxley	L. T. Meade
Guillermo A. Sherwell	J. S. Fletcher	L. Frank Baum
Gulielma Zollinger	J. S. Knowles	Latta Griswold
Gustav Flaubert	J. Storer Clouston	Laura Lee Hope
H. A. Cody	Jack London	Laurence Housman
H. B. Irving	Jacob Abbott	Lawrence Beasley
H.C. Bailey	James Allen	Leo Tolstoy
H. G. Wells	James Andrews	Leonid Andreyev
H. H. Munro	James Baldwin	Lewis Carroll
H. Irving Hancock	James DeMille	Lewis Sperry Chafer
H. Rider Haggard	James Joyce	Lilian Bell
H. W. C. Davis	James Lane Allen	Lloyd Osbourne
Hamilton Wright Mabie	James Lane Allen	Louis Hughes
Hans Christian Andersen	James Oliver Curwood	Louis Tracy
Harold Avery	James Oppenheim	Louisa May Alcott
Harold McGrath	James Otis	Lucy Fitch Perkins
Harriet Beecher Stowe	James R. Driscoll	Lucy Maud Montgomery
Harry Houidini	Jane Austen	Lydia Miller Middleton
Helent Hunt Jackson	Janet Aldridge	Lyndon Orr
Helen Nicolay	Jens Peter Jacobsen	M. Corvus
Hendrik Conscience	Jerome K. Jerome	M. H. Adams
Hendy David Thoreau	John Burroughs	Margaret E. Sangster
Henri Barbusse	John Cournos	Margaret Vandercook
Henrik Ibsen	John F. Kennedy	Margret Penrose
Henry Adams	John Gay	Maria Edgeworth
Henry Ford	John Glasworthy	Maria Thompson Daviess
Henry Frost	John Habberton	Mariano Azuela
Henry James	John Joy Bell	Marion Polk Angellotti
Henry Jones Ford	John Kendrick Bangs	Mark Overton
Henry Seton Merriman	John Milton	Mark Twain
Henry W Longfellow	John Philip Sousa	Mary Austin
Herbert A. Giles	Jonas Lauritz Idemil Lie	Mary Catherine Crowley
Herbert N. Casson	Jonathan Swift	Mary Cole
Herman Hesse	Joseph A. Altsheler	Mary Hastings Bradley
Homer	Joseph Carey	Mary Roberts Rinehart
Honore De Balzac	Joseph Conrad	Mary Rowlandson
Horace Walpole	Joseph E. Badger Jr	M. Wollstonecraft Shelley
Horatio Alger Jr.	Joseph Hergesheimer	Maud Lindsay
Howard Pyle	Joseph Jacobs	Max Beerbohm
Howard R. Garis	Jules Vernes	Myra Kelly
Hugh Lofting	Julian Hawthrone	Nathaniel Hawthrone
Hugh Walpole	Julie A Lippmann	Nicolo Machiavelli
Humphry Ward	Justin Huntly McCarthy	O. F. Walton
Ian Maclaren	Kakuzo Okakura	Oscar Wilde
Inez Haynes Gillmore	Kenneth Grahame	Owen Johnson
Irving Bacheller	Kenneth McGaffey	P.G. Wodehouse
Israel Abrahams	Kate Langley Bosher	Paul and Mabel Thorne
Ivan Turgenev	Kate Langley Bosher	Paul G. Tomlinson
J.G.Austin	Katherine Cecil Thurston	Paul Severing

Percy Brebner	Samuel Hopkins Adams	Various Authors
Peter B. Kyne	Sarah Bernhardt	Vaughan Kester
Plato	Sarah C. Hallowell	Victor Appleton
R. Derby Holmes	Selma Lagerlof	Virginia Woolf
R. L. Stevenson	Sherwood Anderson	Walter Camp
R. S. Ball	Sigmund Freud	Walter Scott
Rabindranath Tagore	Standish O'Grady	Washington Irving
Rahul Alvares	Stanley Weyman	Wilbur Lawton
Ralph Bonehill	Stella Benson	Wilkie Collins
Ralph Henry Barbour	Stephen Crane	Willa Cather
Ralph Victor	Stewart Edward White	Willard F. Baker
Ralph Waldo Emmerson	Stijn Streuvels	William Dean Howells
Rene Descartes	Swami Abhedananda	William le Queux
Rex Beach	Swami Parmananda	W. Makepeace Thackeray
Rex E. Beach	T. S. Ackland	William W. Walter
Richard Harding Davis	T. S. Arthur	Winston Churchill
Richard Jefferies	The Princess Der Ling	Yei Theodora Ozaki
Richard Le Gallienne	Thomas A. Janvier	Yogi Ramacharaka
Robert Barr	Thomas A Kempis	Young E. Allison
Robert Frost	Thomas Anderton	Zane Grey
Robert Gordon Anderson	Thomas Bailey Aldrich	
Robert L. Drake	Thomas Bulfinch	
Robert Lansing	Thomas De Quincey	
Robert Lynd	Thomas H. Huxley	
Robert Michael Ballantyne	Thomas Hardy	
Robert W. Chambers	Thomas More	
Rosa Nouchette Carey	Thornton W. Burgess	
Rudyard Kipling	U. S. Grant	
Samuel B. Allison	Valentine Williams	

www.ingramcontent.com/pod-product-compliance
Lightning Source LLC
Chambersburg PA
CBHW030124180626
46812CB00002B/549